To Uncle Jim and Auntie Jne.

BRITISH JOURNEY

Lots of love,
Joe

BRITISH JOURNEY

JOE HAYMAN

Copyright © 2017 Joe Hayman

The moral right of the author has been asserted.

Apart from any fair dealing for the purposes of research or private study, or criticism or review, as permitted under the Copyright, Designs and Patents Act 1988, this publication may only be reproduced, stored or transmitted, in any form or by any means, with the prior permission in writing of the publishers, or in the case of reprographic reproduction in accordance with the terms of licences issued by the Copyright Licensing Agency. Enquiries concerning reproduction outside those terms should be sent to the publishers.

Matador
9 Priory Business Park,
Wistow Road, Kibworth Beauchamp,
Leicestershire. LE8 0RX
Tel: (+44) 116 279 2299
Fax: (+44) 116 279 2277
Email: books@troubador.co.uk
Web: www.troubador.co.uk/matador

ISBN 978 1788038 751

British Library Cataloguing in Publication Data.
A catalogue record for this book is available from the British Library.

Printed and bound by CPI Group (UK) Ltd, Croydon, CR0 4YY
Typeset in 11pt Adobe Garamond Pro by Troubador Publishing Ltd, Leicester, UK
Cover design by Joe Kenyon

Matador is an imprint of Troubador Publishing Ltd

For Esther, Edith, Isobel and Stanley

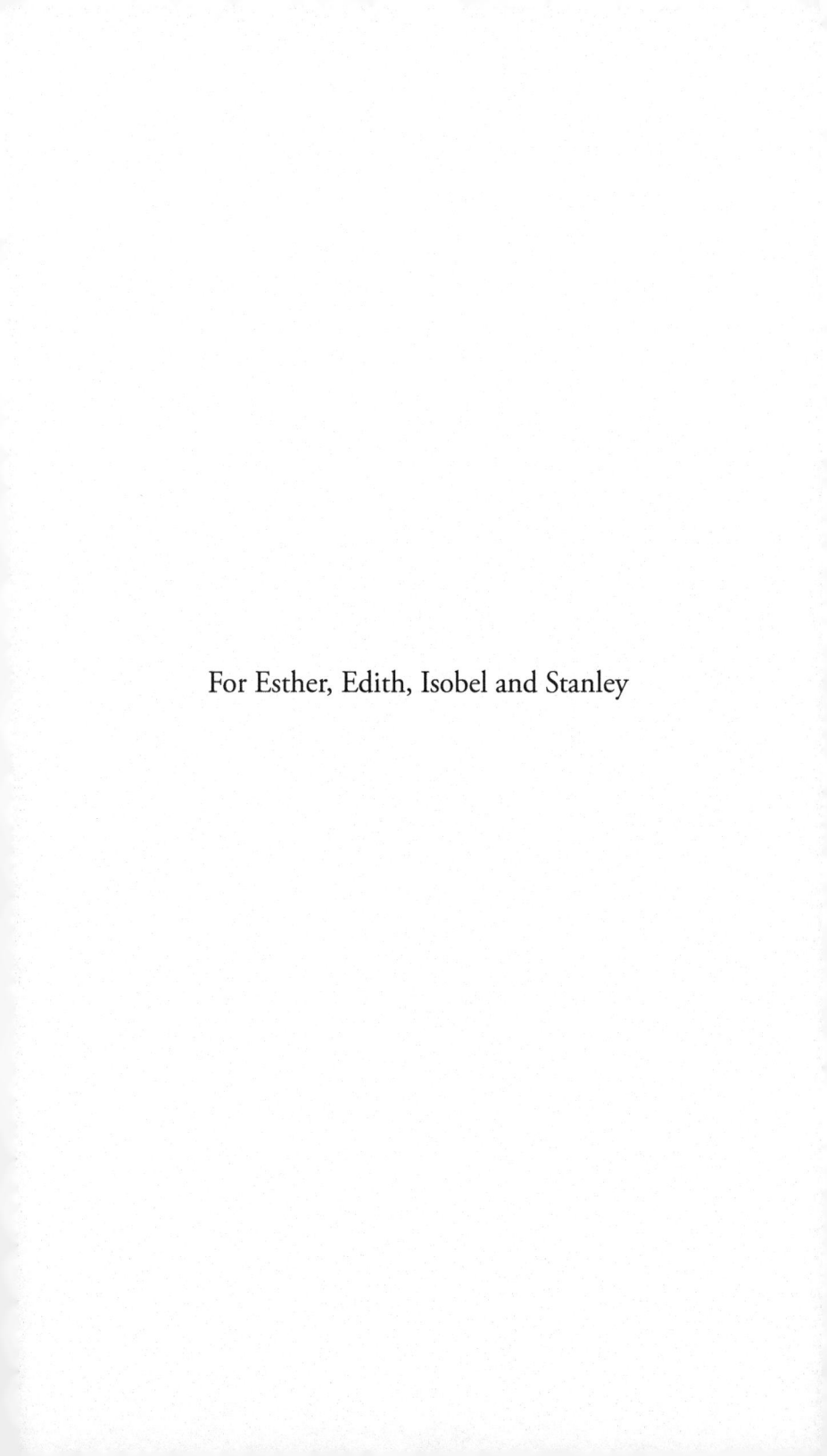

Contents

	Introduction	xi
1	Immigration and integration in Sunderland	1
2	Sovereignty, free movement and religion in Darlington	12
3	Economic and social liberalism in Westminster	24
4	Patriotism and nationalism in Wembley	42
5	Power, prestige and service in Whitehall	59
6	Nostalgia, change and political correctness in Blackpool	79
7	Education, empire and loyalty in Poulton	99
8	Cultural security and Britishness in Preston	111
9	Community, faith and values in Blackburn	122
10	Austerity, solidarity and sharing in Liverpool	140
11	Industry, insecurity and a sense of home in Treforest	151
12	Looking after one's own in Welshpool	173
13	Cultural heritage and national identity in Aberystwyth	192
14	Upholding shared values in Richmond	202
15	Civic nationalism, monarchy and history in Scotland	218
16	Symbols, sectarianism and reconciliation in Northern Ireland	243
	Conclusion	270
	A note for readers	283
	Acknowledgements	285

"You affect to be a patriot. This sentiment can be legitimate and can have resonance but in your mouth it is tainted and made toxic… Your inspiration is not love of country or your fellow citizens, it is an admiration for Nazism and white supremacist creeds where democracy and political persuasion are supplanted by violence and intimidation of opponents and those thought to be different… Our parents' generation made huge sacrifices to defeat those ideas in the Second World War. What you did, and your admiration for those views, betrays the sacrifices of that generation.

You are no patriot.

To her family, friends and colleagues, Jo Cox was a wonderful mother, daughter, sister, partner, and companion… Before being elected as an MP, she had already demonstrated herself to be a credit to herself, her community and her country … devoting herself to seeking to better the lot of those less fortunate than her… She had shown herself to be passionate, open-hearted, inclusive and generous…

In the true meaning of the word, she was a patriot."

Mr Justice Wilkie,
sentencing Thomas Mair for the murder of Jo Cox MP,
23 November 2016

Introduction

"Refugees think England's a good place to come," Joan, a woman in her fifties, told me, "because they think everything will be laid on a plate for them, but we don't have anything ourselves".

We were at a bus stop opposite the Silksworth Sports Centre on the edge of Sunderland on a cold, grey afternoon in November 2016. Five months earlier, the results of the European Union referendum vote in Sunderland had been announced at the centre across the road. The result – a much higher than expected margin of victory for leaving the EU amongst the town's voters – had sent shockwaves around the world. The value of the pound had dropped 3% against the dollar as the result from Sunderland was declared and within eight hours David Cameron had announced his intention to stand down so that a new Prime Minister could lead the Brexit negotiations. A new political era for the UK seemed to have begun, and as I started a journey around the country trying to explore what had brought Britain to this point and what the post-referendum future might hold, Silksworth seemed a good place to begin.

"Doctors and hospitals and schools – there's no room," Joan went on, the lines of time evident on her face. "It's no wonder our country can't cope because there's that many people came here."

As her bus arrived, I asked how she responded to the argument that if the economy deteriorated as a result of Brexit, there might be even less money for services like hospitals and schools.

"We cannae be any worse off than we are now," she said, slowly boarding the bus, her shopping weighing her down.

She took a seat on the bus next to a woman reading the *Daily Mail*. 'Enemies of the People' read the front page headline alongside photographs of the three High Court judges who had ruled that a vote in Parliament was required before the government could trigger Article 50 and formally notify the European Union of its intention to leave. The headline seemed symptomatic of an angry, divided nation. The murder of the MP Jo Cox had been particularly distressing, but there were many other signs that things weren't right in Britain: death threats to the campaigner who had taken the Article 50 case to the High Court; deep cynicism about experts, politicians and other leaders exposed by a divisive referendum campaign; a spike in racist and religious hate crimes after the vote; a schism between those with different views on issues like migration, identity and security, often played out aggressively on social media; growing anger about the gap between rich and poor; an ongoing threat from both Islamist and far-right extremism. Britain's problems had been laid bare and most of those problems seemed to come not from outside, but from within. As someone who cared deeply about the country and wanted to live in a safe and cohesive society, I was really worried.

Five years earlier, I had written a book about the UK in the aftermath of the 2011 riots, visiting different parts of the country and speaking to people from all walks of life about what was going on. It wasn't a representative study by any means but it had enabled me to escape my north London bubble, to see things from the perspective of people who lived different lives to me and to consider the role I might play in addressing the issues the UK faced. I decided to take a similar approach to looking at post-referendum Britain, resolving to speak to a range of different people about the referendum vote and the country's future. I knew this would mean talking to plenty of people I disagreed with and exploring issues,

Introduction

divisions and prejudices I wished didn't exist, but I also knew that if I ignored problems or only listened to people who saw the world the same way that I did, my thinking would not move on. I believed the new era Britain was entering required new thinking and a willingness to listen, particularly from people like me who had been on the losing side of the referendum. With that in mind, I decided that even if I found what I heard upsetting, I would give people the space to talk, reflect on what they told me rather than rushing to judgement, try to find areas of common ground and seek in what they were saying clues about Britain's post-referendum future. This is the story of my journey.

1

Immigration and integration in Sunderland

On the edge of the pedestrian centre of Sunderland the next day a sudden hailstorm hit, and as I sheltered under a shop awning, I met a man in his thirties who had had the same idea. He told me he was originally from Scotland but had lived in the Sunderland for a few years.

"I was gonnae cycle today," he said, "I'm glad I didn't."

We got talking about the referendum.

"I voted to stay in," he told me, "but I still think we've got to respect the vote. Nicola Sturgeon, she's just trying to pull a fast one, saying she wants to stay in Europe. She's a wily one."

"I don't get it," he continued. "Sunderland voted Leave but Newcastle voted Remain. Does that mean Newcastle stays in and we leave? It's bullshit."

I wanted to ask him more about what he had said, whether Sunderland and Newcastle really had the same relationship as England and Scotland and what made a nation, but the hail had stopped as quickly as it had started and he moved on, wishing me luck as he went.

I walked into the town centre. It was a week before Remembrance Sunday, and many people were wearing poppies. Two Royal British Legion stalls were occupied by ex-service personnel, and their volunteers were busy. Much of the market was closed because of the hail, but a cheese stall remained open. It advertised award-winning British cheeses, like the Lancaster Bomber and the Flagship. The Union Flag flew high above the stall.

"It's the attitude towards immigration, that's what it all comes down to," the owner told me. "It's the knee in the jerk. 'Too many foreigners', people think. It's like Enoch Powell, the Rivers of Blood – they should be careful what they wish for."

He told me he had voted to leave the EU and I asked if he regretted his vote given the issues relating to immigration that he had set out.

"It was all about trade, tariffs, exporting for me," he said, "I don't have any truck with anybody."

We got talking about the Union Flag which was flying above his stall.

"I find it quite funny when people equate it with the Far Right," he said. "It's not the National Front's flag, it's ours. If you go anywhere in the world, you see it – the Saltire in Scotland, the Stars and Stripes in the States. It's part of the country and I fly it with pride."

"You shouldn't be bullied into avoiding something you believe in," he went on. "I have my own opinions. People need to study a bit more – education, education, education."

He shook my hand and began to pack up.

Across the road I met a woman having a cigarette outside a shopping centre. She told me she had voted to remain in the EU, but now that we had voted to leave, the result should be respected.

"They messed up the campaign," she said, "now they need to live with it."

She told me that her friends who had voted to leave the EU had done so to try to manage immigration.

"Humans always need someone to blame," she told me, "foreigners are just an easy option."

I asked her for her own view on the issue.

"Immigration does bother me," she said. "I'm not a racist, I'm not a bigot, but I do think that something needs to be done. People who were born and brought up here, they feel like they have to bend over backwards, whereas people who just come here get things on a plate."

I asked whether that was a perception or whether it was true.

"What I do know," she said, "is that I worked in a hotel down south and the agency got caught and fined a lot of money for bringing in illegal workers from abroad."

"Not as much money as they made in profit, mind," she added with a smile.

"Yes, we should take refugees," she continued, "but other countries should do the same – there's got to be a balance… it's like the Gurkhas: they fought for us and then had to fight for years to get in, whereas other people can just come straight in."

"I saw this programme on a guy who had come to the UK from Africa," she went on, "and to pay us back he joined the Armed Forces. He got his limbs blown off and I have every respect for that man – he wanted to repay his adopted country. They're the kind of people we need, not the kind of people who'll trample on your rights. Like round here, there's a Bangladeshi group – if we're all British, these groups shouldn't exist. I know it's a natural instinct, but if we're going to have people in, they need to adapt to our ways."

"I do find some people from certain countries do have quite an attitude about women," she added. "They see English women as easy… I don't just mean Muslims, there are Christians that are the same. Like I know a Lithuanian guy at work – nice guy, but he said that in his country, women didn't work and I just think we've moved on from seeing women as second-class citizens. People from abroad have to be prepared to adapt and adjust to that – I'm not saying completely, but if I went abroad I'd expect to have to fit in."

I asked if there was a political party which reflected her views.

"I'd chop my arm off before I vote for UKIP," she said, "but I do think Labour MPs need to get out and listen to people and allow them to say what they think. It's kind of like censorship – people are very frightened when talking about immigration. But I still wouldn't vote UKIP – for me, that's just a stab in the back for everyone who fought in the Second World War."

She finished her cigarette and headed back inside.

*****

That evening, I had arranged to meet Richard James, a man in his fifties who owned a local company and was a passionate supporter of leaving the EU. He told me that he had been at the count in Silksworth when the result had been announced.

"On Sky News, you could see me in the background," he said. "It was a really good night – we were watching the count and you could see how things were going. They seemed to be very heavily towards the Leave campaign so by the time it was announced, I knew. I'm a season ticket holder at Sunderland and it was like that, cheering away – we were quite ecstatic."

"I don't mind the Europeans," he went on, "but I'm British, I'm proud to be British and I want to remain British – I don't want to be European. We've gone down from having an empire to almost being ruled by the Chancellor of Germany – it's too much of a comedown. When I was in the RAF, we used to have camps all around the world, and now we're being run by Europe."

I asked him whether, as a businessman, he was worried about the economic impact on businesses of Britain leaving the EU.

"Trying to tell people that something is bad for business doesn't cut much ice in this town," he said. "It's their own pockets they're interested in – if they're interested in pockets at all. It's not all about money, there's more to life than that."

Immigration and integration in Sunderland

I suggested that the conventional wisdom was that the economy was the most important thing to people.

"It might be the most important thing in London," he said, "but it's not the case up here. People here are worried about the economy of their household, not the economy of the country."

"I think the people of Sunderland could see all of the people in London, in Parliament, in the banking system, all supporting Remain," he continued. "They were all pretty well-off people, they were all looking after their own pockets. They're scared of losing their cheap labour – any of the people in power, they've nearly all got cheap labour somewhere in the background, and sometimes it's not even legal. You won't find many people in Sunderland employing people as cheap labour on a personal basis."

"I've got a guy working for me from Romania," he went on, "and I can see why some companies will only choose Polish or Romanians – they're totally different, they don't mind getting their hands dirty, but what we should be doing is training our own people. If you go to any hotel in Britain now, you'd struggle to find anybody who's British. That hasn't happened by accident, they do that on purpose, they do it because they can get away with cheap labour. And people round here are looking at it saying 'why does he get a job when I can't get a job myself?' I don't know why Labour is so pro-EU, I really don't…"

"Now having said that," he added, "the immigration which is causing the biggest issues is not necessarily the European immigration, so coming out of Europe won't stop that, but I just think Britain as a country is full."

I wanted to come back to him about what he had said about immigration from Europe not being the biggest issue, as that seemed like a really important point, but first he said he wanted to tell me about a television programme, *The Pledge*, in which commentators with different perspectives debated contentious political issues.

"I love that programme," he said. "There's five people in there, all different types of people... Nick Ferrari, he's me; the Yorkshire girl, the businesswoman, Michelle, she's me – every conversation they have, I'm agreeing with them; and every conversation they have, I'm disagreeing with June Sarpong."

"Last night, I stayed up and watched it," he went on, "and one of the subjects on there was about the fact that some terrorists, after half of their sentence, are being let free. Now why on earth would that happen? They're still terrorists... And now some of them are refusing to go on the rehabilitation programme, or the decontamination programme, whatever they want to call it... and Michelle said that anyone who refuses to do the programme should not be allowed out of prison, they should be kept in there until they're safe and until the terrorist threat has gone. And I'm all for that. But Miss Sarpong, she was saying 'you can't do that'. But I think 'why are their rights as terrorists anywhere near as important as the rights of the people they're going to kill?'"

"I like Nick Clegg and his wife," he continued, "they're nice people, but the Lib Dems were blocking every attempt we had to put more pressure on terrorists a few years ago, they kept blocking it and blocking it and blocking it... Apparently there's thousands of terrorists, or thousands of Muslims, in London who are getting monitored by police, MI5 or whatever – thousands of them. I would do anything, I would bring in any law, to try to prevent an atrocity, and I just don't understand anyone who would want to say 'ah well it's not fair on these people'. These people, the terrorists, they don't want fairness."

"I don't know why the lawmakers can't make a law that people understand where the line is drawn," he added. "We're not allowed to take liquids on planes now, and we spend a lot of time looking into little old ladies' bags for drinks, but they can't put any more effort in for them than they would for young Muslim men looking shifty. We're making ourselves far more in danger than we ought to be."

I asked how he would define people 'looking shifty'.

"If you go through training as a security guard or as airport security or a policeman or whatever," he said, "you'd be trained to spot dangers, to spot the right people, but they're not allowed to do that, because it's discriminating. They can't use their judgment. How often do you hear people talking about interpretation of the law? Why have you got to interpret it? Put it in fucking English in the first place."

I asked what his view would be if the police stopped someone wearing a Union Flag, saying they were worried about far-right terrorism. I suggested that doing so would be discriminatory.

"I don't know," he said, "I don't write the law, but I certainly want to have control of our borders – EU or no EU, immigration into Britain is too much."

I asked if he took the same view in relation to refugees.

"We should take our fair share and we do," he said. "Our geographical area is so much smaller than Germany's and France's and Spain's. It's got to be in proportion to what we can take. I don't know how many China's taking or Russia's taking, or South America's taking – why are we taking them all? Australia – they've got all the space in the world. America – all the space you could want but you can't get in there if you've got a parking fine outstanding. Yet you can't get a mass murderer out of Britain because they might get tortured or hung. It's all back to front."

"You see it in the papers," he went on. "You've got to fight to get Gurkhas to stay here – people who fought for us getting sent back to Nepal, it's just ridiculous. They are British and they should be here, but that guy with a hook – you cannae get rid of him. We're getting rid of the good people and letting the wrong people in. I don't mind immigration, I just don't want people on the streets of London who are a threat – if you think they're a threat, get 'em out, get rid. It's not immigration, it's simply what we can cope with and the right sort of people. I would rather every person from Nepal came here than one terrorist."

I asked him whether what he was saying meant that his main considerations were attitude and contribution to the country as opposed to the number of people coming to Britain.

"When I see an immigrant," he said, "and he's got western clothes on and he speaks English and he's got a job, I never think he shouldn't be here. So I'm not saying we shouldn't look after them, if there needs to be some immigration, we all do our fair bit, but compared to the size of the country, Britain has done too much. And then you've got Merkel – stupidest thing I've ever heard, saying we'll take them all. All of them, well 99%, are young men – they should be over there, putting their country right. Could you do that, leave your country and wife and daughter behind? Whatever dire situation they're in, leaving their family in it can't be the right answer. Why are they all men? *Why are they all men?*"

"I would like an Australian or an American system," he went on, "where you can't come in this country if you've got a criminal record, if you're not the right kind of people. We shouldn't allow people like that Latvian who killed his wife back in Latvia – gets into Britain and kills a girl over here. It's insane how we allow that to happen. So we need to control the kind of people. Refugees are different, they don't have papers, they all claim they're sixteen-year-old Syrians when they're 35-year-old Iraqis or Afghanis. We've got to go over there and get people ourselves, we've got to stop people going across and bring the people we want to help in boats ourselves. We have to have immigration, we have to have refugees, but we've got to control it. For every bad refugee that's come across and become a terrorist or a criminal, we've left a good one there who needs our help. It's not just numbers, it's the type of people that are coming."

"Migration has to be controlled and it has to be at a reasonable level," he continued. "If you walk through London, and 75% are foreign and 25% are English, it's not just because all of these people have come in, it's also because all the people who were there have gone out. My wife and I walked down a street in Birmingham, in Sparkbrook. All the way down, and I mean all the way, every house, every shop, all of it, there wasn't one English person left. Now that's not because all of those people came in, it's because all of them, the English, left. Now why did they leave? They've had to say 'I can't live here, I don't want to be surrounded by these Somalis', and they've had to go. If my street was like that, I would probably want to leave. I wouldn't want to be the last English person out."

"It's too much," he added. "If there's a smattering all over the place it would be fine, but it's too much. First it's a street, next it will be a road and two streets, after that it'll be the whole postcode in Sparkbrook. It's just getting bigger and bigger, we've got to stop it some time, it can't go on forever. Somebody, sometime, has to say 'we're full'."

I suggested to him that given what he had said, this wasn't really about numbers, but about the way culture and power in the country was shifting.

"It's about population for me," he said. "Today we went house-hunting – we went to Silksworth, and they were building a new housing estate by Sainsbury's. It's because we need the houses – there's a housing crisis. We haven't got the space. We don't want to build more houses forever. I like my green country. I like the rolling hills. We are the most populous country in Europe – that's fine, just don't make it worse. Tell them to go somewhere else."

As we prepared to leave, he told me that the big thing that was on his mind was what he called "the Islamisation of Britain and Europe".

"I don't mind Islam, I don't mind Muslims," he said, "but if this keeps happening forever, we will be a Muslim country. I'm not saying that Islam is any worse than Christianity, but if that happens, what happens to Christianity?"

"Things are changing," he continued, "and if it keeps going, and their birth rate is higher than ours, it's just a fact – in 10 or 20 or 50 or 100 or 200 years' time, they will take over. Put it in a spreadsheet if you don't believe me. And if they take over then why wouldn't they vote for Muslim MPs and a Muslim government – and why wouldn't they impose sharia law?"

"If you look at the referendum vote," he went on, "and you take out Scotland and you take out London which has a very high population of immigrants and foreign people, and take out all the other immigrant areas, how many English, white people would have voted Leave? It would have been more like 70-30 or 60-40 in favour of Leave. And that's what I'm saying about having too much immigration: it's like in London, if you take all the Muslims out of London, would you still have a Muslim mayor? If you get too much immigration, eventually they get their way."

*****

My time in Sunderland left me with much to think about. It felt like immigration and integration were big issues locally, including for people who had voted to remain in the EU. The concerns I had heard seemed to be not just economic but also cultural, and I didn't think they would be solved by leaving the EU because doing so would not stop immigration or solve Britain's integration problems.

The conversation with Richard had been unsettling, but while he and I had very different outlooks on the issues we had discussed, I didn't disagree with everything he had said. Like him, I was concerned about the terrorist threat Britain faced; I could see why he was worried that the UK economy had been built on low-paid workers coming to the UK from abroad; and, like him, I was troubled by the way the Gurkha soldiers had been treated, believing their service to Britain merited special treatment in terms of their citizenship. Yet it was his stance on Islam, demographic change and shifting power in the country which stuck with me: the questions he was raising had chilling implications but I knew

I couldn't afford to ignore them. I felt that part of my task for the journey ahead was to develop as full a response to the questions he had posed as I possibly could, and I believed that doing so might help me to find answers to the challenges the UK as a whole was facing. In order to find those answers, I knew I would need to hear a range of perspectives including, crucially, from members of the British Muslim community. First, however, I had organised to go to Darlington to explore the EU referendum a little further.

2

Sovereignty, free movement and religion in Darlington

I had learned a lot about attitudes towards the EU while I was in Sunderland, but I wanted to gather more perspectives so I travelled to Darlington to meet Charlotte Bull, a woman in her sixties who had been closely involved in the Leave campaign in County Durham. In her immaculately-kept home on the edge of the town, she gave me sandwiches and a cup of tea, encouraging me to eat as she talked. I asked her about the night of the referendum result.

"It was absolutely phenomenally exciting," she told me. "We stayed up all night with the television on, and we all had a cheer when we got a 6,000 majority in Darlington. It was like an ending in a way – it felt like we'd been trying for the referendum since 1997, so just to have got one, and especially as people realised that the EU was not the best way of running this country, it was just unbelievably happy. And you were glad it was over – part of me just wishes that I could forget it now and, you know, go on to other things."

"We have been so blooming patient," she went on, "you know, I could have done all sorts of stuff. I could have kept part of my amateur dramatics all these years – lots of people don't want to spend their time campaigning the whole time. People have got involved because it is a cause that they think is worth fighting for. We've done it the slow way, we haven't broken any windows or attacked Parliament, and we've finally got a result against all the odds."

I asked her about her motivations for getting involved with the campaign.

"One thing that particularly made me annoyed and upset," she said, "was if I felt something very important had happened, like a major treaty was signed, and it wasn't on the news. Now you can't say that anyone lied about it, but it was considered by the powers that be – Parliament or the BBC – that it wasn't important enough to talk about. And that was the kind of thing I got really, really annoyed about. I tried terribly hard not to be paranoid, but it felt like there was a conspiracy of silence about it. No doubt things got out on the computers, on the internet, but it's not the same as being forewarned – and I felt that people were being conned."

"The very fact that they kept quiet meant that I felt that as a country we were being deceived," she added. "Now I used to be a teacher, and if a child doesn't tell you something, there's a reason they do that – because they know you won't like it if you found out the truth. And that in itself is at the heart of my feeling that I should be in the Eurosceptic movement."

I asked why she thought that politicians and the media would hide information about the EU.

"I think," she said, "that they thought that over a long period of time we would all get older and gradually accept it as more and more laws were made in the EU and not in our sovereign Parliament – and it nearly worked. They still hid it right up to the last election, when Nick Clegg said only 9% of our law is made in the EU, and then Gordon Brown admitted it was nearer 50%. That's such a basic, mind-boggling thing that we need to know about – it's appalling – because once your MP feels like they have to hide facts from you, they can do anything. This is what I believe that democracy should be about: your MP should be conscious that we know about everything they do and say and vote for. They should think 'well

I must please most people, most of the time, or else I won't get back in'. But they weren't having this fear because they kept the smokescreen up: you know, when the Queen announced things at the beginning of Parliament, she would talk about 'co-operating with our European neighbours' or something like that – they didn't talk about loss of sovereignty, loss of power."

I asked her why Brussels felt so distant but believed that Westminster, which many people also felt was distant, was the right place to make decisions.

"Mmmm," she said, finishing her sandwich, "because before a general election, in a Westminster Parliament, you have to have what's called a manifesto, and that means you know what they're going to do in the next five years. But in a European election, the MEPs have no control whatsoever over what's going to happen over the next five years – they're just someone with a coloured rosette on. The people who decide what the MPs vote on are the Commission, and the Commission are made up mainly of civil servants. We have two representatives from the UK – they can be constantly outvoted by everybody else, and because they don't have to please most of the people most of the time, they are not doing a very good job, they are just concerned with their own survival."

"You might say this is not the most important part," she continued, "but the way they behave is so greedy and arrogant. I mean, you only have to be an MEP for five years and you get this massive pension for life, and somebody proposed that they stop getting limousines, but it was 'oh no, we cannot possibly do that'. Now that might not seem like the most important thing, but it really rubs it in, and it makes you feel like they are acting like a ruling class. They believe in this federal state with superior people at the top who decide what us minions have to put up with."

"I don't want to exaggerate," she went on, "but this evolution of the EU has happened because so many European countries have not had our background of democracy. Within my living memory, you had dictators all over Europe, so I don't blame them, but they just haven't reached the same standard of democracy as we have. I really, really believe in British democracy – it's precious and it needs to be protected. It's the knowledge of those who rule us that if we don't like what they do, they will be voted out. That is the crucial nutcake, the core, of what real democracy is."

"There is a vision of democracy," she added, "which David Attenborough recently talked about. He was saying that we elect people who are so much wiser, so much cleverer than us, and knowing that they have our best interests at heart, we should just let them get on with it. Now, he's very good with animals, but he's not very good at seeing into the human psyche. You could have any dictator saying that – Kim Jong-un could say that. I think we have developed our democracy so painfully and so gradually over hundreds of years – if you go back to the signing of the Magna Carta and the Civil War – and I really think it's precious."

"Maybe I've overstated," she said, "but I like to think that now we get democracy back, i.e. Mrs May is now aware that she has to give us a Brexit – she wouldn't be offering that if we hadn't forced her to do so. It's all a bit bizarre, that somebody that didn't actually campaign for Brexit is now responsible for bringing it about, but once you force people to be aware of the fact that they are responsible and answerable to us, then their natures will become much more honest."

She encouraged me to eat some more of the sandwiches, and as I ate, she talked on.

"My anger with the EU is not really with anybody from a foreign country," she said, "it's with our own people. I'll give you an example: when I was trying to lobby our MP, I went all the way down to London to meet her, and the same day three people had climbed on top of the House of Commons to protest against the runway at Heathrow, and the BBC news was all about that, and because we were well-behaved and we did as we were told and stood there like good little boys and girls, we didn't get a mention. I even spoke to a policeman about this: you misbehave in this country and break things and shout and set fire to things, first people say 'oh, that's dreadful', but then they say 'oh, really it's our fault, people are very upset, we really ought to do something about it'. That makes me so mad because we have done the right thing and we've been ignored so many times… I talk about being a nervous wreck sometimes and that was an example."

"I felt like that when I found that things were being kept secret from my fellow Britons," she continued. "I felt that I had a kind of duty to get things out there, so I started by writing letters to the local paper and joining the Democracy Movement. And, without being too sentimental, that was a little bit because of my dad being a soldier in the Second World War. I've been with him when he was visiting the graves and he got really upset because there were graves with the names of people he knew who disappeared on the beach and he didn't know what happened to them…"

Her voice faltered, and she stopped briefly to try to collect herself.

"I always get sentimental about this," she went on after a moment, her voice now shaking with anger, "but how dare they keep secrets from us, after all people have given to keep us free. *How dare they?* I feel so angry about the way the people of this country have been treated, and that's the fire behind it all, the feeling that we've been tricked, that we've been treated with contempt."

She had a drink and picked up a sandwich. I admired the integrity of her thinking and her passion for her country and fellow citizens. She was, I believed, a democrat in the truest sense of the word and I really respected her motivations and the way she had pursued her cause. It felt like there wasn't much more to say on the points about democracy she had made so I decided to move on to talk about economics.

"Politicians are looking at the interests of banks and multinational businesses," she said, "and kind of thinking 'well, everyone else can be dragged along with it'. Mrs Thatcher said that if you make the country rich enough, all the benefits will dribble down somehow, and benefit everybody – no, that does not happen. Who is it who is losing out and losing their jobs? It's teaching assistants – suddenly, they're not given any pay over the summer holidays – it's even cleaning ladies – suddenly they have to do the same jobs for less money. They are as caring and conscientious about their jobs as anybody who is paid millions in the banks, and it makes me angry to see people exploited, it really does. The people who defend the people who haven't got anyone to defend them, that's what democracy should be for, it's what the Labour Party should be for. They are meant to be there to shout very loudly until nobody wants to vote for the people who support that exploitation."

"Also," she went on, "if there are skills shortages, instead of businesses getting all these desperate people from Poland, who will be willing to work for a great deal less and plonk them into Sunderland and they'll be so grateful they'll never go on strike or anything, why don't they look at their own people in their own country? And we know the answer – it's saving money."

"Free movement," she added, "it sounds so generous, allowing us to go anywhere that we want, but we're actually being manipulated just to jump and go where business people want us."

"Sorry," she added, "I keep going off on tangents!"

It didn't seem like a tangent, it seemed a very important point. Time was running short, however, so I decided to ask whether some of the more challenging cultural issues I'd heard about in Sunderland, particularly relating to immigration and integration, had also been a factor in her decision to campaign to leave the EU.

"That sort of thing isn't my main concern as such," she said, "it is more of a practical question: you have a little boy in the class who doesn't speak English, you have to make special arrangements for him, and there isn't much money for that, so somebody who would normally give children extra help is not giving that: they are dealing with the little boy who doesn't speak any English. I have personal experience of this and it's very hard if you can't communicate; ideally, if we had loads of money, you would have specialists with different language skills, but the reality is that if I'm with the little boy doing maths and handwriting and art, it's a problem."

"It's these little tiny problems buried away that don't hit the headlines," she went on, "like how many people the hospitals can cope with, health tourism and so on… it's just pounds, shillings and pence in the end. You have to sympathise: if you were an impoverished Portuguese, and you couldn't get a job in your country but you knew you could get a job here, of course you'd come over. You can't resent that person, they're coming legally – just like you or I would if we got a job in America. You wouldn't think 'oh God, I'm going to upset an American by taking that job'."

"I know there are also problems a little bit with the terrorism aspect, the Islamic thing," she continued, "and I think we should help Islamic people in this country voice how they feel about things when they don't agree with the notorious comments you get in the newspapers. Anyone who is a nutcase, you get their comments and then everybody thinks 'oh that's dreadful, all these Muslims think this' and they don't. There's nothing in the Koran that forces women to wear the burka. I haven't read it all through or anything, but every chapter starts about how Allah wants everything to be peaceful and happy. They have this phrase, I can't remember it exactly, but they start every chapter – to a boring degree – with it. So you can be a Muslim without wanting to blow anybody up or mistreat women. But the trouble is that the bad aspects, the nutcases, get the publicity."

"I think if we've lost our culture," she added, "it's not been anyone like an immigrant that's caused it."

It seemed a really important point, and I asked what she meant.

"We swept God away rather too quickly," she said. "If we could retain what used to be thought of as Christian values, I think this country would be better off and it would be a much happier place. Imagine we are all brothers and sisters, imagine we don't think selfishly, imagine we think that everyone is just our equal – as far as we can, we should be as nice to anybody as we would be to our own family. That, I believe, is that whole point of what Jesus was telling us. If you think about the actual words from the Lord's Prayer, it starts '*Our* Father' – we are all brothers and sisters."

"The ideal world is a world where we all feel loved," she added, "even if things are going badly – that to me is what Christianity is all about and they don't teach it properly in schools. It's all stories and values – it doesn't work talking about it like that."

I said people used the idea of 'values' to provide some moral framework for a society which had resonance for people from all kinds of different religions and people who weren't religious at all.

"I understand what you're saying," she said, "I just feel having gone into schools that it's not working. Something's been undermined, something's gone. It does sound right that we should all be able to agree together what the values are, but it doesn't work somehow. It's not strong enough."

"I'm sure there could be a shared moral framework," she went on, "and there are certain things that we could learn from Islam, but it just seems people are losing certain things."

I asked what those things were.

"There is a certain amount of pride that we've lost," she said, "we've lost a bit of nitty-gritty. My parents' generation, they had to be so tough and they took great pride in looking on the bright side. They were determined to make the most of themselves and change clothes and turn up hems – if they went out, they always used to wear a hat… I'm expressing myself the wrong way, but they had pride in themselves, they had standards – they'd try and be generous, they would try and be a good person. My grandfather said he didn't want to just live and die, he wanted to live according to some sort of pattern and stick to it and use it to make decisions for his life."

"I think we've lost a certain amount of toughness, of trying to keep things going," she went on, "trying to stay faithful and to stay at it. These are just vague impressions, but it's not to do with immigration. You know, Muslims look after their old people, they live morally, there are certain ways in which we could take lessons from them."

I suggested her Christian values seemed inconsistent with Nigel Farage's poster depicting refugees from the Middle East alongside the words 'Breaking Point'. I asked whether she had found supporting the campaign to leave the EU difficult after the poster was launched.

"I don't know whether they were meant to be Syrians," she said, "but Nigel Farage was one of the first to say with Syrian *refugees*, and I underline that word with bold pen, they're not the same as migrants – we should be looking after refugees fleeing war."

"Some idiot within the EU decided that there was no difference between a refugee and an economic migrant," she went on. "I can't remember exactly when that happened but whoever has done this has caused this massive problem. We've always looked after refugees in this country, we've prided ourselves on it. It's just that there is a difference between migrants and refugees. But I must say I wish the whole blooming thing about migration hadn't been raised, because it so overshadowed the democracy argument. That and the blooming £350m. They weren't the point to me and I think it is a pity that it all became that way."

"Having said that," she continued, "there are people who if you went to a job interview and you can see that three of the people there are not from Britain and you're going for the same job, I think you're entitled to feel, you know, that 'I should have been given priority'. On a personal note, you wouldn't think that – you would think 'no, it should be fair', but this idea of not being loyal to your own group of people is important. You could end up opening your country to the entire world but we cannot house the entire world. We're not a huge continent like Russia or America, and we're already up to our eyes in debt – we can't afford to have just more numbers of people coming in. And I do think that because our ancestors tried to make our lives better, so we should try to make our children's lives better, and I do think we should prioritise that."

"If you start saying that the people of your own country don't matter more than the people of other countries," she added as we said goodbye, "where does it end? It just means that nobody is loyal to anybody and we're all just pawns in a big game."

*****

As I headed for the station, I reflected that even though Charlotte and I had voted differently in the EU referendum, I agreed with her that the economics of the Single Market did not always work in favour of those in low-paid, insecure jobs. While I wasn't religious myself, her description of a society with a shared moral framework and where people cared for one another also appealed to me. I admired her commitment to her fellow citizens and to democracy, while her willingness to learn from Islam was notable in contrast to other views I had heard. Yet as I walked back into the town centre, I still had much to consider, particularly the points she made at the end of our discussion about loyalty to nation and prioritising the wellbeing of British children. She had talked about being loyal to one's own people in the same way that Joan, the woman at the bus stop in Silksworth, had talked about 'looking after our own'. I couldn't help thinking that this was a natural human instinct, but one which created significant tension in an increasingly interconnected world.

As I sat in a pub by the station waiting for my train, a man who was watching a football match on a big screen called over at me.

"Where's your poppy?" he shouted aggressively, "where's your poppy?"

I went over and showed him the poppy on my jacket. We got talking.

"I voted Remain," he told me. "Leaving is a fucking Tory right-wing stitch-up."

I asked him how that could be the case when parts of the country, like Darlington and Sunderland, which were dominated by Labour had voted overwhelmingly to leave the EU.

"Tony fucking Blair," he said. "When them Eastern Bloc countries came in, he could have put a limit on Polish people coming in, but he said no. So these poor Polish came in and flooded working-class areas. I don't blame them, I've nothing against them, but they swamped the working-class areas, and UKIP took advantage."

"That's all," he said, and went back to watching the football as 'Another Day in Paradise' played on the radio.

*****

I headed to the station with his words ringing in my ears. Like Charlotte, he had strongly challenged the principle of free movement from a worker's perspective, and as I thought about what he had said, and my conversation with Joan about 'looking after our own', I reflected that this was not simply about economics, it was also tangled up with a sense of identity and tribe. It was about 'them', in this case people from Eastern Europe, undermining 'us', in this case the British working class, either by taking jobs or putting pressure on public services, and leaders not doing anything to stop it.

It seemed clear to me that there were a range of issues being played out in the country which had much less to do with economics and more to do with culture and identity: a loss of a religious underpinning for society and a challenge to the primacy of the nation state which Charlotte had pointed to; and a fear of a shift in power, religion and culture which Richard in Sunderland had so clearly felt. And somewhere in those issues I felt there was an explanation of why the man I had just met had been so adamant about me showing my poppy. As I headed to London to talk to some Remain voters about what I had heard in Sunderland and Darlington, I wondered whether it would be possible to identify any common ground.

3

Economic and social liberalism in Westminster

I had arranged to meet three young professionals based in London, keen to put to them the views I had heard in Sunderland and Darlington. As I waited for my first appointment, on Whitehall, I saw a group of taxi drivers protesting outside Downing Street. I went over to talk to them and it was clear that while they were officially protesting about air quality in London, they were most worried about competition from firms which enabled customers to hail cabs from their mobile phones and charged much less than black taxis.

"There have been various independent studies," one of the protestors told me, "which have shown that their drivers are earning well below the minimum wage. Obviously, they will contest that, but I read that some drivers are earning less than four pound an hour, which is ridiculous."

"We've never operated like that," another man said, "but they're taking so much business that the only way we make a decent living is by doing overtime, so instead of doing an eight-hour day, you're doing nine, ten and in the end you think, 'you know what, make a day of it, do a twelve-hour day'."

"The fact is that the majority of the public don't really care about that if we're perfectly honest," the first man said, "it's all about having a cheap ride. The question you have to ask yourself from a moral and ethical standpoint is 'what is the cost of that?' Because there is a price to pay."

"Companies in the tech space are circumventing a lot of rules and regulations," he went on, "and the political world is taking too long to catch up. Some of these companies are really stretching it – what they're doing goes in the face of all those rules and regulations and effectively have carte blanche to do whatever they want: consumers want those cheap rides, and with a growing population and a huge demand on public transport, there is a political demand for it."

"People don't think that works and they don't think that works," the second man said, pointing first to Parliament and then to Downing Street.

"The referendum was partly about the corporate world and the increasing influence they have over the political establishment," the first man said, "the fact that companies can now take governments to court if they don't like their policies – if it impacts your profitability, or your potential future profitability, then you can contest it in the law courts."

"Listen," he went on, "governments take revenue from us as taxpayers, and the global businesses, they're cheeky, they say 'we'll set up a little chain of accounting events in the Caribbean, they get to get our tax revenue, and we can trade for free in the UK and Europe and wherever. So they're saying to governments 'we don't pay taxes to you, we're bigger than you'… And they are giving jobs to people, and the government doesn't want to upset the applecart too much because it means that they're lowering welfare spend, and they're able to brag about unemployment statistics and how well they're doing – but the relationships between the political world and the corporate world are becoming very intertangled to say the least."

*****

My first meeting was with Laila Kausar, a woman in her thirties who worked for an international development organisation. I asked her to describe the evening of the referendum from her perspective.

"I thought it was going to be close," she said, "but that it would be Remain in the end. And then we stayed up and watched it until one or two in the morning and we realised it was going the wrong way. And then watching Cameron resign, it just felt really terrifying, and what has terrified me the most is the rise in hate crime, and feeling for the first time that even though I was born and brought up here, I'm not white – and that was really scary. I used to think that wouldn't ever have to be something I would have to worry about, and now I do."

I asked her about her own plans for responding to what was happening in the world.

"I wouldn't actively go into politics," she said. "It's a scary place to be, especially for female politicians with the levels of abuse and bullying they receive. Fortunately I have a job which allows me to respond daily so I do feel like I'm helping. I keep thinking I should do some volunteering, and I feel really bad that I haven't, but I do think there are lots of really good organisations: Hope Not Hate, the Anti-Fascist League. I think there definitely is an outpouring of people who think 'what can I do?' but I'm not really sure we've mobilised particularly well: I think that the Remain campaign could have done a better job, and we didn't really learn from the lessons of lecturing people that the EU was good for them, because people didn't want to be patronised and told that they were stupid. No one does."

I suggested that people might not want to be told they were stupid, but that might mean taking on board what they were saying and some compromise in the future. I asked her to what degree she was willing to compromise on issues like immigration.

"I'm a massive proponent of immigration," she said. "My dad came to this country and benefited from the education system and went back home to Pakistan and brought huge amounts to Pakistani society from what he'd learnt – I think people should have access to the world's resources, no matter where you're from."

"I think it's really scary that the debate about migration and immigration is getting conflated with the refugee issue," she went on. "I think that Britain should be really proud of the fact that we've always opened our doors to people that need us, from Kinder transport to Ugandan Asians in the 1980s, and that now seems to be missing a bit from the national psyche. So I wonder how we can recreate that."

"When the tragic picture of Alan Kurdi lying on the beach in Bodrum was published," she continued, "my charity had such an outpouring from the public, we had people calling up saying 'I want to take a refugee into my home', 'how can I help?', 'how can I donate?' – so I still think people are fundamentally good but there has definitely been such a hardening in relation to immigration that I fear is spilling over into asylum claims and refugees."

"I do feel really passionately that things like science and arts and culture and exchange, making resource available for the global good, is a good thing," she added, "but you've got to balance that with not letting people get left behind from the benefits, and maybe we're guilty of doing that, because who is going on Erasmus programmes, really, and who is able to become a scientist and benefit from EU funding? We've got to make opportunity a bit more equal."

I suggested that in order to boost opportunity, there might be more redistribution of money and opportunity away from people like her to people in other parts of the country. I asked how she felt about that.

"I feel good about that," she said. "I don't believe in life after death – I believe you've only got one chance to do it, so you might as well do it well. If it means we're not hurting ourselves or attacking people on the street, if we're not spreading vile messages of hate, then yeah, I think opportunity does need to be better distributed. And I think there needs to be a bit more listening, trying to work out why people voted the way they voted."

I asked her how she would respond if she 'listened to people' and those people said that they wanted to limit immigration and maintain their version of British culture. I gave her the example of Richard, the man in Sunderland who had talked about having Sadiq Khan becoming Mayor of London as an example of how power could shift in a multicultural society.

"And that was meant in a bad way?" she said with genuine shock and sadness in her voice.

"I don't know," she went on after a moment. "The country I grew up in isn't a racist one and that's what I'm worried that the natural conclusion of all this is. I want to listen, but racism, homophobia, misogyny, they have to be challenged because we've made these gains and we can't afford to lose them. But you can do that while still acknowledging that parts of the society have not connected to the political elite and have not felt the benefits of economic growth and maybe have equated that with jobs going to people coming from the EU – it's not a crazy leap to make."

As we parted, I thought about her reaction to the conversation about Sadiq Khan. It had been a painful moment but I was heartened that she had finished on a positive note, focusing on the perspectives of people who lived very different lives to her own. I believed that was the spirit in which the country as a whole needed to move forward if its divisions were to be healed. Yet while I felt she could look across the economic divide and was clearly willing to put her hand in her own pocket to try to bridge it, the schism in cultural attitudes seemed much more difficult and even discussing it seemed to carry greater potential to cause distress. I imagined there would be further difficult conversations ahead as I explored the issues and I could only hope that the lessons which I would draw from those discussions would make the painful moments worthwhile.

*****

My next meeting was with Dominic Smithson, a man in his thirties who ran an education training business. I asked for his reflections on Britain after the referendum.

"It's funny," he said, "I remember someone saying in 2010 that waking up and finding yourself in a Conservative government was like finding that Father Christmas had been and he'd stolen all your toys. But this is a more permanent thing, like Father Christmas has been assassinated or something – it's an epochal thing that cannot be reversed."

I wanted to know why the vote had made him feel so bad.

"I suppose," he said, "that there's something comforting about being a member of the EU – the sense that they would act as some kind of countervailing force to the more general rightward-leaning instincts in the country. The UK is a very centralised democracy, there are very few checks and balances on a successful leader, and I suppose that the EU was one of those forces that did a lot of good in trying to advance legislation on issues like workers' rights. There's also a sense of camaraderie and connection with Europe that it felt like we were severing – it's like a divorce, it's more than just a 'conscious uncoupling', it's an emotional earthquake."

"You're on this grief cycle," he went on, "shock, anger and then finally through to acceptance. You try to justify how it's happened: how did it come to this?"

I told him that a number of people had mentioned immigration to me as a source of concern.

"But that's the irony isn't it," he said before I had finished the question, "the places that have the most immigration don't care about immigration. It's the places that don't have immigration that worry about it. The people in places like London know that immigrants are people too, that they have the same kinds of dreams and aspirations and they enrich our culture hugely."

"Now that's not to say on something like teacher training," he went on, "that the government hasn't taken a soft option in not working as hard as they could in providing the training they could to UK nationals. Why as a country do we import teachers from abroad, or nurses? It ought to be completely within our power to train the number of nurses that the country needs."

While Dominic had, like Laila, held firm on the value of immigration, his points about education and training for British people resonated with much of what I had heard from Leave voters in the North East. The conversation about education brought us on to his business, which provided training for teachers, and he told me that sales had slowed significantly since the referendum.

"We shouldn't be the kind of business that is affected by a decision like this," he said, "but headteachers are fearing the worst about what they can expect in terms of future government spending. Theoretically, funding hasn't changed between the referendum and now, but the feeling that Britain's got some very difficult decisions ahead has made a world of difference."

I asked how he felt about those who had chosen to leave the EU given the impact their vote had had on his business.

"It feels like it was like the first culture war in Britain of the 21st century," he said, "and as we go through the redundancy process at work and we have to let people go, not solely but in large part because of the collapse in sentiment due to the vote, I haven't yet got to the stage where I can say 'never mind, I think they made the wrong decision but I'm sure they have their reasons'. And of course they do, everyone is making the best decision that they can make, but I do still blame them because it's their fault."

"It's not very scientific," he went on, "but my sense is that the wilful isolationism of Leave voters harks back to a different era, not explicitly but ostensibly of empire when Britain was self-sufficient on the world stage, the Blitz spirit, all of that… I was going to say 'nonsense' and of course that does a disservice to the people who experienced it, but as far we we're concerned in modern Britain, it's irrelevant. The world has changed dramatically even in the last twenty years, let alone since 1945, and that's what I mean about a culture war, because you see Britain increasingly coalescing into different camps – you can predict that your *Daily Mail* reader will be a Leaver, that they'll be a monarchist, and sitting here in multicultural London feels a million miles away from that worldview."

I asked him whether he really felt Britain was in a culture war.

"I think it is a battle," he said. "You know, some people in London may see more in common with Europe than they would with the rest of the UK. You know, London is a global city and does it have more in common with Paris than with Sunderland?"

I asked him what his answer to that question would be.

"I think that's the kind of thing which is easy to say and it sounds pretty," he said, "but I don't actually think it's true. I mean the main difference with London is that it's where the money is, and when you're not having to worry about money the whole time, it's easy to be relaxed about things. When all you see is the evidence of decline, your major industries heading somewhere else… if any of us were born into a family in Sunderland, we would probably be feeling that too."

"I think we're all fundamentally the same," he continued. "Our conditioning, our parents, where we grow up, the people we live with, that's what turns us into who we are, and it's not like one side is clever and one side is stupid – we're all making decisions based on the evidence we have available to us. And actually the evidence that they have available to them is that free trade has not been good for them. That said, they may find out that protectionism works even less well."

"I think that the changes there may have accompanied the time of EU membership," he went on, "but I don't think it's been driven solely by it. You've got the internet revolution and lots of other technological advances that have made high-skill, high-pay jobs increasingly important in the UK economy and eliminated vast swathes of the jobs that used to be the bread and butter of many people's lives. At the turn of the century, with the changes in agricultural policy, those jobs were soaked up, and new jobs were found to create new things and that kept the economy growing. What happens this time round, who knows?"

His comments made me think about the black cab protest and I asked whether he felt the cabbies should be supported.

"You've got to support industries against bumps in the road," he said, "but I suspect that the black cabs are uncompetitive because other people offer a significantly better service than them. So no, I don't think industries like that should be protected. It's like keeping the Beefeaters outside Buckingham Palace – their jobs have been protected even though if someone came in with a rifle, they'd make really short work of them."

I suggested that the cabbies would say that other firms were circumventing rules which they kept to very tightly.

"The contractual point is valid," he said, "but I think with the exception of the payment and the workers' rights issue, it's not about playing by the same rules, they're just outclassed. It's like the person who loses a game and goes 'that's not fair'. And this kind of thing happens all the time, you know, the champion plough-puller in nineteenth century England might be quite upset with the invention of a tractor. But you can't protect that job forever when the world is going in a different direction. Providing it's as fair as possible, you've got to let it go and let it flow."

I asked him what he felt the answer was for people who had seen things 'flow' away from them.

"As far as there is an answer," he said, "it's about making society and the economy work for everyone, which means a more balanced economy between north and south, more funding for those regions that feel neglected and under strain. It's about being able to create the conditions in which people in that area can achieve economically as well as we can here in London, particularly about encouraging small businesses to start up in those areas."

"When people don't feel under pressure in the same way," he went on, "they'll make different decisions, and decisions which seem more natural to us in London because we're already in those conditions. In the meanwhile, if we're more able to spread the benefits across the whole of the UK, we've got to try and continue to make the argument that immigration and free trade supports the economy and creates jobs, because actually it does."

I suggested that some of the redistribution of benefits of being part of the world economy would come out of his pocket either as an individual or as a business owner. I wondered whether he would support that.

"Yeah," he said, "for businesses in particular – though business is a massively broad term: I work in a small family business, we pay all our taxes in the UK, we don't have some kind of offshore shell in Antigua and somehow we need to find a route through to making sure that business is socially responsible, both in terms of the actions that it takes but also in terms of taxation so that the multinationals are fairly taxed. I appreciate that is not easy, but all businesses have a responsibility to help support the country on which they rely. Everyone needs to contribute."

His economic analysis echoed what the taxi drivers had said, but I wasn't sure he accepted the cultural arguments for Brexit which I had heard in Sunderland. I asked if he could see where people were coming from on the cultural issues relating to immigration and integration.

"To some extent, I think the culture is driven by the economics," he said. "It's a bit like Maslow's hierarchy of needs. My kids only get really stressed when they're hungry or tired. It's not meant to be a patronising analogy but people are the same: they get stressed when they're not getting what they want. People in those areas haven't had what they want for too long and that's what drives the behaviour. In London you can get most of what you want most of the time but if you lived in Sunderland you might well be unhappy about the way things are turning out or think the best days are behind you because maybe, actually, they are."

*****

My final meeting of the day was with Dan Naylor, a public affairs specialist in his thirties who felt passionately about remaining in the EU. Over a cup of coffee in a café in Westminster, the taxi protest continuing outside, I asked him about the night of the 23rd of June and the next day.

"I got a text message from my brother saying 'it's Leave'," he told me, "and I remember feeling a bit of disbelief and shock. I'm not just reeling those off as trite descriptions, and I do genuinely remember feeling a sense of bewilderment that the country had voted for this, and my general sense was a lot of what I thought we were as a country was gone."

"I have an image of the country," he went on, "that we are a tolerant nation, that we allow different beliefs, that we allow religious attire and burkas and so forth, that we welcome immigrants to this country. So the belief for me was that we were rejecting that image that I had of the country and that was quite a revelation for me, an upturn of my beliefs about what the nation stands for."

I asked him how that made him feel. He paused for a moment.

"I can pad it in adjectives," he said, "but on a raw emotional level, and I know this is going a bit far, but it feels like that anti-immigration rhetoric that I'm so ashamed of won out. And I know I'm probably going to come across as a caricature of a liberal, metropolitan elite, sitting here drinking my soy latte, but to me, the raw emotion was a bit ashamed that we were no longer this tolerant country, and feeling absolutely gutted that we as a country are not being a beacon of somewhere that promotes the right things – that this is a place where if you play by the rules, you can make a career, you can make a life, and be welcome."

Outside the café where we were meeting, the taxis had taken over Whitehall, driving at a snail's pace in order to bring traffic to a standstill. There was a cacophony of beeping horns. I told Dan what the taxi drivers had said to me and asked for his view.

"Luddites said the same thing when machinery was moved in to help process wool," he said, "they actually destroyed machines in industrial England – so transition is always uneasy… We need to better support people through changes, so through automation and artificial intelligence, they reckon that in the next ten years, 25% of jobs are threatened. And you know, there's two reactions: one of fear and breaking machines, or there's managing the economy to a new economy where it's reformed and changed. And it seems to me that the second one is preferable. Technology is not going to be un-invented, hailing apps are not going to go away. You know, in 200 years' time, would we expect to get a taxi in the same way? I don't think we would."

"I know it's trite for me to say that," he went on, "because I'm somewhere near the top of the food chain doing really well, and I can hear in my head the cabbie saying 'it's alright for you, your job isn't on the line'. I know I am sitting in a privileged position, I have benefited from being in a global city, being flexible, using technology… it's the hardest thing to do, to put yourself in someone else's shoes and honestly ask yourself whether you would feel threatened or angry. And yeah, you probably would. But that doesn't make me wrong in what I'm saying."

"Protectionism is not the answer, it's a race to the bottom," he continued. "Where we will benefit as a country is where we retrain and open new industries, so the government should really put their shoulder behind supporting those factory-workers losing their jobs to prepare them for the modern economy. And with the taxi industry, the answer is not to ban new entrants but to do as recent rulings have said to say drivers are no longer self-employed and firms have to pay a fair living wage."

"I caution," he added, "against staying still or moving towards a mythical 1950s England that was Anglican and mostly white. If we do that, we risk stagnation, we risk demise, we risk irrelevance."

The remark seemed to point to some of the more cultural elements of the discussions I'd been having, and I asked him for his view on those.

"I can see why," he said, "when you get outside London, whether you're in Kent, whether you're in Sunderland, whether you're in Margate or Thanet or all these various places, where the traditional thing is fish and chips, and most people have a similar religion and outlook to you, and most people are broadly like you in terms of appearance, that you would have different worldviews. Those places are fundamentally different in both outlook and culture to London."

"To be frank," he went on, "there's been a campaign within certain parts of the press that immigrants are 'swarms', 'criminals'... if you combine all those factors and stir it in a pot, and this is a terrible generalisation on my part, but if you're in certain industries and read certain press, you can see why people would be concerned and would want to stop immigration."

A woman was reading a copy of the *Daily Mail* on a table next to us, and Dan nodded as if to indicate that that was one of the newspapers he was talking about. I asked if he felt able to compromise on issues relating to immigration given how common concerns about it were.

"Frankly, I think there's a fundamental lack of leadership talking about the benefits of immigration," he said. "I think that people like Tony Blair are right when they say this is a moment where we can't just hide from or duck the big issues. If we accept that the orthodoxy is that all of the problems with society are to do with immigrants then we won't actually fix the real problems – it would be like a doctor diagnosing a patient incorrectly, and we would not cure the patient."

"Since 2008," he went on, "immigrants made a net contribution of £20bn to the UK economy. I don't even hear that case made, and I think that's frankly a dereliction of duty that no opposing case has been made. It's a sign, in fact, of how far things have drifted that we even question 'should be make a case for immigration?' You know, when the Nazis were on the rise in Germany, we took in Jewish immigrants… I do see that some people feel culturally that they want to maintain a more homogenous, more Anglo-Saxon, Christian country but if I've understood correctly, a lot of Christian values are about charity and tolerance and helping people so I don't necessarily think that Christian values are incompatible with immigration."

"So I do accept," he added, "that there are people who feel under siege, who feel threatened… But my question back to them is, on what level is it a racial thing? Because I thought we as a country were getting to a point where race wasn't a determinant. If it's not a racial thing, if they're quite happy to have a multiracial society, is it a values thing? If it is, absolutely, let's talk about how we integrate people. I'm much more comfortable judging some on their values and who they are but I'm uncomfortable that we should make choices on a racial basis."

As we parted, I reflected that his point about values was crucial: Richard in Sunderland had raised questions about the changing demography of the nation, but I agreed with Dan that the discussion should be about values rather than people's ethnicity and heritage. The question was muddied by religion and culture, which were partly grounded in heritage and partly grounded in the values of the faith or culture, and this was clearly an issue to which I would have to return.

More broadly, I agreed with Dan about the need for leadership, but from my conversations I felt that any such leadership would have to be credibly rooted in the values and interests of ordinary people across the country. Dan was clearly a fan of Tony Blair but, rightly or wrongly, in the eyes of people like the man I'd met in Darlington, the former Prime Minister had lost credibility by allowing free movement from Eastern Europe without properly considering the impact on British workers. He had been seen to prioritise free markets over British workers – a charge the taxi drivers had levelled against leaders from across the political spectrum – and from there it seemed a very long road back to any sort of credibility or mandate to lead.

*****

I walked back onto Whitehall. Traffic was beginning to move again, and workmen were beginning to stack metal barriers ahead of the upcoming Remembrance Sunday ceremony at the Cenotaph. Nearby, I spoke to one of the men who had organised the protest. I asked whether he felt that we were seeing a fundamental threat to black cabs.

"Not just to black cabs," he said, "this is a fundamental threat to British workers. Today it's black cabs, tomorrow it could be something else – if you're going to allow companies to come into any industry that's well-trained, that's regulated and you let those companies not pay any tax and use investors all around the world to put in a predatory price to put the British worker out of work, then it's obviously going to have an impact."

"All the British worker wants to do is go to work for a decent wage," he went on, "and all this is doing is driving down the lowest wage to the lowest common denominator. And that's what Brexit was about, because the EU was fantastic for those who own big companies, but the average British worker, for the last twenty or thirty years, it has not been great for them. The establishment have got to realise that I'm proud of my country and I'm proud that we've always been a very fair and tolerant people who quite rightly will take people from all around to give them a better opportunity, but what was happening with the EU was basically undermining British workers and undermining any future for our children."

"We paid massive amounts of taxpayers' money on the Olympic Stadium," he added, "but no British workers were working on it. The kids from that deprived part of London, at sixteen, seventeen, why wasn't they offered apprenticeships so they could become plumbers, electricians?"

I asked what he thought the answer to that question was.

"Because it was all about profit," he said. "It was easier to get someone fully trained from another part of the world than it was to fully train a British kid."

I asked to what degree his concern about maintaining the taxi trade reflected his belief that British workers should be given priority over foreign workers. I knew that black taxis were overwhelmingly driven by white British men whereas some of the new entrants to the market often employed migrants to Britain and people from minority backgrounds.

"As a taxi driver," he said, "you do a thing called the Knowledge and we have many people from ethnic backgrounds, different sexualities, male and female – it's equal opportunities for everybody. The Knowledge doesn't care the colour of your skin, doesn't care your sexuality or religion, you're all of the same standard and that is about being safe to drive a Londoner from A to B – we're not Luddites like we've been accused, we just want them to make sure that the regulations are kept to by everyone."

He told me he'd voted for Brexit, and I asked if he was happy with his choice.

"Most certainly," he said. "As a member of the British working class, I think we've been forgotten for too long and our ambitions have been taken away and that was Brexit was about. How is it good for the working class when free movement is lowering wages and living standards? That's not good for the working class. It's good for companies because the EU are offering them a cheap supply of labour costs. But that's not really fair on the working man or the woman."

"I don't want to be rich," he said as we parted, "all the working man wants to know is he can pay his bills at the end of the week and that he's got a job to wake up to on Monday."

*****

That evening, I reflected that emotions were still running high five months after the referendum. The Remain voters I had met were measured when they spoke to me, but I had felt deep pain from each of them. Laila was very concerned about the rise in hate crime after the vote; Dominic had seen his business suffer and had been forced to make redundancies; Dan's view of the country had been upended. I reflected that the taxi drivers were seeing their world challenged too – albeit in a very different way – and while Dominic and Dan felt strongly that nothing should stand in the way of 'progress', everyone I'd met seemed to agree on the need for rules enforced by the state to ensure a level playing-field. I also felt that both the taxi drivers and the young professionals would support approaches relating to education and training to better prepare British young people for the job market. At the same time, I felt the young professionals would support redistribution of wealth and opportunity around the country even if there was a cost to them, and there seemed to be general agreement that multinational firms operating in Britain should be made to pay their fair share in taxes.

I was pleased to have found plenty of common ground between Remain and Leave voters, centred around the state protecting people from the worst impacts of globalisation. Yet I sensed far more agreement on economic matters than on the social and cultural issues relating to identity, immigration and integration which had been raised with me in the North East. I felt that despite their efforts to see the perspectives of people who had different lives to them, the young professionals did not fully understand the lives or attitudes of the people I had met outside London and found it hard in particular to accept that the views I had heard in the North East were driven by more than economic circumstance. Based on my experience, however, I felt that there was a genuine cultural divide in the country which was about much more than economics. This cultural schism seemed even more complex and emotionally charged than Britain's economic divide and the ways to address it seemed far less obvious to me, so in spite of the dangers which the conversation with Laila had demonstrated, I decided to focus on it for the remainder of my journey.

4

Patriotism and nationalism in Wembley

On the afternoon of Armistice Day, I stood on Bridge Road, in Brent, North West London, just around the corner from Wembley Stadium. People of a range of different backgrounds walked past and a man chatted in Polish on his mobile phone. Three students ate at the local Piri Piri chicken shop, while at the laundrette, a woman read the *Evening Standard*. The front page bore the headline 'Trump backlash' and there was a photograph of an American flag set alight at a protest against Donald Trump's election as President earlier in the week. Two girls in hijabs walked past; one stopped at a cash point. An elderly man got on his mobility scooter outside a halal butcher. The shop next door advertised Mecca Cola – 'the taste of freedom' – and phone cards for cheap calls to Pakistan.

Outside a kebab house, I found the owner smoking a cigarette. He told me he was originally from Kurdistan, and we got talking about the referendum.

"I'm into out," he told me. "I never believe in the EU. It bring nothing, nothing. It was good in the time of the Communists, Russia, but now what can they do? Nothing."

I asked him about the anti-immigration feeling which seemed to have been associated with the referendum.

"Every culture living together in London," he said, "they are dreaming, the people who think no more immigration, no more refugees. They are already part of England, the Jamaican people, the Indian people. What you tell the people? Go back? It's not possible. Fascism is an old idea. It is not possible anymore."

"Democracy has expired," he went on, "everyone doing everything to get in more money, this is mistake. We lost a lot."

I asked what he felt we had lost.

"Identity, culture, profile," he said.

I asked what he meant by profile.

"Who we are," he said, "what we have to do, to which future are we going."

I asked what he felt we should do.

"If I know that," he said, "I will be the new Karl Marx."

He laughed to himself, shook my hand and went back inside. His phrase 'to which future are we going' stuck with me. A vision for a shared future seemed important for any nation, particularly one which was made up of people from a wide range of different cultures and backgrounds, and as I walked down towards Wembley Stadium, I thought about football and the notion of a team working together towards a shared goal.

*****

I was in Wembley for the England-Scotland match that evening, keen to think about the lines between patriotism and nationalism. As I walked down to the stadium, schools were beginning to close and there were children all around. The sun was starting to go down, but it was still warm. On the big screens by the stadium, adverts from the Royal British Legion beamed down.

Scotland fans gathered at the top of Wembley Way, the pedestrian road leading to the stadium, sang 'Flower of Scotland' and waved the Saltire. An Argentinian student came over and talked to them, and they chanted together about Diego Maradona, the Argentinian footballer who scored the infamous 'Hand of

God' goal which helped to knock England out of the 1986 World Cup.

Not far from the stadium, I met two British-Indian men wearing England shirts and poppies. One told me he had voted for Brexit.

"You voted for Brexit?" his friend asked.

"Yeah," the first man said, "didn't you?"

"I didn't know how to vote," his friend said, "but if I had, I would have voted Remain."

"I just think when you have complete open borders as a country, you lose control," the man who had voted for Brexit said.

"As a country," he went on, "we should have the absolute right to allow the immigration we want. If it's good for economy, and good for our growth, then absolutely. But you can't have open borders where anyone can come in – if they add no value to the country and the economy, what's the worth of having them? All they will do is scrounge off the social services, and you don't want that. When my father's generation came over, there was demand for work, and that benefited the economy, but immigration doesn't always necessarily benefit the economy, particularly when it's unchecked. And sometimes I think that's lost on us."

"Who are ya? Who are ya?" A group of fans shouted behind us, and he paused for a second.

"What's nice," he went on when the group had passed, "is that I, as the son of an immigrant, made that same decision as a fourth, fifth, sixth generation normal British person. It's nothing to do with your ethnicity."

Thinking back to Laila, the woman I had met a few days earlier who had been so worried about hate crime, I asked if he felt the referendum had precipitated an increase in racism.

"Of course not," he said, "that's ridiculous – people play that racism card so easily. I'm British-Indian and I've never experienced racism in my life. And if they talk about racism in Britain, they haven't gone to other countries in the outside world – they don't understand what racism really is. Go to India and see what real racism is, you wouldn't believe it."

"The thing is that we're so scared to say stuff," he went on, "it's all become politically correct. So if I call someone black or Chinese or whatever I have to be careful because someone might take it in the wrong way. People can't express their natural differences, they can't express themselves for fears of being called a racist or anti-Semitic or all that nonsense."

I suggested that there were racist and anti-Semitic people in the country.

"I'm sure there are," he said, "but a very, very small minority. They're trying to paint everyone with the same brush. You've got to go to places like India, like America, that's probably worse than us."

I asked him about the poppy he was wearing and what it signified for him.

"Our whole country wears a poppy," he said, "and to me, it means freedom, the ability to live the way you want, no one dictating over you. It's not just a British thing or an American thing – it was a war against evil and the whole world was involved. India was involved, Pakistan was involved – people forget that kind of lost history."

"I think quite a lot of British people have forgotten their history," he went on, "and I think that's quite sad. I don't think they appreciate it – they'll get excited for a game of football against Scotland, but they don't know history, they don't know what's gone on in the world wars, they don't even know who the Chancellor of the Exchequer is in this country."

"I don't know who the Chancellor is," his friend said.

"There you go," the man said, indicating to his friend, "this guy is a prime example of the average British person – they don't pay any attention to politics."

"I've never voted," his friend said, "I wouldn't even know how to vote."

I asked whether Britain at least lived up to his dream of freedom in terms of treatment of migrants to the country and people from ethnic minorities.

"Of course we do," he said, "we've always been a refuge, we've always protected human rights. And in that context, I think we should help people who are in genuine need. I think that's fair, but you can't just have open borders: lots of people want to come here, they're not all in trouble in their own countries. They come over for economic reasons, not for life-saving reasons."

"I'm not a massive supporter of UKIP," he went on, "but I think it is pro-British. I think Nigel Farage wants our country to grow and be more successful – and everyone wants that."

"I don't think Nigel Farage is a racist person," he added as they prepared to head into the stadium. "I think sometimes he says things that aren't politically correct and might get taken out of hand by the media, but our media is like that – they'll make a story out of nothing."

Nearby I found an England fan who had come from Essex to watch the game. We got talking and he told me he didn't recognise the country anymore. I asked him what he meant.

"To have an identity is not just about saying 'oh, we live in a diverse country now'," he said, "so when I look at London now, I do not see my country. I see foreign people in my country who have not integrated. France is going through the same thing – diversity is destroying identity."

"It's just being honest," he added, "you don't have to be a Nazi to say something like that."

I asked what he would like to happen in Britain.

"I'd like to go back to the 1950s," he said, "even though I wasn't born. Going backwards, if you look at people in the East End – there was really terrible hardship, but it made us England."

I asked what he would say to people who said the nation couldn't go backwards and that it had to go forwards.

"Your question is quite stupid, really," he said, "because I know we can't really go back to the 1950s, but traditions have I feel been eroded. I think our culture is actually being taken away, in traditions, music, and that's how I feel today."

"My friend who's married to a Romanian," he went on, "he says 'they just don't understand our sense of humour'. He shouts out 'Mr Grimsdale', which is from the Norman Wisdom time, and they don't like it. But for me, Norman Wisdom and Mr Grimsdale and silly things like that, all that kind of comedy coming up from the music halls, helps us understand where you come from. When you bring in diversity, that's ok, because you're adding, but when diversity takes over…"

I asked whether that meant he wanted to maintain control of British culture.

"Control of the culture doesn't really come into what I'm saying," he said. "It's about something which *is* culture. A tourist I met on a train coming back from the seaside once said to me 'where is your Shakespeare, where is your *Three Men in a Boat*, where is your country?' She was saying that we're being invaded, and that's true from my point of view."

"Most foreign people who come here," he went on, "I think they say they're British, and that's very strange for me. I don't have an association with anything except England and London. People don't seem to be allowed to have an identity which is just being English."

He was wearing a wristband with the poppy on it, and I asked what that signified for him.

"It's about stopping, remembering and understanding," he said. "It's about thinking about people, from my family and others, who actually gave away their freedom for our freedom."

"They were fighting for continuation," he continued, "and that's the point I'm trying to say. We have people in this country who want to attack poppy sellers, and that tells you something – that you've allowed people into your country who are here for a reason and this reason is nothing to do with suffering but is to do with continuing their beliefs without integrating and actually causing trouble to the indigenous people."

He headed in to watch the game.

I had found the conversation challenging, but I didn't want to ignore what he had said. I thought he had conjured a romanticised 1950s England which I suspected had not really existed as he described it, and I felt that part of the response to what he had said was to come up with a vision for Britain's future which was more appealing than his version of its past. I had been troubled when he had said that soldiers were fighting for 'continuity' as opposed to diversity and I wanted to get the views of veterans directly on that question. Yet it was his remark that living in a diverse country was not the same as having a national identity which stayed with me, because while I questioned what underpinned what he was saying, I didn't disagree with the statement. I believed that having a shared national identity in a diverse society was possible, but I felt that if such a shared identity was to be achieved, something beyond ethnicity or religion was needed to bind people. I decided to explore what that might be as I continued my conversations.

*****

Closer to the stadium, I got talking to a woman in her twenties. She told me that in spite of having come to the game to support England, she was not very patriotic.

"I'm half-Italian," she said, "so I tend to edge more towards them."

"I do feel patriotic sometimes," she went on. "I vote and stuff and I care what happens here, but I just don't feel they listen to us."

I asked who 'they' were.

"The Government," she said. "I just don't feel that they put our thoughts into what happens, so that's why I don't support them."

The conversation moved to the referendum, and she told me she felt that Leave voters had been "slightly racist". I asked her why.

"I just think a lot of people voted Leave because they felt like we had too many immigrants," she said, "but actually, if we took everyone away, would England cope? A lot of our workers aren't British, you know? I'm not saying that's 100% the case, but England could fall down…"

I asked if she could see where people who had voted to leave the EU were coming from in terms of their concerns about immigration.

"Do you know what," she said, "I do think it's difficult because living in London is like a mini world, I think we appreciate a lot more cultures – for us, it's normal, whereas I think maybe people from the small villages don't have so many people from other countries, so maybe they just don't understand it which, you know, is fair enough. We live in London, we see so many different people, races and nationalities every day, so for us it's normal."

"Until you experience it," she went on, "you can't understand it, and you realise that people are good, no matter what nationality they come from, no matter what race."

I asked if that meant she worried about nationalism and racism.

"I do," she said, "but I think that's happened for years and I don't think that's ever going to change. I just think that's the way some people are, that's the way they have been brought up. I think saying 'all this racism has come out' – I think it is always there, I just think they chose to show it at that point."

"I think it's going to happen," she went on, "be it that we voted in, be it that we voted out – it happens in every single country. I just think that unfortunately at that time everything was publicised and televised, I think it came out more, but I think it's always there. You know, you see it every day, you see it when you're walking down the street. I just think it's a normal thing."

I said she seemed almost relaxed about it.

"Do you know what," she said, "it's not that I'm relaxed about it, because I think racism is an absolutely disgusting thing and I've experienced it being Italian. But I don't know what you can do to stop it, because that's people's upbringing, that's people's parents who haven't said 'stop, that's wrong', so for them it's probably normal."

I asked whether that meant she would just do her thing and leave other people to do their thing.

"Unfortunately that's just how it is," she said.

She was joined by a friend of the same age, and I asked her what she thought about the referendum.

"I was just massively disappointed by it all really," she said. "Just listening to people's reasons for wanting to leave, people's thoughts on immigration, it made me feel quite sad."

I asked how that made her feel about the country.

"Very divided," she said, "not very unified at all."

I thought back to the owner of the kebab shop, talking about a future that people were working towards together. I asked her whether she thought football matches, where people could come together and express national pride, could help bring people back together.

"It might hinder it a bit," she said as they left. "I mean sport is fine, I don't think there's anything wrong with being here, but things like the EDL mean that national pride has got a bit of a reputation in recent years. It's not necessarily big sporting matches, just big groups of people together, like EDL protests – that's what I'd like to get rid of."

Nearby, a group of Scotland and England fans posed for a photo together, shaking hands warmly as they parted. Next to them, a bagpiper played 'Flower of Scotland' and a woman in a hijab and wearing an England shirt walked by. Next to her, a group of England fans posed for a photo in front of a large England flag. A

Scottish fan ran in front of the group and raised his kilt as the photo was taken.

"Wasn't much to see there," someone shouted.

Behind him, the Scotland fans chanted.

"You are my Scotland, my bonnie Scotland,
You make me happy, when skies are grey,
You are my Scotland, my bonnie Scotland,
Don't you take my Scotland away."

*****

As night fell, the famous Wembley arch lit up in the red and white of England and the atmosphere started to change. A man urinated by the side of the road while another fell into some bushes and had to be helped out by his friends. Scotland fans walking past shouted.

"Let's all laugh at England, let's all laugh at England, la la la la, la la la la."

Another group sang.

"I want to go home, I want to go home, London is a shite-hole, I want to go home."

Kick-off was approaching and the crowds walking down to the stadium thickened. As the fans filed past him, a preacher with a megaphone tried to get their attention.

"God wants us to be playing by the rules on the great pitch of life. God's like the referee on the great pitch of life and he wants us to play by his rules – the Ten Commandments. Read God's rulebook for yourselves, read the Ten Commandments."

"Oh fuck off," someone shouted, and someone else blew a whistle in the preacher's face.

"The devil wants to lead us astray," the preacher continued, "the devil really does exist. Angels and demons, they are around us in the world. Admit that you do need a saviour, that you do indeed need the Lord Jesus in your lives. Do you feel a need for a saviour in your life?"

"No!" someone shouted.

"You don't have time," the preacher went on, "for things that are spiritual. The blood of Jesus was spilled so that we could have community spirit. We do indeed need Jesus in our lives…"

"England!" Some young people shouted over him, "England!"

As the crowd swelled, I moved to the side of the road to let the mass of people pass. Across the road, I noticed a group of young men with a flag bearing the words 'Lest we forget'. One of them saw a woman in a burka walking the other way and shouted "ISIS, ISIS" at her, brandishing his poppy at her before disappearing into the crowd. I tried to find him in the throng, but couldn't.

Nearby, a busker set himself up with a microphone and speakers. As he sang 'Flower of Scotland', an England fan dragged him away from his microphone and others tried to drown him out with a rendition of 'God Save the Queen'. As he moved onto 'Redemption Song', another England fan grabbed his microphone and shouted "Come on England" while his friend kicked at the speakers. Police separated a pair of arguing England and Scotland fans, and as the game neared kick-off, a group of England fans went past singing about the Scottish independence referendum.

> *"We wish you'd said yes,*
> *We wish you'd said yes,*
> *Scotland…*
> *We wish you'd said yes."*

******

In order to try to make sense of what I had seen and heard at Wembley, I arranged to see Alex Smith, a former advisor to Labour leader Ed Miliband and a keen Manchester United fan. We got talking about football rivalry.

"I think it's basically tribal," he told me. "People want to interact with people who are like them, and, to be honest, that's as old as time and even animal in its nature, and I don't think we'll ever be able to avoid it."

"Football historically was a way through which people had a place to rear their own community," he went on, "to feel part of something. I personally derive a huge part of my identity and my character from being exposed to the meaning and the values of Manchester United as a young child. And I think that some of that is in the Manchester United 'myth' – it's anti-establishment, it invests in youth and I always associate myself with those values."

"I'm born and raised in North London," he added, "so that association wasn't derived from a place, it was derived from an idea of what this thing stood for."

This interested me. He had said that tribes were based on groups of people who were like one another, and I reflected that in the past tribes had been based on family, ethnicity, religion, as well as being from the same place. Many football fans considered it totally unacceptable to support any team apart from one's local side, but Alex was talking about something different: values which transcended place, meaning that he could identify with Manchester United even though he wasn't from Manchester. I thought about what the England fan had said about diversity not being the same as national identity and about the idea of multiculturalism, an attitude of 'live and let live' which meant that people in a community or country might live side by side but not be 'bonded' in any particular way. This was, I felt, problematic in terms of creating a sense of community and shared identity, but given that Britain was a country made up of people from different ethnicities and religions, I knew faith and heritage couldn't be the factors which bound everyone together. The values-based approach Alex described, along with the notion of a common future which the kebab shop owner had talked about, seemed to offer a possible way forward.

While I instinctively felt that bonds formed on the basis of shared values and a common future would be richer than bonds relating to ethnicity or heritage, I also knew there were risks in that approach: I wondered what would happen if the reality didn't match up to the values for which the society was supposed to stand and I also knew that there was a danger that a strong sense of common identity – whatever it was based on – would lead to people turning against those who were different. I decided to explore these concerns with Alex, asking first for his thoughts on whether the modern incarnation of Manchester United lived up to the ideals he had described.

"I can't relate to the commercialism of the club," he said, "the fact that it seems to value its support around the world more than its match-going support, because it can monetise that support more easily in selling shirts or through its TV deals around the world. But I also believe because of the heritage of the club that it will continue to be radical and anti-establishment, because it's in its DNA and it's in the supporters' DNA. So right now, most football fans would say 'United is just a huge commercial organisation' but that's not the case for people who believe in the club, the community and what the team is supposed to stand for. For those people, it's a way of life. And if you read the fanzines and you listen to the podcasts or you go to the pubs around the ground before the game, you see all of that founding attitude and that mentality. So it's mythologised because it sells shirts, but it's real for the people who believe it."

I wanted to return to the danger of cynicism developing if a reality didn't match up to a vision, but first, with worries about patriotism boiling over into racism and nationalism in mind, I asked Alex how much of a role rivalry had in creating the sense of identity he had described.

"Football teams always need an opposition," he said. "The reason Manchester United have a rivalry with Liverpool is because it's the other big football powerhouse and it's the other big northern powerhouse city, and therefore there's a natural rivalry between those two. That being said, I'm sure that people in Manchester and Liverpool would for the most part agree that they have something in common – and that's that they're not London. They share an industrial, working-class spirit – so in that sense they're united by values, including being anti-establishment."

"I think of it as sibling rivalry, in some ways," he went on. "Two brothers may spend most of their time at loggerheads but if there's an outside threat, those brothers are completely united against the outside world. The rivalries are only skin-deep – when you have shared values and those values are being attacked, you realise that you have more in common than that sibling rivalry. There's a begrudging understanding and therefore respect between proper United and Liverpool fans – they're all football fans so they don't sing songs about tragedies which have affected the other team like Munich or Hillsborough."

I asked for his reflections on those who did sing such songs.

"It's a minority," he said, "and there's a bit of a mob mentality about it. Pissed up people on a Saturday afternoon will do things that they wouldn't do if they were thinking about it. Also, it's an expression of a broader frustration that's not about Hillsborough or Munich if you really deconstruct it. It's the need to let loose and express your tribal associations in whatever way you can find language for: it's nasty and it's not justifiable but there's a context to why it occurs."

It seemed that he was describing one positive identity based on inclusive values which welcomed anyone and which wasn't bound by place or characterised by hatred of something else, and one less positive identity, defined by anger and confrontation with rivals. Thinking back to my conversations about national identity on

Wembley Way, I asked him if he felt there was a parallel between the positive and negative sides of a shared identity he was describing and the two sides of national identity: patriotism and nationalism.

"Patriotism in my mind is a positive construction," he said, "it is a love for something. It's defined in how you feel about yourself, the people around you, and actually patriotism can extend: some people think of themselves as Londoners or Mancunians, some people think of themselves as English or Scottish or British, some people think of themselves as European or global citizens – and many people think of themselves as many of these identities and more, all at once. And each one of those people can have pride, happiness and patriotism in however they self-identify. Nationalism is different – nationalism is by virtue insular, protectionist, defined against other nations and other people, rather than what you stand for yourself. Maybe there's the possibility that patriotism in one place and patriotism in another place means by extension nationalism as they run up against one another, but in spirit patriotism is positive, it's proud, while nationalism is fearful and small."

"I don't know all the reasons why there is a very nationalistic tone right now," he added, "but I do wish that people were afforded the respect and freedom to feel patriotic. I do suspect that part of the reason for our current nationalism is that patriotism was discouraged for too long – that positive, affirmed shared national identity and that positivity about who we are. There wasn't enough conversation about that at a time when the world was changing faster than it's ever changed before, and denying people that opportunity to talk about how they feel and who they are has led to the fearfulness and the smallness and the insularity of nationalism."

"If people can't feel comfortable with a flag that stands for nothing but the nation then you're in big trouble," he continued. "You know, be offended by the Far Right and the National Front and the organisations that want to stress our differences in a negative, divisive sense, but our job is to take the flag back so it can be a unifier."

"I'm not a big Tony Blair fan," he added, "but his style of communications was much more in line with what the country as a whole believes than anything the Labour Party has managed at any other point in my lifetime. New Labour used the Union Jack in its literature, in its campaigning, in its manifesto, at its conference – the Union Jack was everywhere. Blair was very clever, he was very good on economic security, on physical security – defence, crime – and on cultural security."

Before he left, I asked Alex for his thoughts on cultural security, as this was clearly a major emerging theme. I wondered if he felt there was a danger that building a stronger sense of British culture would mean that Britain turned its back on migrants and on global issues.

"I think while people do associate with tribe," he said as he went, "if they feel secure within that tribe, they're more likely to be less fearful of a different tribe. So I don't think community is in any way a closed thing – on the contrary, I think community is about being hospitable and welcoming and open towards other people – you know, 'you might be from a different culture, but I want you to come round and see how I do Christmas Day'."

It seemed a crucial point. Far from stoking division, there was a case to be made that if people were secure in their identity and their place in the world, they would be more likely to reach out to others. I wondered how that sense of security could be built, and whether a sense of shared values, common endeavour and a shared future could be part of the answer. I still had my concerns, however: I didn't know whether in order to create a sense of a national story, a country needed a common enemy or a romantic notion of the nation – like 1950s England – which might push a country to make bad decisions based not on reality, but on a myth.

As I left Alex, I though back to the young man at Wembley brandishing the poppy at the woman in the burka. It had been a deeply unpleasant moment, and it made me think about the dangers of a sense of common identity boiling over into hatred or exclusion of others and the ways in which symbols could be misused. It seemed that the issue of national identity was highly combustible and should be approached with care, but I also reflected that the evidence from my travels so far was that the risks of prejudice and hate were there whatever I did. Better, I felt, to come up with a positive response than to leave such feelings to fester.

5

Power, prestige and service in Whitehall

In Whitehall on Remembrance Sunday, veterans heading towards the Cenotaph mixed with tourists taking photos. The sun was shining, it was cold and the mood was sombre. Having been full of beeping taxis the last time I was there, Whitehall was now empty of cars and quiet. An elderly veteran slipped over and police officers rushed to help him up. Old friends shook hands and hugged one other. Young cadets mixed with older veterans and a man held a baby wearing a tiny poppy pin. Opposite Downing Street, where I had met the taxi drivers a few days earlier, the press had gathered to take photos, and the crowd applauded politely as the procession of military personnel started to come through, halting just before the Cenotaph. A woman in a wheelchair got up from her seat to try to see. The Union Flag flew high in the sunshine.

It had interested me that people I had met on my travels had summoned what soldiers had fought for in the war as supporting their vision of the kind of country Britain should be. The woman in Sunderland who had told me she would never vote UKIP had said that doing so would have been a betrayal of those who had fought for the country, while the man at Wembley a couple of days earlier had said that British soldiers had been fighting for continuity, not diversity. The argument about what the military had fought for seemed to go to the heart of what the nation was for and about, so I had come to Whitehall hoping to enable veterans to speak for themselves on the issue.

As a marching band went past, people took photos on their mobile phones, and a few parents put their children on their shoulders so that they could see. Big screens showed how packed Whitehall was, the crowds eight or nine deep. Outside the barrier, members of the public mixed with service personnel. A father and his son posed for a selfie: the son complained of the cold and the man rubbed his hands together to keep warm. A young woman clambered up the railings to get a better view.

"It's not comfortable," she said, "but I might get a photo of the Queen."

"There's very few of these World War Two boys now," an older woman said, as a group of older veterans passed by, some pushed in wheelchairs, others walking with guide dogs.

The marching band played Rule Britannia, and next to me someone sang along.

"Rule Britannia! Britannia rule the waves!
Britons never, never, never shall be slaves!"

As it neared eleven, the politicians started to appear.

"Is TB there?" A woman asked, and on cue Tony Blair came into shot on a big screen.

"Boris scrubs up rather well," another woman said as the Foreign Secretary came out.

At eleven, gunfire rang out and a woman in front of me jumped in shock. Whitehall fell silent. The Queen and Duke of Edinburgh appeared and the Lord's Prayer was read. A woman next to me said it to herself, and I could hear it whispered along Whitehall.

*"Our Father, who art in heaven
Hallowed be thy name
Thy kingdom come,
Thy will be done,
On earth, as it is in heaven."*

Having laid their wreaths, the royal family, politicians and other dignitaries disappeared as 'God Save the Queen' was played. The lady next to me sang along. A brass band played 'It's a Long Way to Tipperary' and the crowds began to disperse.

By a nearby pub, I met a veteran who had served in the Falklands and the first Gulf War. We got talking about the nature of being a soldier sent abroad to fight when directed to do so by politicians.

"That's what happens when you're a government employee," he told me. "You're a civil servant – if they say 'go to war', that's what you get paid for. You could be a conscientious objector, but why are you in the Forces if you are?"

"The Iraq one I didn't particularly agree with," he went on, "particularly because we were on the tails of America, in their slipstream, and they haven't found any Weapons of Mass Destruction either. I think Tony Blair is a war criminal and I think he should be accounted for."

"Now on the Falklands," he went on, "they invaded British territory so that's a different thing, but when it's Iraq – they said about Weapons of Mass Destruction and terrorists, but look at it now… It's ten times worse since America, with Britain, went in. So it's wrong, it's wrong."

I asked if he wasn't always in agreement with the politicians, what he was putting his life on the line for.

"Queen and country," he said.

I asked him to expand a little on that.

"Well, it's the people of Britain, isn't it," he said, "it's the British domain. Politicians are politicians, but you're fighting for freedoms, aren't you?"

He seemed uncomfortable, finished his cigarette quickly, thanked me and was gone.

Nearby, I met a man who had served in Northern Ireland four times and in the first Gulf War. I asked him what he'd been fighting for.

"There was no jobs," he said, "so I joined the army."

"I've got a lot of old comrades," he went on, "and reunions and that sort of thing means a lot. It's less about the country and more about the uniform, the camaraderie, that sort of thing."

"All these lads together," he said, pointing at groups of people walking past, "they ain't here for Queen and country, they're here for each other."

"We're not the country we were any more, are we?" he added.

I asked him why he felt that.

"We've lost our place in the world," he said, "politicians are wrecking everything."

"You could fit the British army in Wembley now," he went on. "We had 200,000 people out in Germany for God knows how long, and they were a permanent standing army. Say in the Falklands, if the British said 'we're coming to get it back' then we'd go and get it back. We could never, ever, ever do that now."

"On the international stage," he continued, "I would say that Britain has become a third-rate power after India, China, even Russia... all the older guys are being pensioned out, and the army is shrinking and shrinking and shrinking and it's got no backbone anymore."

"You used to get posted all around the world," he added, "but now if you get posted, you get posted from Catterick to Grantham..."

He laughed to himself.

"When I joined up in 1980," he continued, "there was a petrol strike. Maggie caused it, and they called in the army and they had the resources in the army to provide that sort of service. Now they just wouldn't have the resources. Then they had, I don't know, 600,000 active troops to call upon; now they've got 56,000."

"Every old sweat will tell you that it was different in the old days," he added, "but nowadays I think we are, dare I say, puppets to America. If America wants to go to war, we're the first team they go to, and we validate what they do because they seem to be scared to go by themselves. And we just trail along behind them, borrowing all their equipment."

"Maggie was the last one who was independent," he went on, "and I hated her. She was a horrible bitch, but she was the last one who had any balls about her. The rest of them, they're getting what they can out of it."

As we talked, the conversation moved to his time in Northern Ireland.

"When we were over there," he said, "the motivation was that they were coming for us by killing people at traffic lights, blowing bombs up at barracks, killing people at petrol stations, putting bombs under squaddies' cars outside their homes. They were coming to get us, so we went to get them."

I asked whether the 'us' was the army rather than the country.

"Yes," he said, "it's like when I was in Germany – I brought my family up there, my kids went to squaddie school, and my motivation if we'd had to fight the Russians was to give them time to escape. It wasn't about what was happening in London or Washington, it was all about getting the kids and the missus a chance to get on the train to the coast or wherever it was."

"It's the goldfish bowl looking out," he went on, "whatever happened outside the goldfish bowl wasn't of any interest to you – if they were attacking the next division, then that was fine – they weren't attacking us. My logic was that they could look after themselves and that if we were attacked that we could look after ourselves."

He looked out at the people looking past.

"I see lots of youngsters here," he said, "I wish I was that young again."

"I know it's all about saving money now," he went on, "but some things should be sacrosanct. You've got bases closing and they're going to ruin communities, and once they're gone, they're gone and fallen into tatters and there's not much chance of them coming back."

I asked what he meant by 'ruined communities'.

"Like the Welsh bases," he said, "they've been part of the Welsh community that they've been in in the South of Wales, and they're no longer going to be there. There's going to be no more representation of the British Army in Wales – there'll be a recruiting office in Cardiff maybe. There used to be a lot of Welsh regiments. There's one single Welsh regiment now."

"It's just strange," he went on, "that they think it's ok to sell the barracks to some property owner who's going to make billions out of it by building however many houses. Same with the airbases in Lincolnshire – they closed them down, sold them off for pennies, and somebody is going to make £500m on them. It's just a nonsense, and we're never going to get it back. And if we need it, there's not going to be the backbone there to hold up the rest of the body."

As we parted, a brass band came past playing 'Rule Britannia'.

*****

Further down, three soldiers were enjoying a drink outside a pub. I asked them about what the previous man had said to me about fighting for Queen and country.

"When you're out in these places," one said, "that's at the back of your mind. The people you are there with, your comrades, that's who you want to look after and protect."

"It's a brotherhood," his friend said.

"Yeah," the first man said, "that's the best way to describe it. And you know the bigger picture is that this terrorist organisation could take over the world, ruin Britain – you do think of that, but it comes right at the back of the list."

"We're proud to do what we're being paid to do," the second man said. "We are one of the smallest countries in the world but we're one of the most powerful countries in the world and we're trained as one of the best armies in the world. You sign up because you know the British military is an institution, the best institution I've ever been part of."

I suggested that they were saying that their pride came from the institution rather than the country.

"Both," he said. "We're one of the best armies in the world. Even if it's just marching up and down to Buckingham Palace, there's children from all around the world that know about that. There's a lot of pride in that, you can't beat that."

"But we're less in manpower now than they are in Tesco's," his friend said. "If we went into battle with Tesco's they would probably bean us to death. It sort of makes you think."

"But modern technology is coming along now," the first man said, and they talked for a while about whether technology could replace 'boots on the ground'. I wanted to move the conversation on from what was becoming quite a technical discussion, so I asked them about the man at Wembley who had said that 'continuity' – as opposed to growing diversity – was what soldiers had fought for.

"I'm a firm believer," the first soldier said, "that with the Commonwealth, all them nations that we've worked with, and if you look over the years, we've always worked with these nations, we've come together. There's loads of people who have put their lives down fighting with Britain, and there's loads of history that people forget."

"They don't forget," his friend said, "they're ignorant to it."

"What I'd say though," the third soldier, who had been quiet up until now, said, "is that what an average serviceperson would like to see is for us to look after our own country more."

I asked him what he meant.

"It's a really hard one to explain," he said, "because we know that we've got Commonwealth soldiers coming in and we look after them and we're all part of the same thing, but it's like, sometimes, you see things on telly or on the news about giving away aid to other countries, but there's soldiers on the streets of London that are homeless. If we can't look after them…"

"It's probably just that the news is putting the wrong stuff on there," he added after a moment, "but our foreign policy is sometimes a bit too one way: we're looking after everybody else but we can't look after our own."

I asked him for an example.

"Ok," he said, "well the amount of immigrants we have coming in, and we have all this extra housing. Where I live now, it's one of the biggest towns in the country, we've got all these houses, but yet we've still got homeless people. So why are we building houses to take people from all across Europe when we can't look after our own? It seems wrong."

I suggested that immigration brought people who contributed to the British economy which in turn paid for the armed forces, housing and other infrastructure.

"Well no it doesn't," he said, "because they don't pay tax. I work in an industry where people have been brought in from across Europe to work in the fields and I know they're paid cash-in-hand, there's no tax being regenerated back into the system. It's fine if they're doctors or professional people and they're putting something back and supporting us – which a lot of them do, don't get me wrong – but if they're not paying that tax or the national insurance, then all they're doing is taking."

A member of the public walked over as we were talking.

"Excuse me," he said, "can I just say thank you very much indeed? If it wasn't for your bravery…"

They all shook hands with him, and exchanged a few words. When the man had left, I asked if that happened a lot.

"Quite a few times," he said.

"He felt sorry for you," his friend joked, "he thought you were homeless."

"Just going back to what I was saying," the man continued, ignoring his friend, "I've met people from Kosovo who have come here for a better life and they're contributing towards the UK. They're working hard, they're paying taxes, that's awesome. But then you've got a minority that don't do that… But then you've got a minority who are born and bred British that don't contribute too so it's one of them things…"

"What we see in the papers," he went on, "sometimes it can be so negative – it never puts the positive side like 'some guys have come over from another country, they've contributed, they've set up their own business, they're looking after a little village'. I basically subject myself to the news and the papers very little now because I know that the negative stuff seems to get people in, where the positive stuff doesn't."

A man pushed a woman in full uniform past in a wheelchair, and one of the soldiers I was talking to made a playful joke about stripes the woman had on the wheelchair, which matched the stripes on her uniform.

"Call me ma'am when you say that," she said, and his mates laughed at him.

"You just got owned," one of them said, "pulling rank on you!"

They talked to her for a few minutes about where they had all served. The camaraderie was clear, warm and genuine.

The soldiers I had been talking to had to go.

"It *is* Queen and country," one said as they left, "because when they do the national anthem there's always a lump in my throat, always stand to attention. It's pride and it is the Empire. All I'm trying to say is that when we're out on the ground, in these environments, we're miles away from the UK, we're protecting each other. But the bigger picture is the Empire, because we don't want the Taliban on our streets and all the rest of it. So it is about that, but when you're out in those places, you're protecting the people around you. It's about teamwork…"

"Teamwork makes the dream work," said his friend, and shook my hand.

*****

As the crowds began to disperse, I walked away from Whitehall, looking for more people to speak to. In a cafe at the north-west corner of Trafalgar Square, I got talking to a man in his twenties, Grant, who told me he had set up an organisation working with homeless people and regularly met former members of the Armed Forces sleeping rough on London's streets.

"A lot of these guys' stories are really similar to my story," he told me. "I'm a recovering alcoholic, I've spent nights on the street, and the other night I met a guy who had been in the Royal Scots Guards. He'd suffered with addiction issues, I've suffered with addiction issues; he'd suffered from schizophrenia, people in my family have suffered from schizophrenia. He was an articulate guy and he served in our armed forces, and he said it himself: 'we all wear poppies once a year but do we really help these people the rest of the time?'"

"I'm not saying this in a racist way," he went on, "but we'll look after the Somalian guy who has come in with nine children and when you see a guy who served in the Scots Guards, it makes me think 'actually, is our government really serving the people it should serve?' And I don't say this in a racist way, but I don't see why we should put someone from a Somalian family in a home ahead of someone from our armed forces. I see that and I think 'what the hell are we doing?'"

"People feel that the government are putting more emphasis on people who have never served this country ahead of people who have served this country," he continued, "and once you have that situation, you will see a rise in anger. No-one's addressed it, and it's not because politicians are bad people, it's because they're so protective about being PC now and it's a real problem, because Nigel Farage and Donald Trump are un-PC and people want to hear it. They say things that will make people in the liberal elite go 'oh, that's horrible', but in truth most people out there want to hear it. They want to hear that we are going to be tough on immigration, we are going to be tough on refugees, and unfortunately that's where it's at. And Labour and the moderate Tories like David Cameron have ignored these people for far too long."

He told me that he was from the political Left but he understood why people voted for Donald Trump and supported Nigel Farage.

"I respect Farage," he said. "I don't agree with everything he says but I respect what he's done, I think it's incredible. That guy went around saying it for twenty years when everyone else was too scared. I mean, do you remember the Rotherham kiddie-fiddling scandal with the Asian people? The Labour politicians were saying 'we can't criticise this community, we can't say anything about this'. And that's what's broken the Labour Party's support amongst the working classes. They've gone 'fuck these people, we're not listening to a word they say any more'."

His arguments about political correctness were challenging but important and I resolved to return to them on my journey. Yet it was his argument about 'service' which stuck with me. It seemed to be underpinned by the notion that those who had contributed more – in this case soldiers risking their lives in Britain's armed forces – deserved more than those who weren't British or who had contributed less – in this case, migrants or refugees from Somalia. The idea that those who had risked their lives in service of the country deserved special treatment seemed reasonable to me, but I wondered if that argument could be made without referencing people from a war-torn country like Somalia. In some ways, the question of relative priority of people who had served in the military compared to people from abroad felt like a red herring – as it seemed possible to support both – but I did accept that in a time of scarce resources, choices would have to be made. I knew that before I concluded my travels I would need to address in my own mind the question of 'looking after our own' once and for all.

*****

I'd seen a number of peace campaigners around Whitehall and when I saw them congregated at a pub at the top of Trafalgar Square, I went over. One of the leaders, Andy, told me he had been a soldier and now worked with other veterans in the UK and US to organise campaigns for peace.

"We're trying to speak out against war," he told me, "and against the fact that British Armed Forces have been deployed in almost every country across the globe. We think that British troops should be removed from overseas, that British troops should not be fighting wars of imperialism, or neo-imperialism if you like."

"We're also against the proliferation of nuclear weapons," he went on. "We're against Trident, obviously. And we're against the whole culture of the military, of the armed forces – the 'warfare state' as we call it."

I asked what he meant by the 'warfare state'.

"We believe Britain is a particularly 'war-y' nation," he said, and pointed into Trafalgar Square, towards Nelson's Column. "You only have to look up there to see a statue of a guy who fought in a war – he's commemorated as one of our greatest heroes. Surrounding him are statues of generals from the Indian Mutiny who were really bloodthirsty characters. This is a 'warfare state': it basks in its top killers. We're trying to get people to understand that that's not what life is about, it's what death is about, and we're about life and health and peace."

I asked what he thought about what some of the soldiers I'd met had said about the sense of prestige coming from the military.

"But why should we revel in the prestige of machines and organisations which are made for violence and killing and maiming?" he responded. "There's a lot more to British history and British contemporary society than an organised killing machine. You know, there's literature, there's art, there's culture, there's the National Health Service, there's the efforts that workers put in, there's education. There's all these things when we're talking about British prestige that we can drink from that will be a lot more fulfilling than death and violence. Who benefits from it? Who gets something out of it? We don't. The money that's being spent on the armed forces, on the warfare state, is being diverted from the poorest and most vulnerable in society."

"Let's take Trident," he went on. "It costs billions and billions and billions, and if you ploughed that back into the economy we'd all be a lot healthier and better disposed towards each other, a lot more educated, a lot happier, a more equal society. And there's also the argument about what the armed forces are protecting us from. The French aren't going to invade us any more, Hitler's gone. There's no invasion threat and the harmony of the world doesn't exist because of aggression or armed threats – it exists because of people wanting to help each other out. One of our greatest inventions was the idea of socialism, and arguably the idea of communism. It's that brotherhood, that sisterhood, people working together. It's that social democracy which you could argue was awarded to people in 1945 after fighting two world wars. And now that they're dying off, we're going back 100 or 200 years."

He looked over at the statue of Lord Nelson.

"It's an architectural masterpiece," he said, "but it's phallic as well, isn't it? It's a column for fuck's sake. But it's there, it's blended in – people don't know about the killing and the maiming that happened at the Battle of Trafalgar. You know, it was appalling, utterly terrifying – there were something like 10,000 dead in one afternoon, and these men, they weren't fallen, they were ripped to pieces. And we're celebrating that?"

I asked if he thought it should be taken down. He shook his head.

"Where would you stop?" he asked. "Some of these buildings represent the wealth and power of a tiny elite – the National Gallery was built with money from the slave trade, but it's melted in, it's part of what London is. And if we were taught history in a different way and people learnt about things in a different way, and didn't learn about the glory but learned about the suffering, we could leave it there, but we might think of it a bit differently and learn from it."

I suggested he was talking about a big change in national attitudes and our sense of what the nation was, giving the example of the huge popularity of the Poppy Appeal.

"It never used to be like this," he said. "Soldiers were never seen as heroes: young men would go out to garrison towns and do squaddie bashing. Soldiers were the lowest of the low, and coincidence or not, the remilitarisation of society has coincided with two overseas wars of invasion and occupation. Poppy Sunday used to just be Poppy Sunday, there never used to be a month of it like the build-up to Christmas. It's glorifying war to justify the warfare state."

I asked why, if that was the case, so many people had come out.

"They're tourists," he said. "It's become a festival, a jamboree…"

"That guy," he went on, nodding towards a military officer in full uniform walking past, "he's walking with a swagger, he's very well turned-out. That doesn't look mournful or sorrowful to me. And getting rat-arsed in the pub – that isn't mournful or sorrowful.

In the 1920s, war veterans staged a protest on Armistice Day and marched past Downing Street with pawn tickets in their lapels because they had to sell their medals to feed their children or put a roof over their head. They were protesting against the lie that Britain was 'a land fit for heroes'. That was the original guys who fought at the Somme. They were angry, but now it's turned into a celebration of militarism."

I suggested that many people wanted to thank the soldiers for their bravery.

"But what are we thanking them for?" he said. "For invading Iraq and Afghanistan? Why should we thank them for that? Why would we thank them for going into Northern Ireland, going into people's houses in snatch squads and breaking people's faces open with their rifle butts?"

"If we were to talk about history," he went on, "we could say that arguably the Second World War was the only just war. But how many Second World War vets are actually here? Not many. And how many other wars were actually about the defence of this country? You've got to go back to the Battle of Hastings, and then you've got to ask who the 'we' is? The ethnicity and the make-up of the country has changed completely since 1066, so you've got to ask what are 'we' thanking 'them' for?"

I asked for his view on the Falklands conflict.

"That's an interesting case," he said, "and if you compare and contrast it to the treatment of the people of Diego Garcia, where they were just chucked out of their islands and American planes and listening devices were moved in – the Diego Garcians are still asking for their islands back... But coincidentally or not, the Falklands War got Margaret Thatcher a massive majority in 1983. Her popularity was failing before that, and then it was soaring."

"Everything's politics," he added, "and politicians use the army as their tool."

"It's a cultural tool, too," he went on, "and economic. We're the second biggest arms seller in the world and we do really well out of that. Promoting that doesn't just help politicians, it also helps really powerful businessmen too."

I asked what he'd meant about it being a cultural tool.

"It permeates the kind of cultural thought of society," he said. "At the Cenotaph we read a poem written by Siegfried Sassoon called Suicide in the Trenches, and the last verse is: *You smug-faced crowds with kindling eye/Who cheer when soldier lads march by/Sneak home and pray you'll never know/The hell where youth and laughter go.* And a lot of people are encouraged to cheer – it's a very rousing thing when you see a smart unit of soldiers in uniform, glittering medals and all that kind of stuff, and it does something to the crowd – it makes you think 'hooray' and it creates a kind of groupthink. There's something animalistic about it as well – you know, when you're a little boy, you get very excited about that kind of thing and it's like going back to childhood. It's very subtle, but it's quite base and very seductive."

I asked how soldiers responded when they heard him saying such challenging things.

"This is the only time when we physically mix with them," he said, "and there's a range of human emotion from derision and anger and mockery to bemusement, because we're rocking their world… They've constructed a safe world for themselves where everything is ok: we're in a democracy, the price of fish is good – you know, there's nothing to worry about, apart from immigrants or whatever, and then when they see us it's like 'what the fuck?'"

He needed to go, but he wanted to tell me about another poem before he went.

"It's by Sassoon and it's called 'At the Cenotaph'," he said. "It could have been written in Blair's era, because it's written about the devil who goes to the cenotaph in the guise of an ordinary person, and when he bows at the Cenotaph, he's saying 'oh God, please make these people believe that war is good, that war is purgatory and good for the soul'."

I asked if he meant that Remembrance Sunday was being used that way by modern politicians.

"It's not boots on the ground now," he said, "it's drones and stuff, but it's still out there killing."

As we parted, I looked up the poem on my phone:

'I saw the Prince of Darkness, with his Staff,
Standing bare-headed by the Cenotaph:
Unostentatious and respectful, there
He stood, and offered up the following prayer.
Make them forget, O Lord, what this Memorial
Means; their discredited ideas revive;
Breed new belief that War is purgatorial
Proof of the pride and power of being alive'

*****

At a pub around the corner, I talked to an ex-serviceman called Kevin who was smoking a cigarette outside. He was wearing five medals and he talked me through them.

"The first three are service," he told me. "You've got Kosovo, Afghanistan, Iraq, and then you've got the Diamond Jubilee Medal and the Volunteer Reserve Service medal, and the last two are there purely for show."

I asked him for his view on the peace campaigners I had just met. He told me he wasn't convinced by them and we got talking about the statue of Admiral Nelson.

"When it comes to statues," he said, "they're part of the history. No one saw a statue of a dead general on a horse and thought 'Yeah, I'm going to join the military'."

"Now having said that," he went on, "I think we have taken on from America a bit of this veteran worship thing – it's a bit like America sneezes and we catch a cold. In America it's partially because in the 1960s and 70s, they had conscripts who came home from wars they didn't want to fight in and who were treated in a horrendous manner, and there's a horrendous sense of guilt there, so they now have this sort of veteran worship. They don't have Remembrance Day, they have Veterans Day, and every veteran gets to eat for free in restaurants and so on. And that has started to roll over here, so every military charity refers to everyone who wore a uniform ever as a hero, and that's not healthy."

"A lot of guys who served in Afghan never saw combat," he continued, "but we're starting to venerate people, and I personally don't think it's going to end well, especially as we get into peacetime. Whilst we should honour those who come home and support those with wounds, holding up some guy who just finished his Phase One becoming a truck driver in the Royal Logistics Corps as a hero is probably not where we want to be."

"It's a tough one," he went on, "because there are guys coming back and they need support, but it should be support, it shouldn't be an automatic level of respect. Now don't get me wrong, as a veteran, I'm not going to turn down a 10% discount on BA flights, but then you hear about SeaWorld in the States: the veterans get a separate area to sit and then at the start they ask the veterans to stand up and everyone cheers them. Is that really healthy? I don't think so."

His friends came out and started chatting. One noticed my jacket, which was made by the outdoor company Berghaus. The company's logo was on the breast, about the same place that everyone else was wearing their medals.

"Ah, I remember the battle of Berghaus," he said, gently mocking the lack of medals on my chest.

The jokes continued and everyone seemed happy but when the conversation turned to a friend who had been lost in battle, the mood changed immediately, and a sad silence fell. It was a private moment, and I didn't want to intrude. As I left, a man appeared with a bugle and played 'The Last Post'. Everyone outside the pub stopped talking and stood to attention.

*****

I walked back up to Trafalgar Square, and noticed the military iconography Andy had mentioned. Nelson's Column dominated the square and was surrounded by huge lions. On three of the four plinths there were statues of military figures, and I thought back to what Andy had said. I had disagreed with him on a lot, particularly his suggestion that the soldiers were simply in Whitehall for a 'jamboree', but he, and the other former soldiers I had met, had made me think about the nature of national pride and prestige. While I didn't feel as negative about Britain's military past as he clearly did and I didn't share his view that World War Two was the only just war Britain had fought, I could see why soldiers would be angry with politicians who they mistrusted taking them into foreign wars.

I thought about the implications of the conversations I had had over the course of the day. I felt the country needed to find a way to look after veterans who had been hurt or harmed in service of the country without idolising every member of the armed forces or losing a sense of responsibility to people from outside the UK. I also thought the country needed to be able to look at itself proudly without being defined by size of its armed forces – after all, I felt that Andy was absolutely right that there was much in Britain to be proud of besides the military. In thinking about that military past, I also agreed with Andy that the military statues should remain: they were, for better or worse, part of our history, and I couldn't help thinking that if Britain was to progress, it needed to develop a more nuanced way of thinking about that history which avoided both blanket shame and blanket pride.

In Trafalgar Square, the flags of 75 countries had been chalked on the ground and the artist was inviting tourists from those countries to put a coin down on their flag. The flags included England, Scotland, Wales and Cornwall, as well as Poland, Greece, Trinidad and Tobago, Colombia, the Czech Republic, Latvia, Ukraine, the US, Israel, Australia and New Zealand.

"All the flags is one," he said. "If we combine all the flags the same into one, no anymore war. One flat world and then there will be peace and love."

As tourists came and put their coins down in the shadow of Admiral Nelson, a busker played 'Redemption Song' and the bells of St Martin's Church rang out.

6

Nostalgia, change and political correctness in Blackpool

I headed north, bound for Blackpool, where I wanted to think more about British culture and the country's relationship with its past. There had been heavy storms the night before, and as the train trundled along, the two women in the seats next to me complained about the weather.

"Might see some flooding," one said.

"Yeah, maybe," said the other.

The ticket inspector came past.

"Two returns to Blackpool," one said.

The inspector issued their tickets, large print-outs with a scannable code.

"They're the new kind of tickets," the inspector explained. "Not exactly saving the planet but they'll get you through the barriers. Just scan them like you would at the airport."

"I never go to the airport," one of the women said.

"Well give it a try," said the inspector, "or just ask the staff at the station and they'll help you".

"I guess that's what progress looks like," said the other woman as she looked at the ticket with disdain.

*****

I was in Blackpool to look at British culture and identity and James Bamford, a man in his thirties, had offered to take me around the town.

As we drove towards the seafront, we went past the Comrades Club, a former club for service personnel, now boarded up, and an old church which was being knocked down. We reached the promenade which was packed with cafes, sweet shops and amusement arcades. Fish and chips were advertised for £2.95, while the Merry England was selling pints of McEwan's for £1.95.

"Everyone thinks of Blackpool, they think of the front," James said, "and it is a nice place to go for a walk, look over the Irish Sea and the Bay, see across to the Lakes, North Wales. It's just when you go a few streets back that it gets a bit grim – terraced streets, B&Bs and whatever. A lot of it is very dilapidated."

"As long as you look that way," he added, indicating towards the Tower and out to sea, "it's lovely."

We parked and walked onto the Promenade. It was a cold, sunny Saturday in November, and there was a buzz around the town with a local football derby against Wigan that afternoon and *Strictly Come Dancing* filming in the ballroom at the Blackpool Tower that evening.

At the Tower, the police were out in force as the BBC filmed the programme's judges getting into a gilded horse-drawn carriage and setting off on a trip down the seafront. A police officer shivered in the cold. A car drew up and one of the presenters, Tess Daly, got out and waved to the crowd. While Remembrance Sunday had passed, many of the people watching on still sported poppies.

"Nice to have a bit of glitz and glamour," a woman in the crowd said to her friend. I went over and asked who she was supporting.

"Ed Balls," she replied firmly.

James told me he was a big fan of the show.

"Dancing is a big part of British heritage," he said. "That's what you did on a Saturday, you went to the local dance and that's how you'd socialise. And that way of going out has been lost – it was a bit more of a nicey-nicey affair than in the nightclub after ten shots. But that's what you did, you wanted to try to ask a girl out, you went to the dance."

"*Strictly* mixes that old and new," he went on. "It brings older and younger people together, which I think is important. I watch with my mum, which is a nice way to spend time with her – the classic British thing of all the family watching telly together."

"It's escapism, isn't it?" he added. "You know, if things were different, Ed Balls could be Chancellor living in Number 11. Instead, he's in Blackpool in a sequin shirt, having a great time."

I asked what escapism meant to him.

"Everyone's got things in their lives," he said, "and if they can escape from it for a few hours that's good; whether it's watching *Strictly* or playing football or reading a book, you need a way just to switch off. It doesn't mean the world is going to change or stop. Everyone needs an escape – the glitz and glamour and the showbiz, all that kind of stuff, bit of nostalgia, that's it."

Thinking back to my conversations in London, I asked about his reflections on nostalgia.

"You should celebrate your past," he said, "and learn from it too, because if you don't learn from the mistakes from the past, that's a worry isn't it? You know, airbrushed history, that's not a good thing and obviously Britain's history is not exactly very glittering, and you wonder whether a lot of British people really know about history and our empire-building."

I suggested a lot of people would talk proudly about Britain's history.

"Mmmm," he said, "because their understanding wouldn't connect with the reality that we invaded and took over and said 'here's our flag, we're in charge, thanks very much'. We don't mind imposing on other people but we don't like being imposed on ourselves."

"You saw that in the referendum campaign," he went on. "These are emotive issues and these are what drive a lot of people to vote.

They see it as a threat to their way of life – whether that's true or not I don't know. Obviously in this area it's not because there aren't different cultures living here. I think having people from all over the world to meet, different ways of life, different beliefs, that's a good thing – better than being insular."

The word 'insular', literally describing being 'like an island', struck me as I looked out to sea at the edge of Britain. I wondered if he thought nostalgia was dangerous.

"No-one's perfect," he said, "everyone makes mistakes. The question is do you learn from mistakes or do you repeat them? That's when education comes in – you've got to make sure that youngsters know about the mistakes so that when they grow up and are running the country, they won't make them."

I asked how he thought that was going. He laughed.

"Not very well," he said. "Maybe the people who are running the country now are clinging on to the Empire days. It's not right, but people buy into it because they have insecurities and identify with it, so they vote for it."

"It is very emotional," he added, "because we're all human, we're all stories in the end."

I said that 'we're all stories' was a nice way of putting it.

"It's from *Dr Who*," he said, "but it's true, we're all stories. The Empire, that's a story: it's history, but it's a story. Was it Churchill who said 'history is written by the victors'?"

"We're all humans," he added. "That's the point, and all this time spent putting imaginary borders on the ground… the question is 'who's going to have the balls to change something?'"

*****

I decided to talk to people on the Comedy Carpet, a pedestrian area on the promenade under the Tower where the jokes and songs of comedians who had performed in Blackpool in years gone by were inscribed on the pavement. By a pavestone with the inscription, 'Britain, Britain, Britain, it's been called heaven on earth and it's easy to see why', I met a couple from Coventry who had travelled up for a soul music weekend. They told me they felt that Blackpool comedy was an important part of British national life and I asked them why.

"It's history, it's tradition," the woman said. "It's like the old-fashioned postcard humour."

"Everything's dying out," her husband said. "Everything's being put on the tablet or the internet now. You sit in a pub and all you see is people on their tablets and they don't talk. Whereas this, it's brilliant. I've walked round and laughed me head off at almost every one of the jokes."

I asked whether they felt that the music hall comedy of the past had been sexist and racist.

"That's down to you," the man said. "If you go into one of them shows, like Joey Blower, you've got to go in there with a sense that you're going to get the piss taken out of you, and if you don't, you're going to be offended. If he spots you, he's going to have a go at you and you've just got to ride it. If somebody took the mickey out of me, I'd give them as good back as what I got – see if they said something like 'oh, you're little' – because I'm five-foot-four – I'd have a crack back at them and take it as a joke. I'd enjoy the banter."

I asked about jokes which had been told which had suggested women couldn't play a full and equal role in society. I wondered if they were troubled by that kind of comedy.

"I think people like that are dying out," the man said. "I think that's the kind of thing people like Bernard Manning would do. I think women now have a more equal equality – but then again, it's down to the same thing: if it's meant to make you laugh, you've got to not be offended by it."

"There's that many channels on the telly," his wife said, "if you don't like it, don't watch it. Turn over."

I asked whether they felt that humour contributed to wider social attitudes, for example jokes against Irish people contributing to a situation where Irish immigrants had been treated as second-class citizens.

"Things have changed a lot now," the man said. "You can't pick on the races now."

"I think it was yesterday," he went on, "I saw a Scottish Chinese, I couldn't believe it when she opened her mouth. She was as Chinese as you can imagine, she had the slanty eyes and everything. But then she opened her mouth and she had a Scottish accent and I thought 'I've seen it all now'."

"It's the same as *Porridge*," he went on. "You had that Glaswegian on there, coloured fella – it had never been seen before. And when he come on and everyone went 'they don't have them in Scotland'. But they do."

"It was accepted then," the woman said. "Like the old comedy programmes. You know like, what was that one that was always abusive? Alf Garnett. That just wouldn't be accepted now. And, people watching it now, I can see what they mean, but in our day it was just accepted."

I asked if they thought it was a good thing that times had changed.

"I do," the man said, "because Bernard Manning, in the day, he sold out – people wanted to hear that kind of stuff."

"But equality has just gone wild," he went on. "You've got to watch what you say and watch what you do, because one little word could offend somebody. I think it has got a bit sad because sometimes you could have a laugh but now you have to watch what you say because some people find it abusive. Comedy shouldn't be like that – comedy should be 'if it makes you laugh, then listen to it'."

"Kids now probably wouldn't laugh at what we laughed at in the Sixties and Seventies and Eighties," he added. "They wouldn't

Nostalgia, change and political correctness in Blackpool

get half the jokes, because they've grown up with the idea that the coloureds and the Irish, you've got to treat them equal, where in our day it was totally different. You weren't biased against the Irish, but the Irish got the mickey taken out of them the whole time and it was accepted."

I suggested that that was unfair on Irish people.

"It probably wasn't fair," he said, "but you never heard any of the Irish people I knew complaining. And you've got thingy now, *Mrs Brown's Boys*, and that programme is absolutely hilarious. It's a bloke playing a woman. Absolutely brilliant."

"It's a generation thing," the woman said, "because I love soul music, that's all I bought, and my dad used to say to me 'for God's sake, is there not a bloody white person you can listen to?' And that was offensive to me, and I said 'no, I love their music, I love their dancing' so that again is a generation thing. My dad was biased and proud of it, he was English through and through, and he was prejudiced and proud."

"When we were little," she went on, "we never went to Wales. 'We're never going to bloody Wales' said my dad. That's how he was. And you know when you filled forms in and you were supposed to put British, he'd cross it out and put 'English'. You know, if my dad said to you, 'when is St George's Day?' and you didn't know, you'd be out."

I asked whether there would be any changing in her father's attitude.

"No," she said. "He's just turned ninety and he's got dementia, but he'd still stand there and tell you, if you're offended, tough."

"He'd call a spade a spade," said her husband.

As they spoke, three women wearing hijabs and carrying large suitcases came along behind them. They put down prayer mats ten yards from where we were standing, and on a tile which read 'Samantha's going to spend the evening licking the nuts off a large Neapolitan', they prayed towards Mecca.

"Obviously," the man went on, oblivious to what was happening behind him, "when he was born and brought up, there was no foreigners in England and you could walk from one job to another. So to him, this is all wrong, the influx. He thinks we're not English any more, not through and through English and he'd never back down."

"If he had his faculties about him," the woman said, "I don't know what he'd do."

"I think dementia is the best thing for him," her husband said, "because I don't think he'd cope with it. He'd probably say 'what's this world come to?' To him, England is ruined."

I asked the couple if they felt that England was ruined.

"No," said the man. "I don't agree with all the foreigners coming in, but it's the way the world is. Because we give everything for free, you get a lot of people over here – that's just one of these things, you're never going to stop it."

"But it doesn't change the comedy," he went on. "*Morecambe and Wise, Only Fools and Horses* – if people don't laugh at those programmes, they must have had a sense of humour bypass. I watched an episode of *Only Fools and Horses* the other day and Trigger said 'my dad died a couple of years before I was born'. I just sat on the floor and wet myself laughing."

He laughed again, and they were gone. I was left thinking about the woman's father and what he would have made of Muslim prayers on the Comedy Carpet. I thought about change and whether one simply had to wait for people to die in order to move forward or whether people could be persuaded that things had to move on.

Seagulls swooped and dropped as people took photos and selfies. A group on electric bikes cycled through and children played on skateboards. A man on a Segway went by.

Nearby, I met a couple in their sixties, Len and Dawn, and told them I was writing a book about Britain after the EU referendum. I asked for their views about the Comedy Carpet.

"We were brought up with that sense of humour," Len said, "and I see no problem in it whatsoever."

I asked him what he would say to those who said such humour was racist and sexist.

"Well, in this day and age it probably is," he said, "but it's very difficult when you've been brought up in that way, and I honestly believe some of these things have given rise to what's happened with Brexit, insofar as I think people are concerned about protecting the old traditional values. I wanted to stay in Europe, but it didn't shock me that much, because there are a lot of people, particularly the elderly, who didn't like what's happening in this country."

I asked how this linked to the Comedy Carpet and the EU.

"What I'm saying is that they're resisting a change," Len said.

"It's like if you went to the Midlands and talked about Brexit," Dawn said, "the first word would be 'immigration'. Definitely."

"And we've got friends and relatives," Len said, "and I'm not saying they're racist, but quite a lot of the emails are racist, quite a lot of the jokes are racist, so it still exists and I don't know how long that will exist for, because it seems to be people in my age group and slightly above and slightly below, who feel this way more than younger people."

"It's the same with the comedy," he went on. "If you look at some of the TV shows that were on in the Sixties and Seventies – *Love Thy Neighbour, Till Death Us Do Part* – very racist by today's standards, but honestly, they were the most popular comedy programmes of the day."

"*Love Thy Neighbour* was dreadful," Dawn said. "It was about two families next door to each other, one was white and one was black. And I can't remember what the white person used to call the black person but it would make someone like you cringe."

"I wouldn't be surprised if it won awards, though," she added, "because it was one of the programmes of the time, but unfortunately, a lot of people stay in that time."

"People just don't like change," Len said, "and what you've got now is something that is so totally different to what you had twenty or thirty years ago that I think some of the people don't like that and have rebelled against that via the Brexit situation. In other words, they want to keep the things that they believed in in the past. I don't think they're bothered about the fact that Brexit has caused all sorts of problems, pound against the dollar and so on…"

I said that the people I'd talked to in London saw diversity as enhancing people's lives rather than as something to be resisted.

"Here in Blackpool," Dawn said, "I don't think there's any coloured people at all. But in Nottingham, if I speak to some people from there, they'll say 'we're the only white ones in the street' and they resent that. They don't see it as broadening their lives."

"And I think some of the resentment is as a result of the customs that these people bring to this country," Len said, "which they find it difficult tolerating, because some of the customs are sort of alien as far as we're concerned, they're not the sort of thing that we would expect. And rather than trying to understand and adapt, I think they just want to resist."

"It's like queuing," he went on. "There's nothing so bad as being there first at the bus stop and other people pouring on in front of you. And it does build up some sort of hatred against that individual. And again, it's their customs – they're happy when they're surrounded by people that they appreciate and know more about than people they don't know much about."

I wasn't completely sure whether he was talking about migrants or majorities when he said 'they're happy when they're surrounded by people that they appreciate and know more about' and 'rather than trying to understand and adapt, I just think they want to resist', but it occurred to me that in some ways it didn't matter: whether it was the established population or a migrant population, I felt the instinct to stay within a 'tribe' was natural but problematic in terms of creating a shared culture and building community cohesion.

Nostalgia, change and political correctness in Blackpool

Whether there was greater onus on minorities or majorities to reach out and adapt was a theme to which I would return, but for now, I wanted to understand the resistance to change which I was finding on the Comedy Carpet, as I was really struggling to understand why people found it so difficult to accept that some things in the past – like racist and sexist comedy – had been wrong. I asked Len and Dawn for their thoughts.

"It's a bit like what happened with some of these pop stars and TV presenters," Len said. "All these people who have been accused of groping young girls or whatever it is, things that went on in our day were accepted are not acceptable now."

"You wouldn't go to a boss and say anything about it," Dawn said. "We had a guy who we worked with, and the females did not want to go into his office on their own, so you went with somebody else. It was accepted that he was like that."

"And it wasn't just the men," Len said. "I can remember being chased round the office by girls. And I do have some sympathy – not when it's rape or it's young girls – but in terms of behaving in a manner which is very much inappropriate now but in our day it wasn't seen as inappropriate, it really wasn't. I'm not saying that it was right but it was accepted in those days."

Dawn nodded in agreement.

I was surprised by what they were saying, and I suggested that many of the changes we were talking about – from an end to workplace harassment, to pop stars being challenged for harassment and abuse, to racist comedy being stopped – seemed to me to be hugely positive. I wanted to know why people would resist a change away from that.

"It's embarrassment," said Len. "I just think it is difficult for people if they've been brought up that way, it's difficult to then be told it's not right."

"Say for example," Dawn said, "when we were growing up and the newsagent changed hands, somebody would say 'a Paki's going

89

in' and that was accepted, which you obviously wouldn't do now. Now some people would say it nastily, like 'they're taking over the place'…"

"…or some people would just have said it as a matter of course," Len said, "not intending any offence whatsoever – it was just the culture in those days to talk in that way. I don't honestly believe that it was done in any nasty way whatsoever."

"I think it's about time," he went on. "It's only a matter of time until there are fewer people who are affected by what happened forty years ago. Not everybody, because some people will always believe what their parents believed, but I think it will become less and less over time."

I wondered whether what they were describing was simply a natural human cycle and if the comedy that I myself enjoyed would one day be seen in the same way by future generations.

"I hope it wouldn't go that far," said Len. "I think there's a lot of feeling of 'political correctness gone mad' and there's a lot of support to that comment, including from very well-educated individuals and some younger people as well."

"Whether it's in their culture or whatever, I don't know," Dawn said, "but there's certain communities, and they'll have a new settee, and they throw the old one on the street. And we wouldn't do that, would we?"

"I don't know," said Len, "I think there are some people round here who would do it…"

"Well precisely," said Dawn, "but a *decent* person wouldn't do that, but if somebody knocked on the door and said to them, whether the council or what have you, 'that isn't what you should do', then perhaps we could all get on better. But if they're seen to be overtaking, people don't like it."

I asked what 'overtaking' meant.

"Being the only white one in the street," she said.

"And the problem you've then got is that you haven't got a

Nostalgia, change and political correctness in Blackpool

community," Len said, "or not your sort of community. If you've got a lot of people who don't speak a lot of English, and all of a sudden they take over a community, then the English people would I'm sure feel 'we've lost our community' because we can't even talk to our neighbours. And that's one of those things where in time, providing that immigration doesn't take over, will actually improve – if more and more people who have come into this country learn to speak English and use that as their native tongue, then that's going to improve relations surely."

"I think society and TV is trying to help in this respect," he went on. "I mean the number of times we watch and we say 'ah, there's the statutory gay person on the quiz programme' or 'the statutory coloured person on the gameshow', so you've got a much more multicultural society in terms of the gameshows and things like that, so that can't do any harm can it?"

"I'd never thought about it," said Dawn, "but the fact that you have coloured people doing things like *Bake Off* and the fact that Nadiya's won… but if you don't judge people on the colour of their skin then you probably don't notice. You don't think, 'Oh God, she's Bangladeshi' if you're not like that. Like Nadiya, for example, it's her personality that has shone through, so that's why people have taken her to their hearts, and that's why she's doing more TV work, because people are engaging with her. It's not because she's coloured."

"I think rightly or wrongly," Len said, "you look well upon people who have improved society and improved your country, but unfortunately what people do is look at the negative side – they look at the people who are coming along and not doing much to help your country, those who come along and contribute and make the country a better place to live, then that's far more acceptable that the people who come along and don't do that."

As we drew to a close, I felt like I had got closer to understanding why people found cultural change so troubling. As Len had said, many people wanted to 'keep the things that they believed in the past' and they felt uneasy where there was a sense that new people coming to the country didn't contribute. I asked Len and Dawn whether they felt change should just be allowed to happen naturally, or whether it should be pushed through by politicians and the state.

"Well that's the 64,000 dollar question isn't it?" Len said. "If people wanted to take up the Comedy Carpet and say that's all sexist, that's all racist, that to me would be destroying history, and I think that's wrong. You have to say to people 'that might have been ok ten or twenty years ago, but we've come a long way since then'. I think it's a matter of explaining it properly rather than dismissing it."

*****

As the light began to fade, I saw two sisters in their fifties skip-dancing on the carpet in the style of Morecambe and Wise. I went over to them and told them I was researching a book.

"Oh," said one of them smiling, "and there was me thinking you'd talent-spotted us."

"We're available for casting," her sister said, laughing.

I asked whether they had a view on whether Blackpool comedy was offensive.

"I certainly do," she said.

"Ooh, she's very opinionated," said her sister, "you can be spokesperson."

"Comedy is exactly what it is," the spokesperson sister said. "It makes you laugh. It doesn't make you laugh because it's prejudiced, it doesn't make you laugh because it's dark or rude or anything like that, it makes you laugh because you're a human being and when you're laughing, you're laughing at yourself as much as the comedy. Because all comedy is human – it's human language and it's human antics and it's what we all get up to, whether you want to admit it or not in this age of political correctness."

I asked what political correctness meant to her.

"Political correctness is being aware of cultures and society around you and not stepping over the line of deliberately upsetting other people," she said. "But comedy doesn't deliberately set out to upset people, it sets out to engage people and make the barriers of that political correctness less blurred, so you're all laughing together."

I suggested that there were a lot of jokes directed towards women that could be seen as offensive or demeaning.

"I'm a woman," she said, "and I laugh about it. I recognise within the comedy the fact that we can all behave like this at some time or another. It doesn't mean that I'm an unkind person or that I'm nasty or anything like that, it means that I'm an ordinary human being that's capable of laughing at the smallest things in life, which makes the bigger things easier to deal with."

I suggested there might be a continuum between attitudes towards women promoted in the humour on the Comedy Carpet and deeper prejudice and abuse.

"Well," she said, "when I was being abused by my husband, none of it started it as a joke, and a joke would have just been the excuse for the behaviour. It's not the catalyst, it's the excuse for the behaviour – I don't think it makes the behaviour normalised or anything like that."

"There are obviously grey areas," she went on, "and I mean if you're looking at jokes about, say the slave trade, that's a little bit too difficult, because it affected people directly, so that's really difficult for those people to listen to jokes about it. But equally, I've been abused and I can still laugh at a joke, and within that laughter, you learn to deal with your own pain in your own way, and it's more therapeutic than sitting down in front of a therapist years later. And society has the danger now of removing itself, because of political correctness, from the ability just to have a really good laugh and a chuckle and just to let it go."

"Comedy is escapism, isn't it," her sister said. "It isn't supposed to be taken seriously. But there are cultures in the world that don't get comedy and especially don't get British comedy."

"We're all eccentric at one level of another," she went on, "and I think that's what a lot of people don't get. And I think that the more people that come into the mix, the more difficult it is for them to understand that because of their cultural backgrounds, because what we laugh at in this country, people in other countries might look at it and think 'why are they laughing about that?'"

I asked whether that meant it was the responsibility of the people who came to the UK to learn more about the customs of the country.

"If I go and live in France," she said, "I'd learn about that culture, about the expectations, what's accepted behaviour and what's not accepted behaviour, but you also want to influence the behaviours that are accepted and the norms, because society has to grow, hasn't it?"

It seemed to me that she had set out beautifully a model for an integrated, multicultural society, where people who came in were expected to learn about and adapt to the culture, but where at the same time the culture was open to being influenced by those who came from outside.

"I think we've lived through a curve haven't we," said her sister. "We've gone from like where women couldn't do anything: we didn't have the vote, we were treated like second-class citizens, and then you had the Suffragettes and now we've come through to like empowered women who are independent, work and so on, so we've travelled that journey haven't we?"

"But," she went on, "there are lots of areas of society that are trying to keep women from speaking out, from having an education, from mixing with the men, from having to do all the different things."

I asked who she meant.

"Well," she said, "certain areas of ISIS, interpretations of various texts, whether it's the Bible or Catholic. Various religious beliefs."

"Does comedy have an influence on that," her sister asked her, "or is it so far removed from it that it has no influence?"

"I think if ISIS engaged in comedy," her sister said, "women would have more of a say about following men, what dress they had to wear and all the rest of it because the comedy would challenge the authority."

"Now you've got stories coming out from the First World War," she went on, "of views written by German and British soldiers and the views are remarkably the same, because at the end of the day, they're human beings. And when people saw the humanity in that situation, they got up and played a game of football on Christmas Day and gave a dying soldier a drop of their water, even though he was the enemy. And I think that if you don't have the ability to look outside the box, which I think is what comedy is, then I think you lose that ability to have that kind of reaction to things, and you're more concerned about stepping over the line, so you don't."

As they went on their way, I reflected that I had agreed with much of what they had said. I believed that efforts to address prejudice in society were hugely important, but I agreed that fear of causing offence could be holding back the development of healthy human relationships in which people were able to both laugh with and challenge one another. I also agreed that British society had been through a 'curve' as they had put it, an evolution through which values such as equality had become increasingly central. It seemed reasonable to imagine that people coming from other cultures might be at another point on the curve – or on another curve altogether – and that there was therefore a need for people coming to the country to understand and accept the way in which British society had developed. I felt this was particularly important for people coming from cultures where principles such as equality were not as embedded as they were in Britain. At the same time, I believed that British culture was far from perfect and, just as the sister had said that she would want to contribute to the culture of her new home if she was to move to another country, so Britain should remain open to development and learning from people coming to the UK from other cultures.

*****

As night started to fall I got talking a man called Sam who was selling comedy magazines on the promenade. He told me that he was a former construction worker who was trying to make money selling the magazines and joke books to tourists. I asked him if Blackpool comedy was outdated.

"I'd say the comedy is made for a type of audience which is dwindling away now," he said. "It used to be that you'd got mining places and the mill towns, and the whole town would close down and they would all come here. So they wouldn't be used to any other comedy, because the majority of people were one colour – white – so it wasn't seen as anything wrong."

"The sad thing as well," he went on, "is that this has changed dramatically, where we're standing now, and it's a lot better, but there's less people coming."

I asked why he thought that was happening.

"I don't know," he said. "The weather maybe, or maybe they get better deals going abroad. And it's just like when you've had a taste of something nicer, why would you want to come here?"

"There's Poundland on the seafront right by the Tower," he went on, "and it's just a reflection of the way things are going. And if you go into Blackpool, the town has got a big population, but it's probably the poorest town in the country, and you've got children in really bad poverty. It's Dickensian – you've got whole families in bedsits and I think that's got a lot to do with why the tourists aren't coming."

Nostalgia, change and political correctness in Blackpool

"The communities that did come along," he continued, "they're dying off just because of the age that they are. Them people aren't here anymore because of their age. You know, people who come now aren't going to laugh at the Morecambe and Wise type of things because it's not there anymore, they're not on TV, so people under 30 wouldn't understand all these people here."

"I think people have fond memories of Blackpool from when they were younger," he added, "and that's what's kept it going. You remember things from when you're young and it's always nice. It's always glossed over."

I thought back to what James had said about nostalgia and what Len had said about not making people feel judged. I reflected that people did tend to remember the past fondly and accepting that things which they had enjoyed in years gone past were now considered wrong could be really difficult. Sensitivity to that was, it seemed to me, the key to moving forward.

"This area now is alright," Sam said, pointing towards the promenade and the seafront, "but you go a few streets in and you realise what it's really like… it's like they've painted on rust."

"It's had its day," he added, preparing to leave. "I don't think there's anything dramatic about it – it's like everything, something else will come along."

He went on his way, and I reflected on the conversations over the course of the day. They had reminded me that the issues Britain was grappling with were not simply about immigration, and that part of the cultural challenge the country was facing was that the values and norms of people born and bred in Britain had evolved at different paces, creating a significant tension between people on different points on what the sisters had called 'the curve'. Through the conversations I'd had on the Comedy Carpet, I'd got a strong sense of just how hard it was for people to accept that the culture they had been part of was now seen as 'wrong' and while I didn't think that difficulty meant standing in the way of upholding modern

British values like gender equality, I agreed with Len that making people feel embarrassed and judged was not the way forward. "It's a matter of explaining it properly," he had said, and that seemed reasonable to me.

As I left, the Tower lit up in the colours of the rainbow, the *Strictly Come Dancing* glitter-ball flag flew overhead, a busker hummed on his harmonica and the town's Christmas lights shimmered in the dusk.

7

Education, empire and loyalty in Poulton

A few days later, in a pub in Poulton, a small town ten miles from Blackpool, I had arranged to meet four friends who had agreed to give their views on the book. They were Gary, a civil servant in his forties, Chris, a motorsport mechanic in his twenties, Dave, a man in his thirties who worked on the railways and his colleague Mike, who was in his fifties. By the time I arrived, they had already started talking, and for the most part, I was just able to listen and reflect on what they were saying, with a European Champions League football match between Arsenal and Paris St Germain playing in the background on the pub's big screen.

"He's a twat," said Dave, referring to David Cameron. "I accept the result but what I would not accept was that when he put us forward for this, there was no plan in place for if we were to vote to leave. I don't think he ever thought we were going to leave and I can understand that feeling, but it was his responsibility to ensure there was a plan in place if we did."

"It wasn't his responsibility," said Chris.

"He was the Prime Minister of this country," said Gary, "of course it was his responsibility."

"But he didn't want to leave," said Chris.

"I don't care," said Dave. "It was his government's responsibility to ensure there was a plan in place. We have voted to leave, and someone has just thrown a deck of cards up in the air and no one knows what's going to happen. And that's what I will never forgive that guy for because all the shit that's going on now, it's his fault for not having a plan. And that's my main issue, not who voted in or out or why."

"I voted to exit," said Mike, "but I honestly didn't think it would happen and that's where I feel betrayed."

"By who?" Gary asked.

"By the government," Mike said. "Cameron has betrayed the country."

"But what did you want to happen?" Gary asked him.

"I wanted us to stand as a country on its own terms," said Mike. "Not having to kowtow to Brussels… We would make our own decisions."

"About what?" Dave asked him.

"About everything," said Mike.

"Like what?" said Dave. "Nissan making cars here? Because it seems like it's Nissan making that decision, not us. I'm fascinated because I looked at it, and thought we don't do anything anymore, so I thought we'd be better trading with people who do."

"We still export," said Mike.

"What?" Dave asked. "Cheese?"

"This is the thing," Dave added, turning to me. "Nobody stood up and did what I'm doing right now, which is being a bit of dick and saying 'yeah but what are we going to export? What are we going to sell to the world?'"

"Technology," said Mike.

"Ok," said Dave, "what kind of technology?"

"I don't know," said Mike.

"You see," said Dave. "If someone did this to Nigel Farage, we never would have left."

"Come on Dave," said Chris, "we have one of the biggest

engineering sectors in the world. 90% of all motorsport comes from the UK."

"But how much does that make us?" said Dave.

"A lot," said Chris.

"But how much?" said Dave. "What proportion of our GDP?"

"Sorry," said Chris, "I can't just pull the answer out of my pocket… What I'm saying is that we have a lot of manufacturing going on in this country."

"And that's fine," said Dave, "but it fascinates me because people genuinely believe it's still 1920 or 1940 and we're really great at stuff."

"So how are we surviving then?" Mike said.

"Imports," said Dave, "tourism. Cheap labour. I'm playing devil's advocate in a way, but we just have this idea that we're this jewel in the world crown."

"But who has that view?" said Chris.

"The people who voted Brexit," said Dave.

They began to argue, with Dave particularly angry.

"But it was a protest vote," said Mike, "same in America. Trump got in because people were so pissed off with the mundane politics of America, and so they voted him in."

"You know, Mike," Dave interjected, "you just said that people were sick of mundane politics, but unfortunately that mundane politics normally meant peace."

"Joe public weren't getting listened to," said Mike. "People living on the breadline weren't getting listened to and they went 'fuck it'."

"But I know loads of people who have never really wanted for anything who voted for Brexit," said Dave. "I know they haven't wanted for anything because there has been peace for fifty years and the world where we live has been quite stable for a long time. And I think we take that for granted, and that's what terrifies me. If you look at America now, Trump's got in because people take world peace for granted."

"But we're not at peace," said Chris.

"Well when was the last time a bomb dropped on your house in Poulton?" said Dave.

"Yeah," said Chris, "but when was the last time we weren't involved in a military incident?"

"But that's exactly my point," said Dave. "It's overseas, it's not here."

"Tell that to someone who served in Iraq or Afghanistan," said Chris.

"But that's not my point," said Dave. "Tell me the last time that someone walked up to your door and blew your house up. People in this country take that for granted. So yes, we went off to Afghanistan, we went off to Iraq, but did it affect you personally?"

"I'm a damn sight poorer," Chris said. "We bankrupted ourselves putting our dick about where it didn't belong."

"Alright," said Dave, "but in terms of your peace on your doorstep, the country hasn't changed that much, and I think that's why the Brexit vote happened, except that the world has got more unstable and we blame foreigners for the fact that people have got poorer. When was the last time people in this country were terrified about what was coming to their door or to their village or their town? Genuinely, when? Eighties? Cold War?

"A comedian said this," he went on, "and I genuinely think it's right – right now, terrorists are blowing themselves up in shopping centres, they're just doing people in the streets. Twenty-five to thirty years ago, IRA, Russia, whatever, you knew who the enemy was, and it was easier to deal with. Now, it's harder to identify what the enemy is, because it's like an ideology off the internet… My point is that people actually crave the old days of good and evil. You know, if America did a certain thing, you believed they were good because that's all you knew. They crave the days when they didn't have the information, when there was just a right and a wrong."

"So you crave the days of being subjugated?" Chris asked him.

"I'm not saying *I* do," said Dave, "but I'm saying people who voted for Brexit crave the days of a right and wrong."

"I think you're playing on the idea that people who voted for Brexit are thick," Chris said, "and I don't believe that."

"I didn't say that," said Dave.

They began to argue, and Gary stepped in.

"I think the people who voted for Brexit, they do take for granted the freedoms that they have," Gary said. "You know my dad was in the RAF, and he spent his whole career protecting Britain against the Russians, and now he spends his time telling me how much safer things were during the Cold War. And the EU was in part a product of the Cold War, and what we're doing now is we're heading out of the EU just as we're heading into another Cold War. How stupid does that look in historical terms?"

"So does that mean that we should provide the backbone for a European Army?" said Chris. "We're not the world's police."

"Yeah," said Dave sarcastically, "and why should we go and help all those Jews being burned? 'That's not my problem' – it's the same attitude."

They began to argue again and then a goal was scored in the match on the big screen and for a moment they all turned towards the television.

"But we've caused the problems we're having with terrorism now," said Mike, turning back to me, "because of Blair going into other countries looking for weapons of mass destruction."

"I accept that," said Dave, "and we shouldn't just be going in and removing people without a plan. But doesn't that just sum up the whole thing about Brexit, because we've gone and done something again without a plan. We never learn…"

"Complacency," Gary said.

"The problem," he continued, "is that this whole election

became an issue on race and hate and anger and all the things that divide people."

"Everyone's poorer so let's blame immigrants," Dave added.

"But they could still have the free movement of people outside the European Union," said Mike.

"But Mike," Dave said, "they've decided that people like you who voted to leave did not want any immigration, you wanted to leave the Single Market and close the borders."

"We both work on the railway," he went on, "and I've sat in staff rooms and heard basically lies in mess rooms about statistics and how many immigrants are here, and then if you turn around to people and tell them it's not true, they don't realise… A lot of people on the railway listen to Nigel Farage, and they believe him, and when he stands in front of a poster of a line of immigrants, they believe him that all those immigrants are trying to get into this country."

"That's what fascinates me about the Fylde Coast," he went on, "because I understand people who have had their wages freeze, I understand people who have lost their jobs, I understand people who have lost their pension, I understand people who are sat in a factory, miserable, earning six pound an hour. What I don't understand is how people like you and me, lads who work on the railway up here, basically doing really well for ourselves, could think that immigration is an issue? I don't get that. How is immigration an issue for you?"

"We can't all be NIMBYs," Mike said. "This is about the country as a whole."

"I'm not as well read academically as the others," he continued, turning to me, "but I'm not naïve enough to think you just believe what you read, but then you can only make your opinions based on what you see in front of you. I try to get my news from impartial sources, but the BBC, they're as biased as anyone, and then you think 'what is truth?' As a society, we can't believe everything that is put in front of us, and to me that's so wrong."

"I just think what got me was that there were a lot of people on the railway going on about immigration," said Dave, "and I was like 'you live in Poulton!' Immigration has just made this town fifty times better."

"Yeah," Mike agreed, "and if you get the Jeremy Kyles on minimum wage picking potatoes out of a field or carrots or whatever, they won't do it."

"But that's an issue with Britain as a whole," said Gary. "People seem to think they're better than picking potatoes or cleaning or whatever people think immigrants should do."

"They want the big money," said Mike, "but they don't want to work. Kids today don't want to put the twelve-hour graft in, they don't want to do hard labour bricklaying or whatever, they want to make the money easy by computers."

"Less people are doing engineering degrees," said Chris, "less people are doing science degrees."

"They're all doing performing arts..." said Dave.

They all laughed.

"But seriously," Dave continued, "that's my issue with the current situation, and no one says it: Tony Blair and Gordon Brown, they've made people think that doing a performing arts degree and getting yourself forty grand in debt is a good idea. They've made people think you should still be able to walk out of that and get a thirty grand a year job. And if that doesn't happen, those people feel like they've been hard done to. I'm all for education, education, education, but people have been allowed to go into things they shouldn't have been and they shouldn't have been allowed to get so in debt. We've all been told we're better than ourselves, and we're not. Some people are just meant to go picking potatoes, and no one has the balls to say it."

"But that's the way education works in this country," Chris said, "because it's like private business, they have to sell themselves as the best. I went to Blackpool and Fylde College and did the motorsport course there and they told me 'oh yeah, you're going to go and do Formula One, you're going to do this, you're going to do that, you're going to be amazing.' And I didn't..."

"But you've done something with your qualification and made your career based on it," said Gary, "and that's what formal education should be."

"50% of children now will end up going to college and getting a degree," he went on. "Now are you honestly telling me that they're all going to get the best jobs? If you're bright enough to do a degree, you ought to be bright enough to know that all of you are not going to get the best jobs."

"If you're being sold a lie," said Dave, "it's very easy to take and that's the worst legacy of that government for me. I'm Labour, but people have just been told that you can be anything you want to be and you can't."

"What ruined this country was taking away the polytechnics," said Mike, "where the child who wasn't academic but who had a talent in another area was given the chance to do it. And now we've got a massive skill shortage..."

"When I was at school," said Chris, "I was predicted As for all my subjects, but I knew from a very early age that I wanted to go into engineering, but the college I went to wouldn't let me do an engineering qualification because they wanted me to do GCSEs and get the grades."

"I know someone who just got a first-class degree and he can't spell," said Dave, "and I'm sorry but if you can't spell, you shouldn't be able to get a First. But maybe I'm old fashioned..."

On the big screen, Paris St Germain scored, and the conversation stopped for a moment as they discussed the errors in Arsenal's defence which had led to the goal. I reflected on the conversation: it would have been easy to dismiss what they were saying as pub chat, but I wasn't sure I disagreed with Mike about polytechnics. It seemed to me that vocational education had been undermined, and the drive to provide an academic higher education for more young people had created an inflation of expectations which couldn't necessarily be matched by the jobs that existed.

"I just think people feel entitled," Dave said, turning back to me. "The British feel they are above certain jobs, because we're brought up to believe that we're great, we're British. You know, when I was taught about the Industrial Revolution, we were taught about cotton and about how great we were as a country – no one told you where the cotton came from, no one told you who picked the cotton, and that's a textbook British thing – because 'we're going to make Britain great again'. Well when was Britain great? Well, basically when we had slaves doing all our dirty work for us."

There was anger in his voice, and he took a moment before continuing.

"During the Industrial Revolution," he went on, "slaves were picking the cotton and then slaves in factories were making the money for rich people, so when people talk about making the country great again, all I can get from that is watering down our terms and conditions of employment, getting rid of our pensions, and the rich are getting richer. Us round this table, we've done well for ourselves, and a lot of people aren't like that, and they've blamed foreigners, they blamed immigrants for their problems. But the problems are not caused by immigrants, the problems are caused by the political situation that we've caused ourselves."

"And when people talk about making us great like we were in the Seventies," he continued, "I'm sorry, but from what I've heard about the Seventies, we were not great – we were absolutely on the bones of our arse. That's my favourite Frankie Boyle joke – he said in the old days people used to leave their doors unlocked because nobody had anything worth nicking. Ah yeah, the good old days – the kids were poor, they all had rickets, but we didn't answer to Brussels!"

"We've basically colonised half the world," he added, "and then we get fifteen war refugees turn up on our doorstep and the *Daily*

Mail puts them on the front page and says 'we're not having this, send them back to their own country'."

"But we always knew that we couldn't be self-sufficient," said Mike, "so we went out to countries where we could get the raw materials, and took over the country. That's not great, that's not great at all. But that's why we went into countries – to get something."

"So if we can't do that anymore," said Dave to Mike, "why did you think we could stand on our own two feet? I'm fascinated by that, because it was a conversation that was never had except for Nigel Farage saying 'take back control' – take back control of what? We don't own anything anymore."

While I was keen to avoid rerunning the referendum debate, I was interested in the fact that they were speaking quite negatively not just individual politicians or policies, but about the British psyche. There was an implication in what they were saying that Britain had got above itself, and that Mike had been naïve or superior in thinking the country could stand on its own two feet. While I did think Dave was being excessively negative about Britain's history and present position, I thought he was right to question some elements of the story we told ourselves about the country. I asked the group how they felt these kind of arguments could be made without people dismissing them as unpatriotic.

"I work on the railway," said Dave, "and 80% of people who work on the railway are ex-forces and a lot of people who have a very black or white view on world history. It's impossible to try to argue that the situation is a lot more grey because anyone who does is seen as weird or unpatriotic. So they think it's a bit weird that I might be a bit uncomfortable with the honours system – 'a Member of the British Empire'… And in certain circles, this last two years it's been very noticeable that people treat you differently with my sort of attitude."

"Don't get me wrong," he went on, "I am proud to be British, but I am apologetic for our history. And I just think a lot of people don't feel like that, and obviously the politicians and the strategists play on that and say 'let's make Britain great again'."

"People have been told for so long that they're not allowed to show the St George's Cross because it's racist," he continued, "and I think people jumped on that massively. I don't think there's anything racist about flying the St George's Cross, any more than there is flying the Saltire or anything else, but when I go to the slavery museum in Liverpool, I want people to know that I feel bad about it, because what we have is built on something that was wrong."

I was struck by his statement that 'what we have is built on something that was wrong'. It was one of the most powerful things I had heard on my travels and I reflected on the mixed emotions he must have felt: he had said he was proud to be British, but he also felt that the stability and relative wealth that he enjoyed was based on a history he thought was immoral. The question of how to maintain that balance between feeling positive about one's home and maintaining an awareness of the country's imperfections seemed crucial to resolving the issues and divisions I was exploring.

Around me, the conversation continued.

"We have this rose-tinted view of what it is to be British," Gary said, "and we have an identity crisis going on, of what we actually are, and nobody knows. And we all feel a bit lost."

"Most people under thirty don't care," said Dave. "They're European or they're world citizens. I'm proud to be British, and I think one of the best things about being British is being able to question everything we're doing as a country and saying 'why are we doing that?' And I don't think that's unpatriotic, but you know the last year has been the first time in my life I've been challenged about my patriotism because of that. I accept that we have voted to leave, but it doesn't make me unpatriotic to want the best outcome. And that scares me. I'm a bit of a wuss, and I'm scared about the future, because I'm getting to a point now where I feel I probably shouldn't say what I want to say."

The match on the big screen finished and the conversation came to a close.

"It's the first time in my life I've considered not having kids," Dave said to me as we parted.

That evening, I reflected on what the four friends had said. There was obvious anger at David Cameron about the EU referendum, Tony Blair about the Iraq war, the last Labour government for expanding higher education without thinking through the implications and the previous Conservative government for closing polytechnics. But many of their concerns were much deeper than individual political decisions: they were about a national psyche in which the more negative elements of British history were to some extent ignored and people from abroad were blamed for problems which, the group seemed to agree, were largely of Britain's own making.

Dave's experience of having his patriotism questioned also worried me deeply as this seemed an unacceptable way to quell dissent. Not letting one's own love of the country be questioned seemed an important part of any response to such behaviour but I wondered how someone who held Dave's view that 'what we have is built on something that is wrong' could ever feel truly comfortable with the notion of patriotism.

As I went to bed, I checked the news and saw that in London, the murderer of Jo Cox had been sentenced. In his sentencing remarks, the judge, Mr Justice Wilkie, had told the white supremacist Thomas Mair that patriotic sentiments could be legitimate and have resonance, but in Mair's mouth such sentiments were "made toxic". Cox, the judge said, had been a wonderful mother, partner and friend and had made a real contribution to her community and to the country. She, the judge said, had been the true patriot.

8

Cultural security and Britishness in Preston

My next stop was Preston and on the train I got talking to a woman in her sixties from a market town in Suffolk who was visiting her daughter who lived in the North West. She was warm, friendly and softly spoken.

"It's just not going well is it?" she said when I told her I was writing a book about modern Britain. "My son's in the navy and it is basically bankrupt: we've got these two aircraft carriers and no aircraft to fly from them. You've got a health system which is going to run out of money and you've got us sending billions overseas when we can't look after ourselves properly."

"I voted not to be in," she went on. "I just think it was a chance for a bit of protectionism. Like where I live, it's a small market town and they want to build all these new homes on the edge and it's suddenly not going to be the same place any more. All the schools are under pressure, the sewerage is from another age – and the roads… there's this single carriageway road, they're going to put 600 homes on it, that's 1,200 cars every day."

I suggested we needed to build new homes to solve the housing crisis.

"I know we do," she said, "but these aren't even the right kind of houses; these are three and four and five-bedroom houses – local young people can't even afford them."

I asked why, if that was the case, such houses were being built. She gestured with her fingers to indicate that it was all about money.

"Rich getting richer, poor getting poorer," she said. "I guess it was probably always like this but I think we're more conscious of it now."

"Besides, no one likes change, do they?" she went on. "It's my town and it's going to be a different town from the one it was before, and no one asked me if I was alright with that. They're just building houses anywhere nowadays, no one has a say about it, and in my area, it's all people flooding out of London, because they're the last person on their street who's not white. White flight, they call it."

"I'd do the same if I was them," she added. "I think it's difficult being a Christian in England now – I just feel like we're under pressure".

I asked her what she meant by that.

"I guess I just feel like the British identity, the country is under threat," she said. "You have all these people coming over here from Syria or whatever and that just worries me. You feel like we're a bit of a soft touch."

"I know you can't believe everything you read in that paper," she went on, pointing at the copy of the *Daily Mail* in front of her. "My husband calls it a comic – but like those people from Calais, it was obvious that they weren't children, you just had to look at the photos. If they had been before puberty that would've been fine but I don't like that it's all young men."

I asked what it was about young men that worried her.

"I just think that when young men get together, they can get into groups," she said. "They don't integrate and you just wonder what they're here for. I don't think they've always got a good attitude towards women – you see what's happened in Germany and the problems they've got. And that's before you've got onto ISIS…"

I suggested that part of Britain's heritage was taking in refugees.

"I don't have a problem with that," she said, "but then you've got migrants in with them, and then other people and you don't know what their motivations are."

I said that I assumed that migrants' motivation was to earn some money.

"But how do we know they will leave?" she asked. "How do we know that they won't just blend in? I just think we've got a country, and we need to protect it."

I suggested that her conception of the country was different from Londoners I had met who really valued a multicultural society.

"I can see that," she said, "and I can see that if you like that kind of thing then you wouldn't feel like the country is under threat. But the country I know feels like it's under threat, and that worries me. You know that the white population is falling and that other people are rising. Nothing you can do will stop it, but it does make you feel worried, like one day there'll be more of them than there are of us."

*****

I had arranged to meet an accountant called Chris in a pub by the train station at Preston. Since my conversations in Sunderland, I had wanted to get to the bottom of the question of shifting demography and power, typified by the woman on the train's worry about there being 'more of them than there are of us', and I decided to try to explore this with Chris. I started by asking him for his view on immigration.

"If you want to have trade with other countries," he said, "you have to embrace that there will be some movement of people. You can't have your cake and eat it, so in that sense we have to allow for a measure of controlled immigration. What a lot of people feel, whether it's based on true fact or whether it's just a feeling whipped up by the media, is that immigration is out of control, and that it's eroding some elements of our culture."

I asked him what he meant by 'erosion'.

"It's about respect," he said. "By all means come to the UK but you have to marry with the laws and customs of the country. For example, you couldn't just come and adopt sharia law – it's inconsistent with our values… People in some cases even openly preach malice against the country, and I think that's what worries people. And what further compounds it is people's perception that the authorities don't deal with it and allow it to flourish."

"If you want a poster boy for what I'm talking about," he said, "Abu Hamza would probably be it. And how long did Theresa May try and fail to get rid of him, and how much did that cost the taxpayer? It's a tricky one, because I personally think it's a good thing, the Human Rights Act, but from a common sense point of view, there do seem to be some bizarre rulings that come out of it that seem to call its use into question. Abu Hamza is a prime example where you just think 'this just does not seem to stack up – this man should be deported'. It just seems to fly in the face of the British mentality."

"A lot of immigrants are tarred with the same brush unfortunately," he went on. "I've met plenty of people who have come here from other cultures who are much more willing to integrate and honour our culture and to work hard than people who were actually born here. But by the same token, there are people who don't do that, and they're the ones the media focuses on, because no one ever focuses on the good, it's always on the bad."

I asked him if he agreed with the woman on the train that British culture was being eroded.

"Yeah," he said, "I couldn't disagree with that. I think it's quite a sweeping statement and I think there's many elements to it, but if you just look at some really deprived areas in the North, where there's a huge number of refugees and asylum seekers just been dropped into communities, and they've become the majority of the population in that area. A lot of them have certainly not thought 'we need to come in and embrace the cultures of the land that is offering us refuge and a place to live' – they're very insular and they've almost created their own community. And that to me feels a little bit wrong if I'm honest."

"That's why the likes of Farage have prospered," he went on, "because even though he is part of the elite, his ability to peddle this image that he's for the common man has resonated, especially in those types of areas. He taps into people's feelings, people's emotions, and it resonates with people. And that's where he finds rich pickings."

I wanted to address what Chris felt that Nigel Farage was tapping into. I asked him whether it was the number of people coming to the country, whether they integrated, whether it was language or whether it was about ethnicity.

"I don't think it's the last one," he said, "but I think it's probably all of the others you've mentioned to a degree. This country is like a sponge isn't it, we are just a small island and there's only so many people we can absorb: some of them are born here, some of them are not. So the number of people is absolutely a factor. If you were in a community where the ratio was 90:10 British and then over a ten-year period you were in the minority, you would feel that things have changed seismically. And if all those new arrivals were law-abiding and willing to integrate, you might not think too much of it, but the reality is that they're not all law-abiding and not all willing to integrate, and that exacerbates things even further. That behaviour spoils things for everyone."

"For everyone who does that," he went on, "there's probably a thousand who are fantastic citizens, but it only takes a couple of negative instances to inform people's mind-set. I think if the state was a bit more forthcoming and robust about dealing with it when it does occur, it wouldn't get people's backs up so much."

"It's the same principle in a work context," he added. "If you get someone who is a bad apple, if you deal with them swiftly then you find the rest of the workforce respect that and respond well and feel more motivated. But if that doesn't happen, and people are allowed to disrupt and cause problems and be a subversive influence, then you end up in total chaos."

I suggested that a lot of examples he had given related to the Muslim community in particular. This was a clear trend I had found on my travels and I asked why he thought there was so much focus on that community in particular.

"For me," he said, "it's about taking a reality check: look at suicide attacks that have taken place over the last ten years, and how many of the perpetrators were Muslim – if you were looking at this from a purely common-sense point of view, you'd think that's where you'd have to focus because that's where the predominant threat lies. You can't let political correctness get in the way of rational thinking on such matters."

I suggested that this wasn't simply to do with terrorism.

"No," he said, "it's also about a willingness to integrate – a person's willingness to come into our society and to embrace it and to behave in line with the community spirit and ideals of this country. For some immigrants it's almost like 'we're here, but we don't want to make any effort to embrace the culture and ideas of this country' and they just become very insular. I'm not saying that's universally the case, but I'm saying that has happened and that it is what some people are worried about."

"It's innocuous but far-reaching things," he went on, "so you get scenarios where, for example, the way that schools might operate start to change. Schools might become a lot more careful about what they celebrate, when they celebrate it and how prominently they celebrate it. If your child is going to school and all of a sudden they're being told 'you've got to be careful on this day' or 'you can't celebrate this because it might offend people', it's a prime example: it's the crux of it."

I suggested that statistically the proportion of people who were practising Christians had gone down significantly over recent years. I asked what he felt non-Christians were protecting.

"Personally, religion doesn't play that big a part in my life," he said, "but I think it's about Britishness, it's about the identity, it's not about religion. If you asked ten people what they're concerned about in the context of this question you're asking me, I think you'd be hard pressed to find a significant number of them to say it's about religion: I think this is about Britishness and British identity."

I asked him what Britishness meant to him.

"I think you can boil it down to two words: freedom and respect. And if you've not got one of them, you've got a problem. That freedom is so important, that ability to make your own life, to live up to whatever you aspire to, but by the same token, you need to respect that freedom and the norms that enable it."

I asked how that fitted with people like British Muslims being free to practise their own faith and being respected when they did.

"That's absolutely fine," he said, "if that person practises their own faith but by the same token respects our customs, then that is the utopia for me. But far too frequently that's not the case."

"It's change as well isn't it," he went on. "People just don't like change – it's just human nature. It's not even necessarily that it's change for the worse, although it may well be in some cases, but change in itself is also disruptive to people. And if it's perceived to be detrimental then that's a particularly bitter pill to swallow."

"I think the other thing about some elements of Islam," he continued, "is that in my experience with the most extreme preachers is that you're either a believer in Islam or you're the enemy. There's no middle ground for compromise, no willingness to respect that other people have their own views. You see people saying 'this is the way it should be done', and 'if you're not doing that, you're a direct enemy'. And obviously not every Muslim is like that but it only takes one or two to detract from the good others do. And if the authorities were to take a firmer stand on it and say 'hang on a minute, you can't operate like that in this country', then people would have a lot more confidence in the state to deal with the issue and those perpetrating the hate wouldn't be able to peddle it in the first place."

"If you went to some other countries," he added, "and you practised Christianity, you'd be shut down. Just look at the woman who's been arrested in Dubai for reporting a rape, and you can bet your bottom dollar that there are people in this country who will see that being reported and be thinking 'that's right'. So even though they are living here, with the rights and freedoms that this country gives to them, they're probably still sympathetic to a way of doing things which you have to say is contrary to British ways of doing things."

I suggested that the police couldn't arrest people for thought crimes.

"It's about applying the law consistently," he said. "How can it be right that you are told that your child can't celebrate this festival or special day as much as they once did in order to respect others' beliefs, but by the same token hate preachers can stand up in a British street and encourage people to kill British soldiers? From a common-sense point of view that cannot be correct."

I asked how this view on hate preachers was consistent with his view on freedom being a pillar of our society.

"But I also said 'respect' was a pillar of our society," he said. "If we just focused a little bit more on upholding the respect we might get the balance right."

"For a lot of people," he went on, "the law seems to crack down on people expressing their national identity when they're British, but where someone who is not British wants to express their views contrary to ours, they can do it even to a point where it's pretty extreme without any intervention from the law."

I suggested that perhaps this was about ethnicity – that people felt threatened by the skin colour of people changing.

"I think it's a bit simplistic to say that," he said. "I just think it comes back to this respect thing that I keep going on about. The sheer number of people coming into the country is a factor, but that is offset if people are respectful and integrating and embrace the British way of life. It depends on the behaviour of the contingent in question. It's the perceived loss of that identity which is the root cause of all this."

"What really gets people's backs up," he went on, "is when people on the Left say 'anyone who speaks up against immigration is a Luddite', and then when it does come to an election, those people, their backs are up and they are already coming from a skewed position of wanting to stick one on the establishment. Lots of people in government are in a bubble, devoid from the reality of the pure emotional basis upon which a lot of people will cast their vote."

I asked how he thought politicians should respond.

"I think it's about treating people with respect," he said. "I think there are a lot of politicians who believe that ordinary people aren't intelligent enough to comprehend the facts – 'we'll rule and you follow'. And I'm not suggesting that that's everyone, but I think it is a significant proportion of the political class."

"It's the way they talk to people," he went on. "One programme I watch is *Question Time* on a Thursday night. And you've only got to watch one episode of that to see it: you'll see someone in the audience speak up with quite opinionated views, someone who is obviously not great at articulating themselves, but they've got a strong view, and the response from some members of the panel is as if they're looking down their nose at them. They always have an air of superiority about them, and that in itself can be quite demeaning. And that's the sort of thing that fuels a mind-set in some people that they have to kick up against it."

"There was a chap in the audience last night," he continued, "I thought he came across quite well. They were in Stirling, and he said to a guy on the panel from the SNP in reference to recent referendums 'I was on the side of staying in the UK and I was on the winning side of that, and I was on the side of leaving the EU, and I was on the winning side of that, and now you're trying to undo it all'. The way that the panel got stuck into him I thought was shocking. They tried to belittle him – it's subversive, it wasn't as simple as to say 'you're wrong', it's more subtle than that. But you've got to bear in mind that this programme is watched by millions of people and even that kind of subtle message is going to get across to the population. They were dismissing him from a position of power – it wasn't like stepping toe-to-toe with someone, it was almost like 'we don't need to entertain that', we're up here and you're not, you and your views are going to be forgotten about in ten seconds."

"To be honest," he added, "I had to be tough with myself during the referendum and tell myself 'make the judgement based on fact' because even someone like me, who isn't that put out by the issues we're talking about, there was an element within me thinking 'let's stick it to the elite because we're not being taken seriously by them'. I'm not suggesting that it was a really strong emotion, but make no mistake about it, it was there and I had to be very mindful not to let that cloud my decision."

*****

The conversations had been illuminating, and had brought me back to some of the key cultural issues relating to immigration and integration from earlier in my travels. The woman on the train had talked about there being more of 'them' than of 'us', Christianity being under threat and 'white flight'. Chris had been more focused on values, stressing that skin colour and religion didn't matter if people were respectful of British culture and made a contribution to UK society. He had talked about his 'utopia' being migrants and people from religious minorities respecting Britain's customs and values but also feeling free to practise their own faith. This was, in my mind, an unspoken understanding, but clearly for Chris and many others, news stories of hate preachers and extremist views had had a hugely corrosive impact. This, it seemed, meant that they did not take for granted that migrants or people from minority backgrounds, particularly people of Muslim faith, would necessarily share or respect the values of the country.

As I thought about what a response to the concerns he had raised might look like, I was drawn to his focus on Britishness, as I could see how this concept could help to bring people together without relying on a shared religion or ethnicity. If Britishness was to unite people of a country which was still at least nominally Christian, I felt it had to take lessons from the country's religious heritage as well as from the other faiths, cultures and value-systems which made up modern Britain; I also believed that it should not be defined in such a fixed way that it was not open to further development, including the possibility of influence from people who came to Britain from abroad. I felt that if a shared sense of Britishness could be established and accepted across all parts of British society, then the woman on the train did not need to worry about there being 'more of them than there are of us', unless her true concern was about ethnicity.

It struck me that there were huge challenges inherent in trying to build a stronger sense of Britishness. I felt, for example, that if the values which underpinned Britishness were not upheld, then the concept was worthless, yet the idea of 'policing' people's values seemed to run against the freedom which was itself so intrinsic in the country's culture. At the same time, I felt that efforts to define and defend a set of values risked turning into the exclusionary and illiberal nationalism which I felt had been evident in the referendum campaign. These were difficult issues and as my journey continued I wanted to think about how best to address them.

9

Community, faith and values in Blackburn

The next day, I headed to Blackburn. It felt like I had identified many schisms within British society, and I wanted to think about the role of faith, community and state organisations in holding society together. I also wanted to look at shared values as a way of bringing different communities together and Blackburn, which I knew had a large British-Asian community, seemed a good place to do so. Having heard a lot said about Islam on my travels, much of it negative, I was keen to hear from practising Muslims, and I wanted to think about the role of Christianity in British society too.

As I left the station, I saw the magnificent cathedral which dominated the town centre and, nearby, I met Lil, a pensioner in her eighties, who told me she was in town to pick up her pension and do some shopping. We got talking about the way the town had changed. She told me that it was a former mill town, which in its day had been a global centre of the cotton industry. The mills had been closed for a long time, she said, but many of the people who had come from India, Pakistan and Bangladesh to work in the cotton industry had stayed in Blackburn and created a large South Asian community in the town.

"You'll see people going about their lives side by side," she told me, "but you won't see them mixing much."

"You see them doing their shopping," she went on, indicating towards a group of women of wearing burkas. "Just a slit and nothing else. This woman the other day was wearing sunglasses over the slit, so you literally couldn't see anything of her. Someone said to me 'you don't know what she's got under there – it could be a man, it could be anything'."

I walked into the market and past a stall which sold sweets from all over the world and had a separate section of 'Halal approved' sweets. A few stalls down, there was a bacon stall. Nearby Eastern Eye offered eyebrow threading, waxing and Jignasha tints. In the food hall, a deli advertised 'exquisite Halal cuisine' while around the corner, Spindle's Dinner offered roast chicken dinners with peas and gravy and Spuds and Puds café promoted 'delicious heart-warming hot food'. The café was decked with St George's Crosses, Remembrance Day flags, wreaths and poppies, and all the tablecloths were covered in poppies. 'England, England, England', read the flags. As I looked around, I noticed many people were still wearing poppies, more than a week after Remembrance Sunday.

Next to me, two men – one in torn jeans, the other in a suit – were arguing about whether Parliament should have a role in the triggering of Article 50.

"So it's my fault," the man in torn jeans said, "because people like me don't know exactly what the law is? The government should have educated me. They don't teach this stuff in schools."

"Yes they do," the man in the suit said.

"Not in my lad's school they don't. I've never heard him come home and talk about it."

"They do. Maybe not in your day, but now they do."

"But that's what I'm saying, people like me don't know about the referendum, the ins and outs…"

"It's in statute, it's the law that referendums are advisory."

"But I've never heard of that."

"Well that's ignorance."

"You calling me ignorant?"

"No. I'm just saying it's the law of the land."

"So you've got a book about all the laws of the land at home?"

"No of course not."

"Well nor have I."

Around the corner, I got talking to a couple of men, one in his fifties, one in his twenties, working at an Asian jewellery store.

"It actually became more intolerant since the referendum," the younger man told me. "It's stopped now, but when the referendum happened, you could hear people using the word 'Paki' – not looking at you directly, but you knew they were talking to you."

I asked how it made him feel.

"Nobody would like to be targeted," he said. "We all like to be part of the society, and what's happened here is like dividing us up. Instead of integration, they're throwing everybody out. Instead of becoming a cosmopolitan society, it's broken the whole society."

"It is kind of sad when you think about it," he added. "It's like family being separated. Everyone's got different opinions and they've got the right to those opinions, but not on the basis of skin colour."

I asked whether that meant he thought that people would keep to themselves more as a result of what had happened.

"If you look at the bigger picture," he said, "you're not really keeping to yourselves. Anyone would feel comfortable with their own comfort zones. So anybody coming from a non-English speaking country, a Polish guy for example, he's going to feel more comfortable liaising with Polish-speaking people."

"Another example," he went on, "fifty or sixty years ago, when the Asian community came here, it wasn't like they said 'oh, this is my area,' but when an Asian person bought a house, a second Asian person bought a house, and then the local person started to sell their houses, so who's got integration problems?"

He seemed to be suggesting that the integration problem came from the established, predominantly-white community rather than from minority communities or new migrants, but I suspected that the instinct to 'be more comfortable in their comfort zones' ran across all communities. While it was a natural reaction, however, I did think it was problematic in somewhere like Blackburn because of the kind of separation it could lead to, with people 'living side by side but not mixing', as Lil had put it. I asked the two men what they felt should be done.

"We should all be working together," the older man said. "There is no Asian community, they should forget about the skin colour, there is no difference."

"Put the differences aside, come together as a community," the younger man said.

"Because we are all from Blackburn," the older man said, "that's what we all should be. Doesn't have to be black, white, yellow, pink."

"Maybe my father had a problem liaising," he continued, "because he didn't speak English. But we don't have that problem. Everyone has a responsibility, everyone."

I asked what he felt should happen next.

"Honestly," the younger man said, "I haven't got a clue."

"By Brexit, we've gone sixty years back," the older man said. "It took us so long to get everyone together, friends, English friends, Asian friends, Chinese – Brexit has spoilt everything."

"One step forward, two step backwards," he added.

As they went back to serving their customers, I reflected on what they had said. They had talked a lot about skin colour as the basis for the divisions they had described, but I couldn't help wondering whether the issues were more complicated and related more to perceived differences of values and customs than to ethnicity. I decided to look into this more over the course of the day.

*****

Wanting to explore more about community cohesion and integration, I headed towards the cathedral. The clock struck ten as I reached it and the sun shone on the magnificent new development around it, which included a piazza, a café and a set of new offices and gardens. In the gardens, there was a sign up for the Blackburn Cathedral Flower Festival with a photo of Nadiya Hussein, the winner of the *Great British Bake Off*, smiling down.

"This is the House of God and the gate of Heaven," read the inscription above the cathedral's main entrance.

Inside, I got talking to one of the Canons, Ian Stockton. He invited me for a further discussion, and over a cup of tea in his office, he told me about the cathedral's efforts to build cohesion.

"We have an outward-looking-ness," he told me, "the sense that the cathedral is a place for all. We have community spaces here, the courtyard where people can sit on their lunch break or in the summer, meeting rooms, we have a high standard of music, lots of groups come to use the building for all sorts of events, for exhibitions, for dinners."

"The cathedral has done a lot with regard to community cohesion", he went on, "and over the last ten years we have done a lot with the Asian community. The cathedral has been a space where difficult conversations could be held – conversations involving police and Muslim leaders, about difficult issues – but inevitably, I think we may have been dealing with just one section of the Muslim community. Those who are more disillusioned, or much more questioning about Western values, they may be all the harder to engage with. But that would also be true of the disillusioned white working class, who would be more difficult for us to engage."

He told me that two colleagues who had led the cathedral's work on community cohesion had both left their roles because there were no funds to cover their salaries. I asked whether that meant they couldn't do as much community cohesion work as he would want.

"We certainly could do more," he said. "Many churches, not

just the Church of England, have fewer resources, human resources in terms of leadership, and aged and dwindling populations, and of course there are some churches closing and parishes coming together. So there may be a lack of political realism with regard to faith communities – or at least a measure of wishful thinking from both church and state: there has to be that question – has the church got sufficient resources to step up?"

"Now on the one hand," he continued, "when there is imaginative thinking, you'd be surprised about the gifts and the resources that they have and what can be achieved. But the interfaith work, that needs money."

We got talking about David Cameron's 'Big Society' vision of the state stepping back and churches and other faith and community bodies stepping up. I asked if he felt that was realistic.

"People warm to that vision and there's something in it," he said, "but it can't and it shouldn't be an excuse for the state failing in its responsibility. The church has to be the church and the state has to be the state."

"One danger for the church is an inward-looking-ness when they're up against it," he went on, "and what I say is that if the church is involved in transforming communities, it is more likely to be a healthy church, and that means working with others… The church-orientated work, the bible study and so on, is vital, as is the growth of churches, but there does seem to be a bit of an obsession about the numbers."

I asked if a growth in numbers was a realistic expectation at a time when the role of Christianity seemed to be diminishing in British society.

"I think that has to be a question," he said. "Theologically, we have to ask where is God in this? It's easy to say God is in the success, but when numbers go down, where is God in that? Now the Bishop has used the image of the Lancashire cotton industry, and he said that because that industry didn't change, it died, and if the church doesn't change, it may die. Now this is true, but if we as a church simply look after our own health, that's not sufficient, because life is about engagement with others. 'Seek first the Kingdom of God and all these things should be added unto you'."

*****

I was in Blackburn to meet Emma Lawler, a local youth worker. As we talked in her office in the centre of the town, she told me that she was working with an increasing number of young people of South Asian heritage, some of whom were seeking to get away from what they felt to be restrictive families who, for example, wanted to prevent them going to the local college.

"We had one mum come in asking if her son was here," she said, "and because we're a confidential service we didn't tell her anything, but she tracked him down anyway. I think she thought he'd just go home in a few days, but we did a good job with him and we found him a place to live and got him on benefits, and got him to college. And I guess that message came to the family that there is a life outside their community and if they make it too difficult and too strict then there is a way out for young people and they can lead a different lifestyle. And I think there is a shock for the parents that they need to take a step back and accept that."

"I don't know how I would react to that as a parent," she continued, "if my child made a choice which was so different to what I had in mind for them, but I suppose I'm very laid back and I'm quite happy so long as my children are happy, and I know that's different, particularly for the Asian culture. I know that the local college is frowned upon because it's mixed, there's boys and girls there, and I think that's seen as a threat not just for the girls but for the boys too. But I can't understand why any parent wouldn't be proud for their child to want to go to college to do an educational programme… And I'm sure the Islamic Schools provide a very good education, but if the young people choose something different, is that not their right?"

She told me about a young woman who had been banned by her family from going to the local college because it would mean mixing with young men.

"She had gone to an all-girls school and wanted to study for a job in a caring profession," she told me. "She'd said that she wanted to go to Blackburn College, and she was told in no uncertain terms that she couldn't go there, to the point of being told to leave the house. I think it was probably an idle threat, but she took it up to go to Blackburn College. She subsequently returned home; I assume that meant that she left the college, and it just felt like such a shame really. And when I asked her 'when does this change?' she said 'when I'm married' and that brings up a whole load of other questions. Now I don't know if this is just a strong-minded young woman who is putting her foot down or whether indeed it is a young woman who is being forced to do something she doesn't want to do and I think that's something for children's services to look at."

"My view is that we shouldn't try to push young people to go against their family and their community," she went on, "but I think we should enable it if that is what they wish. It's about their choice. And certainly from the Asian young people I've worked with, it seems to be very small things that trigger that debate and discussion, to the point of control. I do feel for the parents, because in many cases they obviously care deeply about their children, but in many cases it's reputation and family honour which they are dealing with."

I thought back to the sisters on the Comedy Carpet in Blackpool. They had talked about Britain having been on a 'curve' in relation to social attitudes, and I reflected that the families Emma was referring to might be at a different point on the curve from the majority of people in Britain in relation to young people of different genders and backgrounds being educated together. While I was well aware that my knowledge of the South Asian community was superficial, I instinctively felt that the threat of a child being cast out by their family for wanting to be educated in a mixed environment merited Emma's intervention of involving children's services. In doing so, I felt she was protecting the child in question by standing up for the freedoms to which everyone living in the UK was entitled, whatever their background. But my own instinctive reaction aside, I didn't feel I had a strong objective basis for making that judgement, and that was something I wanted to explore further.

"These are things I just want to know more about," Emma went on, "because my husband is a courier, and he delivers things he has to get signatures for, and that's the absolute bane of his life because if he knocks on the door in Asian communities, women won't come to the door because they can't speak to a white bloke. He says women never, ever come to the door. From what you hear, that's their expectation and they're happy with that, but I would want to be able to answer my own door."

"Is it a comfort, not having to open the door?" she asked herself. "I just don't know enough about the culture behind it and why they do what they do. It's those kind of things that I would be fascinated to find out more about."

"I would also say," she added, "that the Asian community are extremely generous to us. On at least a weekly basis there is someone at the door, handing over food, particularly during religious festivals, they'll come and help us. They appear to have a much more close-knit community than I see in the Church of England, which I find a bit more 'po-faced', more talking about doing good, while the mosque is actually doing good."

It felt like an important point. The discussions about the South Asian community showed the potential for a close community to be supportive and generous, but also to be constrictive. It seemed to me that the challenge for Britain more broadly, as a country which valued individual liberty greatly, was to build a strong sense of community and solidarity while not losing the freedom the nation prized for people to live the lives that they wanted to lead.

As Emma and I talked on, she told me that there had been some resentment amongst white young people of people from migrant and minority backgrounds taking 'their' jobs.

"It's ignorance in the true sense of the word," she said, "because if you ask them 'which job have you applied for that you think someone else has taken?' they can't answer."

"I'm not saying 'open up the floodgates and let everybody in'," she went on, "but I don't think for one minute that people are coming here to take our jobs – because what they're doing is trying to come here to try to survive, first and foremost. And so what if they can use or develop their skills to be doctors, dentist, binmen, whatever? The bottom line is that some of the people who shout the loudest are the people who don't want the jobs."

I asked what she meant by that.

"Some of the young people I work with," she said, "they don't think they could do a job. They're from the second, third, fourth generation of families who have mostly been unemployed, and I don't think they believe they can work. It's that shock: how would you do at work, how would you turn up every day? It's hard for somebody who has never had anyone in their family who works, who doesn't know how to maintain a job… It's hard for people for whom Sunday is the same as Wednesday and three o'clock in the morning is the same as three o'clock in the afternoon. If you've not been to school or you've not had anybody in your family who works, what would you do?"

"I think it also comes back to what a job is defined as these days," she went on, "because it's all about zero-hour contracts, less and less money, jobs through agencies which give you two days' work and then you don't work for the rest of the week. So on the one hand you can say to these young people, 'come on, they're not taking your jobs' but on the other hand there is a reality check because there's not that much work around. I do fear for the younger generation – if you're raising the aspiration of these young people and there's nothing at the end of it, what have you done it for? Does it make life worse when you show young people what they could have had and then it turns out it's not there?"

It was a view I had heard a number of times, most recently in the pub in Poulton, but I felt that Emma, as someone working directly with young people making the transition from education to work, was more informed about the issues than most. Her question was unsettling: had we as a society created a set of circumstances in which young people felt compelled to spend significant time and money studying for qualifications for jobs which didn't necessarily exist?

"I left school at fifteen," she went on, "and I went to work at the factory office, because that's what you did and those jobs were ten a penny. And the difference between me leaving school with nothing and young people leaving school today with nothing is that they are forced into education. I went back to education when I wanted to, but young people today have to do that. I understand it – we're trying to build our national resources and trying to make our country better and wealthier, but there will always be young people who, if they were just allowed to have a bog-standard job, it would give them the self-esteem and the routine they need, and if we could give them confidence and self-worth, some of their other more offensive views would trickle away."

I asked her to expand on that last point.

"It sounds a bit simplistic," she said, "but the blame culture is what they use to hide the fact that they've got no idea how to get a job, and I think if we could address that bit, explain to them what the job search is, help them through attending work each day, then I do think those views would reduce."

Her point seemed to mirror what Alex Smith back in London had said about addressing insecurity being the route to reducing nationalism. Yet I didn't think we could or should rely on creating economic opportunities alone to solve the social and cultural problems the country faced. I had met enough people who weren't out of work but were still worried about immigration and integration to know that jobs alone would not be the answer. Addressing cultural insecurity alongside economic insecurity seemed crucial.

"The services which provide that kind of support to young people have gone," Emma continued. "People have lost their jobs, or they're filling two jobs so their capacity is less – so there's nobody who is going to be bothered when Joe Bloggs doesn't turn up into college, or when Susan Whoever doesn't get her benefits."

I wondered whether she felt that if the state stepped back, communities would step up.

"That's Mr Cameron's Big Society," Emma said. "I understand why he said that – you look at pensions, we just don't have the money. The welfare state clearly needed to be redrawn, we couldn't go on the way we were, and I'm a great believer that you shouldn't criticise unless you have an alternative, and I really don't know what the alternative is, but I just think we need to look after our most vulnerable, and I don't think we do that well – I don't think we do that at all."

"We had a young mum with us who was feeling dizzy," she went on, "and I said to her 'when did you last eat?' and she said 'Sunday' and I said 'why haven't you eaten?' and she said 'I fed him' and pointed at her baby…"

"I remember the Eighties," she continued, "and I think it's worse than that, because at least in the Eighties there was an expectation that people would help, and I don't think there's even that now. Well, we see it with the Asian community coming round with the curries, but I don't see that as a society as a whole. We're still quite divided and I think that's definitely hardened over the past five years."

"It's not that people don't care," she said, "it's just that there's not the capacity to care anymore."

*****

Her words rang in my ears as I walked out of the town centre, crossing the inner ring-road, Barbara Castle Way, and heading north. On the skyline, I could see a number of mosques in amongst the tight, terraced streets, and a beautiful old church, which I decided would be my first port of call. As I walked up, I reflected on what Emma had said: for all her concerns about freedom for young people of South Asian heritage to make their own choices, she recognised both the neighbourly spirit within their community and how it contrasted with the rest of British society. I wondered why people in the South Asian community apparently had the 'capacity to care', as Emma had put it, while the rest of society didn't in her view. I thought back to the Canon at Blackburn Cathedral, and reflected on diminishing numbers of worshippers and his downbeat assessment of the capacity of churches to do everything they wanted to do in terms of community cohesion.

When I reached the church I had seen on the skyline, I found it boarded up, a few beer bottles strewn by its entrance and a broken vodka bottle by a couple of piles of burnt-out rubbish. The police were attending an incident at a nearby house, so I left, heading west into the Whalley Range area of the town, where I'd seen a number of mosques on the skyline.

Whalley Range seemed a very different area to where I had just been. Women wore hijabs, niqabs and burkas, and the shops sold Asian clothes and jewellery. A business advertised local halal cuisine and a parcel firm offered a service delivering packages to India, Pakistan and Bangladesh. Above a shop I saw a sign which said 'Aid Convey Drop-off Point'. I walked past the local school, a Church of England primary. It was lunchtime and the pupils played outside in the sunshine. On a new sports pitch, every child I saw appeared to be of South Asian heritage. Next to the school, a sign advertised the Blackburn weekly Ijtema every Thursday at 8pm. Below it, the sign read 'I must strive to reform myself and the people of the entire world'. There were three mosques, an Islamic school and an Islamic centre within a few hundred yards. I thought back to the people I had met who had talked about areas of the country where the demographics had completely changed and guessed that this was exactly the kind of area they had meant.

I headed up to one of the mosques I had seen on the skyline, keen to talk to members of the Muslim community about the issues which had been raised on my travels. I knocked on the door of the main office and got talking to two volunteers, one of whom was in his forties, the other in his seventies. They welcomed me warmly and were keen to answer my questions.

They told me the mosque had been completely rebuilt and a school had been built alongside it. I asked where the funding came from, and they told me it was predominantly from local people.

"We have receivers," the younger man explained, showing me a machine I'd never seen before, a cross between a walkie-talkie and a radio. "It's like a radio, but only for communications from the mosque. We sent out a message saying that we needed funding from the community. That's how it works."

"We received some contributions from Qatar as well," he went on. "That helped with the building but the local needs that we require, we just put a message out on the receiver and people give."

He showed me a laminated sheet of paper with the prayer times for the next month. It had on it the frequency and receiver numbers, which enabled people to tune in. He explained that the receiver was tightly controlled to ensure only messages from the mosque went out through it. Anyone in the community could buy a receiver, and it enabled them to listen into broadcasts from visiting speakers. There were also translations of Friday prayers for those who wanted to listen in.

"We monitor everything," he said, "so we say when an outsider comes in, we might give him a spot if there is one for giving a speech, and we ask him what he's going to be speaking about and one thing and another, and we warn him about the context, so we know what he's going to say. So the speech must only be about religion, no politics, no asking for money – nothing about anything except religion, and if he does say something else, we stop him straight away."

I asked if this was a response to concerns about extremism and hate speech.

"Yes, yes, yes," he said, "anything to do with hate, anything to do with politics, we don't want it. This is a place of community and faith, nothing but that."

I asked if there was good interfaith work in the area.

"As we are based within the community," he said, "we're obviously going to serve the community which needs it. When other communities ask for our help, such as the recent Syria problem, we must have collected 250 tonnes of items: food, donations, clothes, hospital things."

"We're already sending five containers," the older man said.

"Five big massive containers," the younger man said, "and the young people have been helping with that. These lads are all working, and they're asking for donations, and people package it and sort it out. There was a company which has given 700 bags of rice – a big company. It doesn't matter if it is an Asian or an English company, they give."

"At the present time it is Syria," he added, "but it was also Cumbria – we had volunteers going there, helping with the floods. They went and cleaned their houses, and they were very happy, and they sent us a letter to say thank you. This is what we do."

I asked if he felt there wasn't enough coverage of the positive things done by the Muslim community.

"Well, to be quite honest, you're right," he said, "but we don't like to say anything about it. Let people talk, we can't fight them, so let them say what they want. We know what we're doing, we're not doing it for them, we're doing for ourselves, to please the Almighty. To show somebody, to be boasting about it, that's wasted then."

I smiled at the parallel with what the Canon had told me – 'seek first the kingdom of God'.

"We focus within the community," the man went on, "we want to be good citizens. Our faith says that if you live in the country, you follow their laws. You follow your own religion, but you follow their laws as well. To be a good Muslim, you've got to be a good citizen, and to be a good citizen, you've got to be a good Muslim. It works both ways."

I asked if there was any tension between British law and custom and being a good Muslim.

"No, no," he said. "The council has been very good with us, and we help them if there are any issues or situations. There aren't any at the moment, touch wood, but there have always been good relations. The cohesion between the two is good. There's no tension, there's no friction, there's nothing – everyone is happy with what they are and life goes on."

I asked about the people I had met who had raised concerns about sharia law.

"This community here," the older man said, "we don't bring the sharia law in here, it does not apply to the people living in this country. British law applies here. If you want to go to that side, that's extremist to me."

I asked the younger man what his message would be to the people who said Muslim people didn't want to play a full role in British society.

"I think they don't know the whole history of it," he said. "I think we as a community, we have a lot of input in this country. We feel that we abide by the rules, we are integrated with it. I mean the percentage of people who own their own house, their own businesses – maybe about just 2% of people have free housing, otherwise they are all working in textiles and other industry. And I think the young people are more educated than the host, the mainstream population, the white people like yourself…"

I asked why he thought that was.

"Because they want to be educated," he said, "education is the main part. Now people are saying 'these people are getting the jobs' but I'm saying the effort is put in for the Asian community to have an input in this country – you've got the Mayor in London, so there must be an effort he's putting in. Put people into a melting pot and this is what you get."

I thought back to Richard, the man I'd met in Sunderland who felt that Christianity and British culture were under threat from what he referred to as the Islamisation of Britain. The men in the mosque were holding Sadiq Khan up as a model of successful integration, while Richard had seen his election as a portent of a shift in power as the demographics of the country changed. It was that sense of a power shift which I wanted to explore further: the men in the mosque had referred to the white population as the 'mainstream population', and I asked whether they thought that the South Asian population would always be a minority.

"Minority in population, definitely," the younger man said, "but in the sense of progress, you can never tell. In education, the white child is not performing so well and the Asian child, he wants to put the effort in and be something and someone in life."

It was almost time for prayers, and as they got up to leave, I asked the younger man if he was worried about resentment about the success of Asian pupils amongst the white community.

"If you want to get somewhere, you have to put in the effort," he said. "This country has given an opportunity to everyone – if someone doesn't want to take advantage of that opportunity, then whose fault is it?"

*****

I walked back down into the centre of town, towards the railway station. In front of BBC Radio Lancashire, opposite the cathedral, a couple rowed loudly. A man argued with a group of teenagers walking the other way. A couple of teenagers sat under the statue of Queen Victoria and drank energy drinks; they laughed and joked but I was really worried about what I'd heard in the town.

Like Emma, I was conscious of my lack of knowledge about the South Asian community and I imagined the issues she had described might be exceptional given that she worked with some of the most vulnerable young people in the town. Nevertheless, I was troubled by the idea of children being threatened with being cast out for wanting to attend the local college just because it was mixed. Further, while the volunteers at the mosque were clearly very active members of British society, their tight monitoring of external speakers was a reminder of their awareness of the risk of vulnerable and alienated people within their community being radicalised by external preachers.

I also thought that the many strengths of the South Asian community – a clear sense of community spirit and shared values, active institutions at the heart of the community and a strong work ethic and attitude towards education – highlighted some of the challenges facing much of the rest of British society. I thought of Emma's remarks about people not having the capacity to care, the struggle for funding which the Canon had described, and the beautiful church at the top of the hill, derelict and surrounded by rubbish, and I wondered who was in a position to respond to the challenges I had identified in non-Muslim areas in the way that the mosque would have done for the community it served. There were outstanding leaders in the voluntary sector like Emma, trying her best to balance respect for all communities with upholding the freedoms which she believed all British young people deserved, but cuts to local budgets seemed to be putting such work at risk. Based on my conversation with the Canon, the church seemed to be facing similar challenges. I decided to look into the impact of cuts on social solidarity and community cohesion on my next stop, Liverpool.

10

Austerity, solidarity and sharing in Liverpool

The following day, I headed to Liverpool to meet Peter Brennan, a local Labour councillor in the Old Swan area of the city. After my experience in Blackburn, where I had seen the impact of great financial pressure on faith and community bodies, I was wondering what role there was for local government in responding to some of the challenges I'd identified.

We met in the Joseph Lappin Centre, a youth and community hub named after a teenager who had been murdered in the city a few years earlier. The heating wasn't working on a cold day in late November, and as we talked I could see my breath. I asked him how local government and the community organisations he worked with were responding to the challenges I had identified and whether they could play a role in building a stronger sense of community.

"With the cuts that have happened in Liverpool," he said, "we need places like this centre more than ever. As the council funding diminishes, the likes of this have got to step up to the mark. They're doing their very best, but it's a very competitive market for funding out there and everybody is in the same boat. There's important community organisations in this city and their future is in doubt because of the question marks over the funding: sometimes their funding is European, so what replaces that kind of funding? We don't know. Same with the

£90m cuts from the government to the council which are coming. What replaces that? The community can step up insofar as the energy and the enthusiasm is there, but it needs the finances to back it up. If you haven't got the finances, what do you do?"

I asked if he could give an example where money was critical.

"Our social care budget has gone down from £218m to £178m," he said, "and now we're around about the £152m mark and that's going to have to be reduced further. And to put that into perspective, if we're looking at adult social care, we're spending £152m on social care, and we only bring in £128m in council tax receipts in total across the whole city for everything. So we're something like £30m short just to cover social services, never mind anything else."

"That money goes on the care packages for our elderly," he went on. "Paying people to get them up, making sure they have their breakfast, giving them their lunch, going back at night-time to make sure they get to bed. And the workers will tell you, they're run ragged, because they're getting fifteen, twenty minutes per person – what can you do for that?"

I asked him if families could take a greater responsibility for their own relatives.

"They do," he said, "but what we often find is that we're asking vulnerable people to work with even more vulnerable people. It's just not easy, it's not easy."

"It's fine for me," he went on. "My mother is nearly 83, she lives alone, and thank God she's able to look after herself, but her knees are going and the day's going to come when she can't get out, her mobility is going to decrease – she's getting older, I can see her slowing down, but at least she's got me. If she didn't have me… me dad's gone, me sister lives in California, would she get the care that she needs? And there's lots of people in much worse states than my mother. There's people who haven't got a soul in the world."

"Just this year," he added, "in this centre, we're looking on Christmas Day at a lunch with entertainment for local elderly living alone, the homeless and vulnerable families. We've got a space for one hundred people and that's going to be replicated times ten across the city... we're hoping to feed 1,000 people across the city on Christmas Day. I've never experienced it like this in my lifetime – people are coming to us in our surgeries and crying because they can't pay a bill."

"We're not talking about hundreds of pounds," he went on, "we're talking about the very basics that people need to live on. These people are desperate: 'where do I turn? Where do I turn?'"

I asked what he felt should be done, given the size of Britain's national debt. I wondered if he felt we should be cutting our cloth differently given the hole in the public finances.

"We're not hitting the ones who can afford to cut back the cloth," he said. "It's the people who didn't have the cloth to begin with. We're hitting the most vulnerable all the time. It's the ones who can't afford it, not the ones who created it in the first place – the bankers, your tax evaders or avoiders. We should be chasing them to bring more money in. You know, if we brought in all of the offshore money which is stashed away, I don't think we'd be one of the six richest countries, I think we'd be one of the three."

"We've had our government grant cut by 58% since 2010," he went on, "so what I put across to some people who say 'well, we're sick of hearing about these cuts, we want new street lamps' or whatever, I say 'there's no money' and they say 'well that's your problem, you're the council.' But if it continues as it has done, and we have cuts of a further £90m, what do we do? The Mayor said by next year we won't have the money even for our statutory services."

I asked what that would mean in practice.

"The worst is going to happen," he said, "dare I say it, people could die. We've cut back on everything – reduced library hours, street cleaning... in most of the city, we've gone to fortnightly bin collections... some authorities have gone up to three-weekly or even monthly collections, and with that has come the problem of fly-tipping. There's a health and safety risk too, because when people want to get rid of rubbish which is piled up, they set fire to it. You get rats running round, and where's the money going to come from for pest control?"

"There's only so much we can do," he added. "We're asking voluntary sector organisations to do more and more and more, but the support has still got to be there for that. So, yeah, you can clean the streets yourself, you can pile the rubbish up, but who comes along to take it away?"

I asked how the communities had responded to what was happening.

"We've had UKIP standing in the wards that might be struggling a bit," he said, "and they'll say 'it's all the immigrants' fault – if we didn't have all the immigrants coming over, we wouldn't have all these problems, it's them that dump the rubbish, it's them that take the jobs, blah blah blah' – the usual bile. And to be fair it does get raised on the doorstep a lot, immigration."

"Immigration and dog shit," he added, "they're probably the biggest things people complain about."

I found myself making a note to myself for later – 'immigration and dog shit' – and as I did, I asked how he responded to the testing circumstances he was in.

"Keep smiling," he said, "keep going. Because if we all go moping around with long faces, it doesn't help anyone. But it's also telling people 'this is the way it is – you want a pound's worth of goods, but you've only got 42 pence. What do you decide you're going to buy?'"

*****

We left the centre and headed out into Old Swan, Peter talking to me about the area as we drove. We went past a church, and I asked him what role he thought there was for religious and faith communities to fill the gaps in society.

"The clergy and the different faiths have always been quite outspoken on social justice and poverty," he said. "They're all helping out with foodbanks or running foodbanks. They're on our side, they'll publicise our stuff, they'll give us rooms – whatever we need, they are there. So it's good in that sense, but you know, the churches have got dwindling congregations, they're largely older people. There aren't many younger people going to churches, so even the funds they're getting in on the plate, they're not getting much in. But, you know, they do try their best."

We drove on, through row after row of long terraced streets, perhaps one hundred houses per street. As we drove on, we saw leaves piled on the side of the road.

"I'm not happy with all these leaves," he said, "these should be well gone. That should have been swept up."

As we drove on, we saw more and more leaves which had accumulated at the side of the streets.

"Bloody hell," he said, "someone's been very naughty – leaf fall was meant to have been done in Old Swan. They told me it's been done."

He stopped the car, and phoned an officer in the council. He left a message, asking for someone to give him a call. A minute later, the phone rang.

"I'm just on Broad Green Road," Peter told his colleague, "and to be honest, the dead leaves are everywhere. All over the pavement, it hasn't been touched. We're talking from Oak Hill Park, right the way down, and the roads off it… alright, thanks for that… ta-ra lad, ta-ra."

He put the phone down and explained to me that the man he'd spoken to was one of the council bosses, and had said that he would look into it and call straight back. We drove on.

"It's just basic stuff," he said. "It only takes one elderly person to slip and break their hip…"

I asked if the problem was a result of the cutbacks.

"We've lost of 2,000 staff," he explained, "so yeah, it's cutbacks, but we've got a programme, so Old Swan will get done on certain days, but if another councillor in another part of the city has complained because someone in their area has had a fall, the team might go there."

His phone rang again.

"Here we go," he said, picking up the phone and then speaking to his colleague. "Alright mate, yeah... yeah, that's brilliant... alright."

It was agreed that the leaves would be taken away the following day, and we continued down towards the city. We saw another huge church lying derelict, and a series of charity shops and 'cash for clothes' shops, which advertised payment of 50p per kilo for old clothes.

"What you're seeing now is some people taking clothes off other people's lines to sell for 50p per kilo," Peter told me as we drove on, "that's just how desperate people are."

*****

We drove into the city centre, where Peter introduced me to his colleague, Councillor Gary Millar. We talked about local politics and the severe budget cuts which had been taking place. I said that from what I understood, Liverpool's budget was being subsidised by tax income from other parts of the country, and Gary clearly disagreed with my assessment.

"I don't think people are being subsidised just because they're poor," he said firmly. "I come from a working-class background, I grew up in a room and kitchen in Easter Road in Edinburgh. My mum and dad were paying their taxes and people like them have as much right for the hard work that they put into what they do as anybody living in a leafy suburb. It's all about fairness. Being poor doesn't mean you don't work – being poor means that you've got food and fuel poverty because things are so expensive. There are some things, like water and electricity and gas that maybe sometimes are artificially too high."

"It's about sharing it equally," he went on, "so I don't agree that because I'm living in a poorer area, I'm being subsidised by a richer area, and I don't go along with the idea that I might be poor because I haven't got a job, but do you know up until last year, that person might have had a job, and been paying taxes and national insurance for all their life, but for whatever reasons, whether it is bankers or the change in the economy, that my business has closed down or they've reduced their numbers. I've still got a mind, I've still got a soul, I've still got a heart, I've still got a family. It's incumbent on us all, whether we're rich or poor, to share what we've got."

What he said made me think hard. My mind went back to some of my earlier conversations, where people I had met had focused on 'looking after our own'. In this context, Gary was talking about the national community sharing its wealth and making sure that deprived areas like Old Swan got their fair share. Yet my sense from my travels was that the bonds of solidarity were being stretched in the UK, decreasing the likelihood that Gary's vision of national redistribution would be achieved. Why, some of the people I had met might have asked, should I share with a young person who didn't want to work hard or a migrant who they felt made no contribution to society? I began to recognise another huge potential cost of failure to build a cohesive society: a lack of solidarity undermining the kind of sharing within the nation which Gary was talking about, just at a time when people needed to come together. It struck me that the challenge for anybody who cared about building a sharing society was to create and maintain the conditions under which people came together and recognised how important it was to support one another.

I asked how he felt the case for redistribution could be made in such divided times.

"It needs us all to be passionate," he said. "We need to get rid of apathy – in Old Swan, only 34% of people vote. 66% are not voting. Why?"

"The ones that are voting now," he went on, "are the ones that are feeling affronted, upset – 'they're taking our jobs, they're coming over here and getting our benefits'. Factually incorrect, but that's what they're hearing. Fake news. So we have to fight against that propaganda – it's our job to make sure we get as many people out there and voting as possible, but if they don't think we can make any difference, then they ain't going to vote."

"So some of our biggest issues are dog fouling," he continued, "and people say 'Peter, you've got to get that cleared up'. It's not his job, but he's told to do it. He's sworn at by residents. And we're never going to get voted for if we can't get rid of dogs pooing in the street. Is that realistic? For them it is, but for us we know that practicality-wise, we can't do it."

"We've somehow got to find a way to change respect," he added, "and it's not just dog fouling: it's street-cleaning, it's putting your bins out on time, it's not parking on pavements, it's not cycling your bike on the pavement or down a one-way road. Those are just little references to what's wrong."

I said that I had understood that Liverpool was a close-knit community, but I suggested by fly-tipping or not cleaning up after their dogs, people weren't contributing to their community.

"No," he said, "and the reason why that's increasing is those communities are being destroyed. Let's take one area: Norris Green. In Norris Green, housing associations came along and offered three-bedroom houses for people to move into, because they wanted to repopulate what was a deprived area. So people moved in, but along comes the government a few years later and says 'you shouldn't be living there, you've got extra bedrooms, get out'. What's happened in the meantime is that a fantastic community has been built, where granny lives in the same street as her daughter, and the daughter wants to go to college and do better, and granny looks after the grandkids until mum gets home from college. Same when she wants to get a job – granny picks the kids up from school, maybe takes them to school. But then the bedroom tax comes along and you've got them then moving into private terraced accommodation, which they hate, because they're now living in a place which is too small. So what could then happen is that they argue with the next door neighbours, some could become neighbours from hell because they're angry, they're disenfranchised because in this case they've been moved from Norris Green to Toxteth – as an example. They've moved from nice, comfortable, warm, central heating, double-glazing into private landlords, possibly creating a lot of anger, breaking up communities…"

"The same thing happened in the Seventies," he went on, "when the Tories did slum clearances in Liverpool, when there were 60,000 people living in Everton, Scotty Road and Anfield. The docks went from 30,000 staff to 1,500 because it went from many people taking stuff off big boats and manhandling it onto trucks. Liverpool's docking industry was decimated but you still had all the families living in the area; no income, on the dole, they were becoming second and third generation unemployed because granddad worked on the docks, dad worked on the docks, and the kids were about to go and work on the docks, but now there weren't any jobs. So what happened? They moved them out to new towns like Skelmersdale, Kirby and Runcorn. 200,000 people were moved out of Liverpool to other local authorities. And that's seriously affected some local communities – so some of the history of Liverpool's historic communities was decimated by the Tories."

"The EU would say to us, 'do you want some money?'" he added as we prepared to part, "and we would say 'yes, what do we need to do?' They were *asking* us to bid – do you think the Tory government is going to ask us to bid or are they going to say to us 'beg for it'? And we should never have to beg, we should be offered – that's fairness, that's justice."

*****

It had been an interesting day: it was clear that cutbacks were biting, and while I had been inspired by Peter's valiant attempts to provide leadership in spite of difficult financial circumstances, I couldn't help but feel that his hands were tied by lack of money. Having seen evidence that faith and community organisations were similarly struggling, I did wonder who would step up to help at a time of financial strife. Yet as I left, it was Gary's comments that Liverpool should never have to beg the rest of the country for money and that poorer people weren't being subsidised by richer people which stuck with me. His view seemed to be predicated on a sense of solidarity within the nation which I felt needed strengthening. In a divided society, I didn't think that public consent for the kind of redistribution he was talking about could be taken for granted – it depended on a sense of mutual obligation and responsibility across the country, a sense of the nation as a community, of which I had seen little evidence on my travels.

I thought about Peter's comment that his constituents were most concerned about 'immigration and dog shit'. Even in the context of the severe poverty Peter had described, it was hard to justify those who didn't clean up after their dogs: they weren't exercising their responsibility to the community and I could see how a sense of social solidarity could be undermined as a result. Gary had said that communities had been disrupted by government policy such as the bedroom tax but I couldn't help thinking that some of the issues I had explored on my travels relating to immigration and integration might have played a role too. If there was a sense that Britain was a country where not everyone worked together – where people stole each other's laundry, or didn't clean up after their dogs, or took from the public purse without contributing to it, or held worldviews which were not in line with shared values, or didn't feel a sense of loyalty to the country as a whole – then I could see why some people might not want to share with others. It seemed to me that rebuilding a sense of shared values and common endeavour was essential but as I headed to Wales for the next stage of my journey, I wondered how domestic solidarity could be rebuilt without losing a sense of responsibility to those beyond Britain's borders.

11

Industry, insecurity and a sense of home in Treforest

I headed to the Welsh Valleys, focused on beginning to answer the questions I had been grappling with. I was going to meet students at the University of South Wales, and their course leader, Professor Howard Williamson. It was 9.30 in the morning, and students from across the world streamed onto the university campus from the former miners' houses which lined the surrounding streets.

I had an hour before I was due to meet Howard and his students, so I headed into Treforest, the small mining town in which the university was based. The old miners' houses, two-up two-down homes lining long, terraced streets, were now full of students from all over the world. There was a 'To Let' sign up at every second or third house. A Chinese food store along the road was the only shop I could see, apart from the takeaways down towards the station. I walked through an alleyway: along with abandoned beer bottles and pizza boxes, used fireworks, an empty condom packet and general rubbish, I saw a bible study book lying on the ground.

Two hundred yards from the university, I found a builder working on an extension to a house and got talking to him.

"The mining village has gone," he told me, "it's a student village now."

I asked him what had happened to the people who used to live in the town.

"God knows," he said. "They've passed on I suppose, and they leave the houses and their kids sell them on to people like him across the road."

He pointed to a letting agency.

"You look at everything that's closing down," he went on, "pubs and churches, all sorts of things are closing down. They convert them into flats for students, because that's where your money is."

A group of students from different backgrounds walked past.

"It's like the League of Nations round here," he said. "I'm telling you, trainload after trainload after trainload, going up to the college here. There's one fella I see who looks local to me. All the rest are students."

I asked what hope there was for the town beyond students.

"None," he said, laughing, "we're all doomed."

I suggested he'd been able to find work at least.

"Yeah," he said, "but this place belongs to our boss – we're working on an extension at the back so he can have more students in…"

"It's mad," he added, heading back to work, "money, money, money."

I walked on and met a man in a flat cap who told me he had lived in the town for 50 years.

"I moved here in 1965," he told me, "August, it was the Bank Holiday and it was the first year that the August Bank Holiday went from the first Monday of the month to the last Monday of the month. I'd got married just before that, and when I got here, there wasn't any students here at all. Now I don't think 10% of the houses are residents, they're all students. Though I have been told now that it's going to be very difficult to buy a house and put students in. Apparently you've got to apply to the council for permission, and they're not giving it. They're trying to regenerate the area, but whether that'll happen, I don't know."

We looked up the road and counted ten 'To Let' signs outside houses on a single street.

A car pulled over.

"Can you tell me where Princess Street is?" the woman inside asked.

"Yes, I can," the man said, "you'll have to reverse, and then you'll have to go down there."

He helped the woman to turn her car around and then he came back to me.

I asked him to describe the town when he moved to it.

"Well, it was just a village," he said, "the pits had shut. I was working on a building site in Cardiff, and there were builders here and ex-miners – a working class area."

I asked what had happened to the people who lived here.

"A lot of them moved, to be honest," he said. "After the first lot went, and then students started coming in, and people sold just because there were students here."

I asked why he had stayed.

"I had my wife," he said, "I had my children, and they wouldn't have wanted to move I don't think. My wife would have gone, but she passed away, a long time ago now. But I didn't want to move, I didn't want to take another mortgage out."

I asked whether he felt like he was in a minority in the town.

"Round here, yes," he said. "Yes we are, because you look there, across the road. The first house without students in is that house by the yellowy car."

The car that he pointed to was at least five houses down.

"And then you've got to go a fair way up to see any more," he went on. "I doubt there's more than five or six families live from there to the end."

"To be honest," he went on, "I would like to see more families, but what's the odds of people wanting to come and buy a house here when it's only students here?"

"That place was a shop," he continued, pointing up the road. "That place was a shop, there were shops at the bottom. Gone. And you go down to the bottom, and it's all fast-food, and I don't think they'd be there if it wasn't for the students."

I asked whether he was happy about the change.

"In a way, it's not so good," he said. "Like 1977, the Silver Jubilee for the Queen, there was a party up here, a street party, there was a party up there – the number of parties that was around. The streets were closed, the tables were out… I doubt that you'd get one party now. That's all gone. The community as such is not here now."

I asked what it was like in university holidays.

"It's very quiet," he said. "Well you don't see many, do you? There used to be a school up there – been closed for years now. Actually – those people in that house here, they've got children, but they're the only ones."

"The school building is houses now," he added as we parted. "That building up the top. No kids, no children round here. Now on Halloween, nobody knocks the door."

I reflected as I walked away that I felt nothing but sympathy for him – his community had changed around him, and no one had asked him if that was what he wanted. The university had undoubtedly brought a huge amount to the area, but the fast-food shops and higher rental fees meant little to him. It was no longer his place. I felt it was right for the council to try to limit the number of student houses on the basis that economic gain should not outweigh people's right to live in their own community, and I thought it was reasonable for those people who didn't want to live in a student town to move away if they wanted to.

I thought back to Richard, the man in Sunderland who had been so concerned about demographic changes in British communities, and I asked myself why I had more sympathy for a man in a town suddenly dominated by students than I would have had if the change had been about people from a different culture, religion or nationality coming to the area. I reflected that there was no judgment conferred on the students for being students – they were simply at a different stage of life to the older man and their lifestyles were just different from his. There was no sense that one was 'right' or one was 'wrong': they just wanted different things from the community. Yet questions relating to culture seemed much more complicated: was it reasonable for people to want to leave an area if it changed as a result of people of a different religion or culture coming to it? Was it reasonable for people to try to maintain their culture so that the place they called home didn't change? And did the answers to these questions for individual communities translate to a national level? These were difficult questions which I knew I had to try to answer.

*****

At the university, I met up with Howard and headed inside to meet the first of two groups of undergraduates studying his course on youth and social policy. The group of around fifteen was all female except for one young man, and included students from Poland and Jamaica, while the rest were from South Wales or nearby. I knew the area had received substantial funding from the EU, and I asked the group why they thought so many people in the area had voted to leave.

"In Ebbw Vale," the young man said, "we've got a new college and a new road linking it to Merthyr. So these places have been getting funding from the EU, but it's not like people feel any better for it."

"People can't get jobs," agreed a young woman. "All my friends who have graduated, they've gone to Cardiff or further afield so even with all the new things, there's still nothing there."

"The only way you can get a job these days is if you have experience," the young man said, "but you can't get experience unless you have a job. You're just stuck in that loop, in a dead-end job on a till and you think 'I'm going to go somewhere where there is jobs'."

"And the jobs that do exist, they're insecure," someone else said, "so my partner, he's in a job but it's only part-time hours, but he's afraid to leave it just in case, if he goes somewhere else, they might go bust."

"I think you've got to look at culture as well," said the young man. "If you turn the clocks back, say 40, 50 years, there was industry. But now the industry has gone abroad, and there's nothing to replace it. What you've got here is a service nation, not an industry nation. If you're an industry nation, you can build, grow, sell it on, but if you're just providing services, you're just selling someone else's product. It's all very well building town centres, but nobody wants to work selling cheap clothes for the rest of their life."

"These firms take on people at Christmas time," someone else said, "people are there for like seven weeks, and then they just throw 'em because they don't need them no more. So people who are on Jobseeker's Allowance, they sign off Jobseeker's for like seven weeks of work, and then they've got to wait six weeks to sign back on and get money, so what's the point?"

I said that many people I had spoken to had suggested that immigration was the big issue they were concerned about and I asked why there might be concern about immigration in an area like South Wales which didn't have a huge number of people coming to it from abroad.

"Look at this way," the young man said, "you might not have a job, but you've still got free health care, better living quality, we're not getting shot at every day, we've got a stable government, a stable police system, we live in a very lucky country. And people want to protect what they've got, and they don't want to feel like it's being corrupted."

The word 'corrupted' caused a ripple around the room, and the Jamaican student winced. I asked what he meant by 'corrupted'.

"That's a good question," he said. "Like lowering the standards. How can I put this? It's fear of the unknown."

"I disagree with you," someone else said. "This is a secular society and if people want to come here and better their lives and are willing to work for it, I'm for it. And they can, like, do as they please – people should be more accepting of it."

"People just stick to their own, wherever you go," the young woman next to her said. "You know, it's like the Brits staying together when they live in Spain, or London Welsh. People go, but they stick."

I asked whether either of the overseas students wanted to give their perspective.

"I think people voted for immigrants to be kicked out," said the Polish student. "I'm not from here and I can see how they treat me differently after the Brexit vote. For me, people are not interested in politics, they just want immigrants to leave the country, but they have to learn how to recognise immigrants who came here to work, to study – because I work, I pay taxes for this country, I didn't come here to get benefits and stuff."

She had suggested that she felt she had been treated differently after the vote and I asked if she was willing to talk more about that.

"I've noticed, like, when I came to work," she said, "and someone know I'm Polish, they treat me like 'it's about time to leave,' something like that – cheeky comments. I don't do anything bad in this country…"

She trailed off. Someone asked her if the comments hurt her.

"Yeah," she said, "of course."

There was silence in the room.

"People keep saying that immigrants, they take the jobs," she said after a moment, "but I used to work in a cake factory in Cardiff, and over there I used to work with loads of people who were not from here. The majority of people were immigrants, so British people don't want to work for five pounds an hour, and somebody like me, I came here and it's enough for me. But British people don't want to work for five pounds, six pounds…"

"We're a snobbish people," the young man said.

Everyone laughed, and I asked him what he meant.

"Put it this way," he said, "in my area, most of the people who work in the factories are from abroad, because most of the local people say 'ooh, I don't want to get dirty and stinky for that job'. But then we go 'ooh, we don't have any jobs – it's unfair, you've got a job, I don't have one' – but it's because we don't want to get our hands dirty."

"It's like if you went now, 'who wants to dig a hole for five pounds an hour?'" he continued. "Most people here would say 'get lost' but you find someone who is desperate, and they'll say 'yeah, I'll dig the hole'. We're in a privileged state here, we have a very lovely lifestyle, whereas if you've got someone from somewhere like Somalia, gets a job for a fiver, he thinks 'happy days'."

*****

The next group was also all female aside from one young man, but this time all the participants were from South Wales. I started by asking them why they felt people in the area had voted for Brexit.

"The biggest amount of voters were the elderly," one young woman said, "and they had the view of 'make Britain great again'. You know, when we made our own things…"

I asked what people thought about the idea of making Britain great again.

"To us, Britain has never been great," a young woman said. "What does that mean to us? I don't know the meaning of that caption."

"We've got one of the biggest inequalities of wealth anywhere around the world," the young man said, "so I don't really understand where the concept of 'Great' Britain comes from – I don't know what's so great about it."

I asked if there was anyone who had a different view.

"I think you should be proud of where you come from," a young woman said. "I think you should want your place to be great – I think Britain could be great, I just don't think it is right now."

I asked what would make it great.

"I don't know," she said, "but I do think people forget that back in the times where there were the mines, when Britain was 'great', there were also problems, and the problems are just different now, but we're like 'uh-oh, Great Britain is no longer great, we're just Britain'."

"Similar to the mining," someone said. "People get nostalgic about it but it was dirty, it was dangerous, people died… So is it just that we know more about the modern day so we realise it's not great?'

"I don't think it's ever been great," someone else said. "It's always had issues. I just think they need to stop the panic, sit down, have a little cup of tea and just talk about it. I remember when I was younger, I always thought 'why are they worried about money? Just go and make some more'. The Royal Mint makes more money – just print it off, it would solve a lot of problems…"

There was silence for a moment and I asked what, aside from printing more money, would make things better in the UK.

"I think cutting down on intolerance," the young man said. "I think people are really intolerant of other people's cultures and don't really respect or understand each other. I think if you got racism and intolerance out the way, it would solve a lot of problems in our society."

A young woman, who had been sat quietly, raised her head.

"I think sometimes, though," she said, "we are so… this might sound absolutely awful… but we're so scared to upset someone that we actually become racist on ourselves. I'm thinking of a really stupid example, but at work I'm a lifeguard, and if a white female comes in with clothes on, the rule is we've got to send them out.

However, if a Muslim lady comes in with clothes on, we have to accept them. But hang on, the white person might feel a bit insecure so why can't they come in? And you stand back and you say actually, that's racist to the white person because we're stopping them from doing something because we're just so scared to say anything that could be politically incorrect."

"It's not right, is it?" she went on, "and things like that, they don't make Britain great. I'm not saying that we should kick anyone out, but equality is leaning back to not being equality."

I asked what other people thought about that.

"I totally agree with you 100%," another young woman said, "because – I was amazed, I couldn't believe it – one of my friends went to KFC in Birmingham and asked for a Big Daddy with bacon, and they said 'we don't serve bacon in this branch'. And I just think that is ridiculous."

"We've lost our culture by trying to serve everyone else's culture," the lifeguard said.

"If they don't want bacon, that's fine," her friend said, "and I know there's the kosher thing that it can't be served in the same place, but the majority of British people like bacon."

"It's probably a business-decision," another young woman said. "In that area, they probably sell less bacon, so it probably makes sense not to offer it than it does round here. Because if there's no one eating bacon there…"

"Yeah," the young woman said, "but even if they bought two packs of bacon…"

"But serving bacon could lose them customers," someone else said, "so they're not going to do that, are they?"

"But if we go to Dubai," the lifeguard said, "I can't drink or I can't dance in the street… not that that's my daily thing to do, but you know… but we bring people back here, and it's like 'of course we'll do this for you, yes sir, no sir, three bags full sir'."

"I know that Newport is opening a halal burger kitchen," she went on, "and do I think that's wrong? No. Do you think we should accommodate for them? Yeah, but don't change what we've got in place to do it. Make them have their own... You know, I might want to try a halal burger one day, just because I want to. Do you know what I mean? But if I want a bit of bacon in my Big Daddy, don't stop me."

"I do think that we are very tolerant where many countries aren't," she added.

"But in this country, the church used to run the country," another young woman said, "and it wasn't that long ago that if a woman had a baby out of wedlock, she'd be locked in an asylum, so isn't that the same?"

There was no response to her question, and everyone seemed to agree with her. I thought back to the sisters in Blackpool who had talked about Britain being on a 'curve' of cultural development in relation to issues like equality: the young woman's point about women in the past being placed in asylums for having babies out of wedlock seemed to be that Britain shouldn't judge other cultures because it had a history where extreme religious orthodoxy and gender inequality had been dominant. Yet it seemed to me that Britain had worked its way through those times and reached a more balanced position which rejected such treatment of women and promoted gender equality. On that basis, while I thought the young woman who had made the point was right, I didn't think that Britain's imperfect past should stop the country standing up for the values people in modern Britain largely shared. Around me, the conversation was moving on.

"All I'm saying is that I think they should have a place where their culture eats," the lifeguard said.

I asked who she meant be 'they'.

"Anyone," she said, and then paused for a moment before continuing. "Whoever wants to eat how their culture eats. I guess I mean the bigger ethnic minorities, if that's not contradicting myself. Muslims…"

She drifted off and the session ended with few answers.

*****

That evening, Howard and I reflected on the conversation with the group.

"I think you've got racist people over here and cosmopolitan liberal people over here," he said, gesturing to one hand and then gesturing to the other, "and then you've got a huge swathe of people in the middle with a range of views, like the views we heard about KFC or the swimming pool. I thought they were quite brave to express those views, because in universities, you should perhaps not express those views that things have gone a bit too far."

I reflected that it was an incredible thing to consider that in a university, a place of free thought, she should be considered brave for expressing what was, in my experience, a pretty commonly-held view. I asked Howard what his own view was.

"I went to the University of Copenhagen in 2001," he said, "and I was shocked by some of the comments made about immigrants made by the staff there – they were the sorts of comments which in respectable circles in Britain, you would not have heard. But as I spent time in Denmark – which is fundamentally a very boring, safe place – I saw that there were small things which started to undermine this steady, respectful Danish culture. And it was nearly always immigrants: immigrant taxi drivers who didn't respect traffic lights, walkers who would just shoot across the road whatever the lights said. And then on the bus: Danish buses are designed so there's a bit in the middle for mums with prams. And you'd notice that white Danish kids, if a mum with a pram got on, they'd move out of that space, but a bunch of immigrant kids – just schoolkids, noisy, having fun – they'd stay huddled there together in that space, and a mum with a pram wouldn't be able to get on. And there was this view that it was a slow corrosion of what the Danes had built up over time."

"The Danes have an approach," he went on, "which is a bit like that bacon story earlier, which is that it doesn't matter where you come from, it doesn't matter about your skin colour, what faith you subscribe to, as long as you act like a good Dane, you are welcome. So it's not multiculturalism, it's integration. So the argument is that there is a test of being a good Dane, and it's compliance with some of these kind of standards of public behaviour, and if you don't comply with those standards, you are seen as unacceptable in our country. It's partly an arrogant position and partly a position I started to understand better as each day went by. As I say, I was completely shocked by some of the remarks made, but if you looked at criminal statistics, a really significant proportion of sexual assaults on white Danish girls were perpetrated by minority ethnic young men, because they see these women as legitimate targets because their clothes are too skimpy and so on, so these are very difficult issues to unravel."

I asked whether he had a view about whether the more multiculturalist or integrationist approach was a better way to build a strong society. He laughed.

"I don't know what is preferable," he said, "and it's not just those two options, there's acculturation, culturalism... Because I value difference and I value learning about other people's lives, I personally favour multiculturalism, but I can also empathise with people who tend to feel that the mosque that's been built in their community has taken something away. Not that they're Christians themselves, so they don't feel that it has undermined their local church, but they feel that they're being dominated by another people and another way of life."

"I don't know," he said, "but some people round here would argue that in places like Bradford, sharia law already exists. They'd be saying 'if they want to live by effing sharia law, why don't they eff-off to their countries where sharia law is practised and then they'd discover what sharia law is really like – you know, you nick something and you get your hand cut off'. And they'd say 'this is alive and kicking in Bradford' and they say 'if we don't stop it there, it's going to be here soon', and these are complete myths, but it does give weight to the argument that there needs to be a secular code of ethics, code of standards, that people should subscribe to."

As he talked on, I reflected that this code of ethics or standards could be the same or similar to the notion of Britishness which Chris in Preston had described, and could be based on the values which Dan in London had talked about. Emma in Blackburn had given me some ideas about ways in which those values could be brought to life while being sensitive to the traditions of different communities, but I still felt much more work needed to be done to make the idea a reality.

"I thought the point about swimming costumes was interesting," Howard went on, "and I think she had a point: why should we discriminate against white women who, for different reasons, not reasons of faith, would rather be more covered up than less covered up?"

"There was a huge issue for motorcyclists when the helmet law came in," he continued, "and there was a legal case about Sikhs being allowed not to wear helmets because of their turbans. The judge said that if it was a matter of faith, you can be exempted from the law. A lot of serious motorcyclists hated the idea of wearing a helmet, they wanted to be free in the wind, and they wanted to know why the Sikhs got preferential treatment. That's the way it's often seen, it's not seen as respect, it's seen as privileged treatment for minorities, and people would ask 'why should they get privileged treatment in 'our' country?'"

I asked whether that approach belied the welcoming attitude that the country prided itself on.

"I don't think that there's an attitude that we want to make people welcome," he said. "I think that there's an attitude that we're too full. We accept a small group of people who suffer from political discrimination and threats to their life and so on, but I don't think that liberal acceptance prevails in most people's minds. It prevails significantly amongst middle-class minds, some of the people who are least 'threatened' by these other people coming in."

"I think that progressive civilisation is a very fragile thing," he went on. "You only have to see it in something like some announcement on the news that Marmite is in scarce supply, and suddenly everyone is dashing off to Sainsbury's to buy ten jars of Marmite, and not really thinking about a neighbour who might not have any. I think that as soon as there's any kind of threat or indication of scarcity, most people, their default position is very selfish. And I think immigration is one of those things, one of those fear factors."

"Of course, you see tales of great heroism and great altruism," he continued, "but I don't think they're the norm in humanity, sadly. The person on the *Herald of Free Enterprise* who was six-foot-six and was able to become a human bridge and got loads of people to safety when he could have leapt across the gap himself and saved himself – that was a phenomenal act of courage, but I think that most people, as soon as things get tight, they buy twenty jars of Marmite and put them in the cupboard and don't tell anyone that they've got them."

I asked how he felt that people like him who supported a multicultural society should respond to these issues.

"You've always got to listen to people's concerns," he said. "You have to have a proper discussion about migration, immigration, cultural tolerance and borders to what is acceptable. You know, female genital mutilation is something which we say should not be part of a civilised society, so it's not like we haven't put any borders up, it's just where we draw those lines. But in the past if you even raised that as an issue, in some circles you were immediately branded a racist."

I asked about South Wales, an area where there had been scarcity for a long time, but there had also been a strong sense of community. I asked what the secret was.

"There's still a sense of community," he said, "but all around you you're aware that it's decaying and declining. You know, the meetings we have about the football team I'm involved in are in a workingmen's club that probably once had Freddy and the Dreamers or Gerry and the Pacemakers playing on a Friday night, and it was probably full. Now it's got two people drinking at the bar, and the big social function room is used rarely. The lounge that we tend to sit in has sticky carpets that nobody can afford to replace because there's no money around. Taff Street, the centre of Pontypridd, is full of payday loan companies, pound shops, charity shops, and I think there's a sort of muted anger that is played out and expressed a lot towards immigrants. You know, where else do people turn?"

"The market that Tony Blair visited," he went on, "Pontypridd Market, you walk in that most days and nearly all the stalls are shut. Occasionally it's buzzing a bit more but not often. People are living modest, humble lives. Most of the students with any ability go to Cardiff or Bristol or London, so you end up with an ageing, less skilled and less talented population."

"My students are working hard to give themselves a competitive edge," he continued, "but the tragedy is that most of them don't have a competitive edge because they don't have any social capital apart from me. But they don't see it like that – they see it as that if they position themselves the right way, they'll have a chance, which is maybe the only way, the only comfort."

"This word anxiety has come up a lot," he added. "Students round here are desperately uncertain, scared about the future, you know, and if you ask them why they're at university, they wouldn't know, but they know that if they weren't at university, getting a degree, they wouldn't have any chance. At least if you are at university and you do get a degree then you do have a bit of a chance, but not much of a chance still because you live in the Valleys, there's nothing here, you haven't got any contacts, any networks, so they're privately quite despondent, but as I always say, if you don't die, you've got to carry on living and if you carry on living, you've got to try to keep living in a positive spirit. There's not much point waking up in the morning thinking 'my life is terrible' because if you do, you'll probably end up on heroin."

I asked if he had heard any convincing plans for creating new jobs in the area.

"The reality is that employment opportunities that are created here are likely to be small employment opportunities," he said. "The Valleys do not lend themselves in any way towards economic development and investment because the hills are very steep, they're very deep and they're very long, and there's one way in and one way out. There's very few roads through the mountains, and it's all headed to Cardiff and the M4 corridor. You know, if there wasn't coal in this geographical environment…"

He didn't need to finish the sentence. He was speaking a truth which was hard to admit, that these areas wouldn't have been populated so heavily if it wasn't for the mines. The communities had remained, but redistribution from Westminster and grants from the EU had helped to keep them afloat. I thought back to the points made by Gary Millar in Liverpool about reallocation of resources and I wondered whether, if British society became more divided, support for subsidising post-industrial areas would waver.

"In a different generation," Howard continued, "most of these students would not have been in university. It's a terrible thing to say, but some of them should not be at university, and they should be working in textile and clothing factories in Aberdare, and their parents probably did. But, those factories don't exist anymore, so they follow their friends to uni, but they don't seem to have any engagement or attachment to learning."

"According to a BBC report I saw a few years ago," he went on, "nearly all the bus companies which run through Pontypridd bus station employ Latvian drivers. And apparently they do because Latvian men of 21, 22, 23 tend to be family men with small children, reliable, turn up, whereas it was alleged that 'Ponty boys or girls' get pissed on Sunday, don't turn up on Monday. I see that in my life: people do occasionally take days off even though they're not unwell – just because you can't be bothered to go into work that day."

"So I think workforce-wise," he added, "it's a struggle and I think it is quite a low morale place, and I think that's where the immigration thing kicks in. It's very reminiscent of the view that if we're going to help people, we're going to help people locally. There's a lot of hostility to the Romanian *Big Issue* sellers in Taff Street – 'why are they here begging from us?' I see that kind of attitude a lot."

I asked what he felt the response should be.

"It's at our peril that we dismiss the oppositional views as out-of-date, antiquated, dinosaurish," he said. "You know, 'this is the brave new world that we're moving towards and these people, we need to leave them behind' and we need not engage with their views on things."

"If we close down debate, it will find other outlets," he went on. "We have to find ways of enabling people to express their anger and express it loudly in a setting where you can start to unravel and understand why that person holds that view. The problem with a lot of this kind of work is that it's done in a circle and people say 'let's not raise our voices, show respect for other people, let's be nice and gentle'. But if you're nice and gentle then that person never gets a chance to let off their vitriol. You know, the clever thing that the Right have done is to rid themselves of the jackboot association and to recast themselves as the defenders of cultural traditions. They speak to that anger that other parts of the political spectrum have dismissed almost as irrelevant. And it might be a relatively small proportion of the population who freely and willingly articulate those angry views, but there's a much bigger proportion of the population that feels those views, even if they'd be reluctant to express them openly."

I couldn't help but agree based on what I'd heard on my travels, but I was wary about causing offence to people. I mentioned the moment in the first group when the Jamaican student had bristled at the young man talking about immigration and the potential 'corruption' of British culture.

"Maybe you have to jolt people sometimes," he said. "If we're in the business of having a discussion with a view to a resolution that works, we've got to have those things that do hurt sometimes, we've got to speak it as it really is otherwise you get a response that's inadequate and inappropriate because you haven't had a proper discussion about the issues."

It was almost time for us to finish, but before we did Howard had a story he wanted to tell me.

"When I was Iran," he said, "my friend and I met these illegal Afghan immigrants, and I shook their hands and I said 'can I have a photograph with you?' And they didn't mind and then they invited me for food. These guys, they spend three months of their income being smuggled back into Iran – they go home for a month, and then they spend eight months in the orchards. They've got nothing and they were willing to share their food with me. And I just thought 'God, am I so lucky to be exposed to this hospitality and generosity and sort of trustingness', and I don't know where it comes from. You know, I'm a white bloke, and I've probably got more money in my pocket than these guys earn in a year…"

I asked why he felt they had been able to be so generous, while in the UK he had said there was more of an attitude of 'looking after our own'.

"I don't know," he said, "and that's why I get very angry with my son when he won't share his sweets. 'They're mine', he says. It's difficult to know, and I'm guessing here, but Afghan culture is very hospitable. And these guys are probably very lonely, very isolated, and they'd probably never met anybody from the United Kingdom. Plus my friend introduced me to them in Farsi, which no doubt helped. You know, I cause them no anxiety, no threat, it's their turf, their patch – they're in control, and they're extending an invitation to me. Perhaps it's that they didn't feel anxious – it's this issue of anxiety."

I asked why they wouldn't feel anxious while British people, who apparently had much more than them, would.

"Because we feel that people are coming in and taking over something," he said. "You know, 'they're taking over our jobs our culture or our women'. It's been written about in terms of the cotton industry in the North West, the triple whammy: first, India and Pakistan produce cheaper cotton, which puts our industry at risk; the second whammy, you've got people from India and Pakistan go to the North West to work in the cotton mills. And the third whammy is that they come as men on their own and they 'take all the women'. And that's what Geoff Pearson wrote about in his seminal paper on 'Paki-bashing in a Lancashire town'. He argued that there's a build-up of things that create not just this mythical threat, but a real threat to culture and livelihoods – whereas those fruit-pickers, they have no reason at all to be anxious about me."

"All my life I've been exposed to these differences that have allowed me to be relaxed with other cultures, other peoples," he continued, "and I've been happy to twist and turn, sleeping in Soviet bunkhouses one day, five-star hotels the next day. I can adapt – I have immense cultural capital and I would wish that to be conferred on more people and I think that really would make a difference to our interpersonal communications and interpersonal feelings about things."

"Although," he added as we prepared to finish, "a woman in a burka came into my lecture the other day and it really phased me. I hadn't seen her before, I had to have a conversation with her afterwards, and I felt discomforted by that. I'm used to mouths moving and smiling teeth…"

"If I was a dictator," he went on, "would I allow people to wear burkas? I don't know. And is that my selfishness, or is it something else? I don't know, but I do find it difficult seeing lots of women in full cover, including their faces… so we've all got our own different lines in the sand. So going back to the Afghan fruit pickers, I can't think of a reason why half a dozen Afghan fruit-pickers should feel anxious about an encounter with a white western British man in Iran, whereas over here I can see all kinds of reasons why an encounter with a Muslim, female, burka-clad woman might be anxiety-producing to a white working-class man or a white working-class woman."

"Or even," he added as we concluded, "a white, middle-class professional academic, like me."

*****

As I walked down to the station, I reflected on the conversations with the students, wide-ranging discussions in which economics, politics, education and culture interplayed. They faced many challenges relating to their futures, with few jobs in their home communities and few guarantees beyond significant debt even if they gained good results from their studies. They had been born in a place which had once been a world centre but which did not lend itself well to the modern economy. Money from Cardiff, London and Brussels had brought some improvements to the area but could not alter the sense of being on a downward trajectory, and what the future held for people who lived in the area seemed like an open, simmering question.

Yet what struck me most about the conversations with the students was the way that they spoke about religion and culture. Young people had been portrayed in the media as being politically-correct 'snowflakes', unwilling to engage in any conversation which might cause offence to anyone. Yet the students I had met had raised hard cultural issues and not pulled their punches. Based on my conversations with them, I did not feel that their attitudes were solely a result of their anxieties about the future: rightly or wrongly, I thought they were genuinely concerned about the issues they had raised and would have been even if their own personal prospects were more secure. What Howard had said seemed to reinforce that: he had travelled across the world and had every reason to feel secure in himself, yet he had still been troubled by the interaction with a woman wearing a burka. His questions about whether he would ban the burka forced me to think hard about my own values and the extent to which I, as a white man, was entitled to a view on cultural questions within other British communities.

Before I sought to address that question, I headed for mid-Wales with a view to answering two other questions which were outstanding: whether it was possible for people to protect and uphold their culture without excluding others, and whether the attitude of 'looking after one's own' could be compatible with being welcoming to others and fulfilling global responsibilities.

12

Looking after one's own in Welshpool

As I arrived in the heart of Welshpool, a town in mid-Wales near the border with England, I saw Welsh dragons on bunting all around the town centre and many local independent shops: Powys Carpets, which advertised the widest choice of carpets and vinyl in Wales, BJ's Electrical, WR Davies newsagent, Owen's family butcher. Every sign was in English and Welsh and on Severn Street, a shop called Pethe Powys advertised cups, tea towels, scarves, bow ties and decks of cards with the Welsh dragon on them, alongside Welsh Rugby Union shirts. One of the coasters read 'anyone can cuddle but only the Welsh can catch' and was positioned next to a rugby ball; another read 'happiness is having Welsh friends'. I went inside, and found a treasure trove of books on Wales and Welsh heritage.

"If you really want to learn more," the woman in the shop told me, "you should head to Aberystwyth and visit the National Library."

I decided it would be my next stop, but first I wanted to hear more from the people of Welshpool. In the town centre, the Christmas Fayre was in full swing.

"Bora Da, hello," people said to each other as carol singers gathered to turn on the lights at the town's Christmas tree.

"We're here to formally launch the tree of light this year, which is fundraising for Hope Powys, a home for terminally-ill children," the President of the local Rotary Club announced.

"We're now going to ask the Mayor to switch on the Christmas lights," he went on, before adding, "well actually we're not because we don't know where the switch is."

They fumbled around for a minute, and then they found it and the mayor switched it on. They began singing Christmas carols, starting with 'Oh Come All Ye Faithful'. A mother and her daughter joined the group gathered to sing, along with a younger man, and there was a calm and beautiful hum as they sang.

"Oh come let us adore Him
Oh come let us adore Him
Oh come let us adore Him
Christ, the Lord"

As they sang 'Oh Little Town of Bethlehem', a few more people joined, and an old open-top bus taking people on a tour of the town rounded the corner. A steward from the town council joined. As they sang 'Silent Night', the music of the band was interrupted by a mobility scooter beeping as it reversed, and everyone smiled. They wound up shortly afterwards, with a few people staying around to sell raffle tickets and to talk with the mayor.

I walked through the Christmas Fayre: a pub offered homemade food and real ale and stalls sold local jams, marmalades, pickled onions, chutneys and homemade cakes. Locally-made candles and Christmas decorations were on sale, along with handmade local jewellery. Everywhere I looked, I could see the Welsh flag. It made me think about community and national identity, so when I walked past an organic store with the Welsh dragon in the window, I went inside and asked the manager whether it was a symbol of nationalism for him.

"Oh no," he said, clearly perturbed that I'd even asked the question, "for us it's just about buying from the workers' co-operative and trying to sell more stuff made by smaller, local producers. But we stock food from all over the world – we totally embrace that."

"But when you speak to the people who come in here," he went on, "you do get your casual racism, and people do say sort of casual things about immigrants, you know, which I hadn't really come across before I came here."

I asked how he responded when people said things which didn't accord with his own values.

"It's difficult," he said. "I mean, there was a lady who used to work here, and she used to say some outrageous things, and I'd normally just say something like 'well, I've had good experiences with these people' or 'I like a bit of cultural diversity'. You know, she read a lot of things in the tabloids, so I'd try and do it in a kind way. One day she said something awful, and I bit my tongue, and she died a couple of days later, and I kind of felt glad that I hadn't been too aggressive with her."

"It's normally not hateful," he went on, "it's just a negative idea that people have. And it's normally the old folks that have that idea, and they have seen things get so much worse in their lifetime, and I think, for a lot of them, the EU vote, it was very much a rejection of the way things were going maybe, I feel like they want more control in this unpredictable world we live in."

A couple of customers came in so I left him with them, *'No Particular Place to Go'* by Chuck Berry playing on the radio.

"Nice to talk to you, good luck," he said to me as I left.

I headed into a nearby butcher, which also had Welsh dragons in the window and which advertised Welsh beef and local lamb. All of their advertising focused on the fact that the meat was locally-reared. 'High-class family butcher' the sign read, and beneath it there was a sign from the National Farmers Union with a Union Flag on it and the slogan 'thanks for backing British farming'. I headed inside.

"It's all local," the owner told me. "Everything we buy, we buy from the Welshpool Livestock Market, and we like to say 'keep it in the community' because Welshpool is quite a small area, and we know a lot of the farmers so we tend to advertise by saying we know all the people we buy our lambs from, the same as the cattle, we keep it local."

I asked why that was important.

"We just find it tends to be better quality," he said, "but also we like to keep it local because it just keeps it all together – the farmers who have sold us the meat come and buy it back from us, so it's just like a circle, we help the farmers out and they come and shop with us."

He went to help a customer who wanted some lamb.

"Hello Bev."

"Hello Bob, I'm going to have some lamb today."

"What would you like, a leg? How many you feeding?"

"Four."

"Here you go, you might have a little left over for a butty."

"Perfect, thank you very much."

"Sorry mate," he said, returning to me, "if we're not busy at this time of year then we'll never be busy."

"All the Christmas turkeys we buy in," he went on, "we deal directly with the farmer, same with the geese and ducks, so everything is kept local."

I asked if that was important to his customers.

"Yes, definitely," he said, his eyes lighting up. "They want to know where it's come from, they want to know if it's English, Welsh, Irish, you know what I mean? Being a small community like this, it's the word – somebody says 'I've had a lovely piece of beef and it's all local' and we seem to get busier and busier and busier."

"A town like this," he went on, "it's a small farming community, and if you advertise that it's local beef, Welsh beef, then people tend to come and support everybody else. You know, you might be the sister or the brother or the cousin of somebody that we buy the lambs off, so everyone looks out for each other."

"People will say 'it's cheaper in Morrisons'," he continued, "but I'll say it's a farming community here in Welshpool, and shipping in meat from Botswana doesn't seem right."

I left him to his customers and walked down the street and headed to the indoor market. There, I got talking to two women, one of whom worked at a stall selling woollen products.

"On a daily basis," the wool store owner told me, "we must have twenty old people who come in and just chat. They don't come in to buy anything, we don't expect them to, but if one of them doesn't come in for a couple of days, we'll all be saying 'I haven't seen so and so for a little while'. We even have phone numbers for some of them so we can check on them. That's what community is all about, looking out for people, but it seems to stop at the doors of the market at the moment."

"People at the big superstores are just a number," her friend said, "they're just a profit margin – they're not people. Whereas in smaller communities, you've got local conveniences and people know each other by name and can have a conversation about personal lives as well as business lives."

They told me that they felt the sense of community they had described was being put at risk by people moving away to find work and because of out-of-town shopping centres.

"The people who come in here are lonely," said the first woman, "and if you go round Tesco's with your trolley you're equally lonely, but if you come in here and see us, people recognise you and they'll stop and talk to you. You never want to think of anybody being lonely, do you?"

"Growing up," the second woman said, "everybody knew everybody else – us as kids, we didn't get away with anything because our nan and grandad would find out."

"When I'm really old," the first woman said, "I'd want to think there will still be a community here – the way we look after the old people who come in to us, just sitting and listening to them and making sure they don't feel lonely, and watching out for the young kids and making sure they don't get into stupid trouble – but I don't think there will be."

I asked why she felt that sense of responsibility to those who were local to her.

"Because I'm a decent human being," she said.

They had to get back to their customers, and I left them to it.

As I walked away, I thought about the sense of community they and the butcher had described, of people looking out for one another. That was the kind of community I wanted to be part of myself, but I could see how economic and technological change – from out-of-town shopping centres to changing employment opportunities to people shopping online – could put a sense of community at risk.

Outside an out-of-town shopping centre, I found a woman having a cigarette.

"You have to go out of town," she told me, "there's nothing in the town centre."

I asked whether she felt people should support their local community by shopping locally.

"Yeah," she said, "but they need to bring more tidy shops into Welshpool so you haven't got to go out of town. It's mostly charity shops and hairdressers and cafes – that's no good to anybody, is it? We've got nowhere to go for shoes have we – people have to go to Telford or Shrewsbury. So they're basically not looking after the locals because we have to go out of town to clothes shop."

I asked who she meant by 'they'.

"The council," she said. "If they want to keep the people in Welshpool here, then they have got a responsibility haven't they?"

I asked why it was important that people should shop locally.

"Well," she said, "it's your home, so you should try to support it, but if there's nothing here to support, you're wasting your time."

*****

My next meeting was with Dean Hammond, the owner of one the biggest businesses in the town, a builders' merchant and staircase manufacturer. As I entered, I read the sign above the entrance – 'one life, build it'. In his office, he showed me his desk, which was surrounded by photos of his daughter on the wall.

"I live and breathe this company," he told me. "When I'm on holiday, I go and visit other companies and benchmark against them. I can't tell you how many builders' merchants I went to when we were in America recently. It drives my missus nuts."

"We're going for growth," he went on, "we do a staircase once every 24 minutes, 24 hours a day. Sixteen years ago, it took four and a half days to make a staircase. Now, if you phone up 7.30 in the morning from London, we can quote it by 8.30, if you sign off the drawings, we can design it by 10.30, and if you're a really good company and you're desperate, we'll make that staircase, pack and wrap it and have it in London by 2am the next day."

We got talking about government regulation and he told me how he felt it was impeding businesses like his. He gave the regulation of timber as an example, telling me that he was compelled by government to track every piece of timber the company used in order to ensure that no more than 30% of their stock was hardwood from abroad.

"It's a joke," he said. "I've got a guy, a quarter of his time is spent in tracking timber. But the fact that we're tracing it all doesn't mean a thing. We can't make a difference – they're still pulling down the rainforests. The only way to stop it is to regulate and stop hardwoods coming into the country. I was a member of Greenpeace and God knows what else – you have to regulate."

I asked why his business could not simply stop making hardwood staircases unilaterally.

"I can't do that," he said, "I'd have to sack twenty people. 20% of what we do is hardwood, so if I said 'no more hardwoods', then all that work's gone. And I've toyed with it, because I feel absolutely sick and terrible about it, but other staircase companies will just come and take it up – it will make no difference just because I make a stand."

"I was young and naïve when I joined Greenpeace," he went on, "and at that age you believe that you can change the world, but when you're actually in it, and you realise you've got to fire twenty staff, and you live in the community and you know all their families and their children and their pets and stuff… The last time I had to sack people, I didn't sleep for a couple of days afterwards. That's the horrible bit of the job."

"The government needs to make a stand, that's what it's there for," he continued. "If companies like us aren't protected, you'll just have these companies which set up accounts in the Cayman Islands and they say all the profit is made there and they don't pay any tax. It's diabolical. We shouldn't let them get away with it. It's insane. They're making an absolute fortune – the amount of money we'd be able to make in tax would be phenomenal."

I asked whether it was right for governments to interfere in the practice of businesses in the way he had described.

"There's nothing wrong with interference," he said. "We have to interfere in markets as a society, we have to regulate people like them. These large corporations are ripping this country off and they shouldn't be allowed to. Do we want to be ripped off as a country? It's billions of pounds we're talking about."

"The Conservatives need to pull their bloody finger out," he went on, "get out of Europe, halve government organisations. God knows why they aren't more worried about the one point six *trillion* pounds that we're in debt that's getting worse and worse and worse."

"Everybody should be tested," he continued. "They should have a passport when they go to the hospital to make sure we're not subbing other people, anybody who produces crime should go. We've got a Polish lad here in Welshpool who hasn't done a drip of work, is pissed up, shits everywhere, pisses everywhere, exposes himself, has done criminal damage – he should go back to Poland. I'm not racist, we've just got a number of Polish that spend their time up town getting pissed and throwing their bottles around in what was a clean, tidy place."

"A lot of them are really lovely," he added as we prepared to part, "it's just the one or two."

As he showed me out, he gave me a demonstration on his Segway, riding around the office past his colleagues with a broad smile on his face.

As I left, I wondered whether the conversation with him had taken me off on a tangent from my earlier conversations, but I did see something which linked his views on environmental regulation, tax and immigration to the discussions I'd had earlier in the day about 'looking after one's own'. He wanted to protect his staff, his community and those close to him: from redundancy, from being 'ripped off' by big multinationals and from anti-social people from abroad. These were tougher examples than I'd heard earlier in the day – the idea of forcing people to leave the country felt more challenging than the idea of shopping locally – but I couldn't help thinking that the decisions were all based on looking out for those closest to him. That instinct clearly trumped his desire to do good in the world: when it came to the crunch, he would not make redundancies in order to protect the environment, even though his membership of Greenpeace showed he clearly cared about it. It didn't seem impossible to imagine a society in which people felt a responsibility both to those who were local and to the wider world but as I reflected of the scores of photos of his daughter above his desk, and the pain in his voice as he had described making people redundant, I guessed that what was closest would always come first. That was an instinct which I felt should be worked with, not against.

*****

That evening, in a pub in the nearby village of Berriew, I talked to a couple from England, Ed and Naomi, who had recently relocated to the area to open an ethical tourism business. I asked them what they thought of the idea of 'looking out for one's own'.

"But what does it mean to 'look after your own'?" Ed asked. "In my best frame of mind, I don't think of anyone as 'not my own'... I don't have a strong feeling of looking after my own, beyond what I think of as natural groups, like my family, close neighbours and people I know, and even with that, I don't think of my clan as being better than your clan and I don't want my clan to do better at the expense of your clan. I think everyone should be in one clan working for mutual benefit."

I asked if they felt any particularly affinity to the community in Welshpool.

"When we moved here," Naomi said, "we looked at hundreds of places across the country but there was nothing that drove us here particularly except for a set of circumstances which fitted the criteria which we were looking for."

"And those criteria didn't include 'I already feel connected to the community'," Ed said. "We moved here because of the amount of land we could afford and the setting and the proximity to things like the station: quite unemotional things."

"Yeah," Naomi said, "but your community connection grows as you live in a place. I don't think anyone really feels it before they move there, and if they do, it's probably slightly illusory unless you have a family connection there."

"I wonder about sense of community generally," Ed said, "because I lived in a flat in London for thirteen years and I didn't have a massive community feel there – I didn't feel massively protective of those human beings who happened to live close to me. I liked to try to build a sense of community in small ways, and to not be isolated from other people. I find it interesting that in some circumstances, the thing you want to stick up for can be defined most clearly in your head when it's attacked. Until then it's something you're more relaxed about and maybe more positive about, and then something threatens that, and it's natural to react. And I think you see that culturally where people put up a barrier to keep something out: it doesn't mean you care about the thing that's inside, it's just being protective."

"I hear a lot of people who are anti-something without being particularly pro-anything," he went on, "and that worries me because that feels purely negative: 'I don't want these people coming here, we shouldn't be spending money on them, we should be looking after our ex-servicemen'. But you know they're not going out and lobbying for more money for housing for service-people either."

"It's like people who phone up Comic Relief and say 'why are you giving money to Africans?'" Naomi added.

"And that didn't mean they were donating to Help for Heroes or anything else," Ed went on, "they just meant 'you shouldn't be giving money to them' – it's an insular negative view."

"It's almost like a historical nostalgia for a community," said Naomi, "which doesn't really exist. People aren't looking out for each other, not really – I don't think it's about that, I don't think it's about something positive that's an alternative to the fear…"

"I do think it's natural, though, to be concerned about what's around you," Ed said, "because if they told us they were going to build 100 new homes round the corner, you'd still think 'is that going to work, is that going to be good? Is that going to be sustainable?'"

"Essentially you're talking about distance," he went on. "I think it's human nature to be more concerned about stuff that is close to you, but I think that gets spun or gets twisted – so I think it's normal to get more worried about a bus crash just down the road than if there's a bus crash in Nigeria, but there's a difference in noting how it registers differently with you and then ascribing different value to those people as individuals. There's some sort of twisted extrapolation which gets used to say that these people are more important – I hear people talking as if people closer to you are more important people than people coming in from other countries, and I think some evolution needs to happen there so we can help each other to think that no matter where you're from, you're of the same value, while retaining all the normal things about caring about your neighbours and people around you because it's practical and real."

I believed that he was right that there was no additional value to one life over another, but I did wonder if a sense of community had any more to it than simply the practicality of people living near to each other, which didn't seem a particularly strong basis for a sense of solidarity. I asked if they felt any more affinity to someone local than to someone halfway round the world.

"Well," Ed said, "if you said to me I could choose whether a Bangladeshi person I've never met dies now or you die now, I'd say the Bangladeshi person, and not because I'm a racist and I hate Bangladeshi people… there's something about proximity and personal relationships which makes that valid."

I asked whether he therefore felt it was legitimate to feel a sense of loyalty to someone because they were from the same nation.

"I don't really, no," he said. "I mean I don't feel defensive about people in Norwich, just because they're on the same island as me."

"I also feel an acute sense of our negative influence all over the world," Naomi said, "an awareness of the consequences of British actions which have led to the realities that people internationally are living with now. You know, we are still selling arms to countries whose refugees are trying to come to our borders. And for me our responsibility as a consequence of that is at least as important as taking care of your own local community."

It felt like a really important point: while Ed was challenging the basis of seeing a nation state as a community and clearly felt that doing so undermined a wider sense of global responsibility, Naomi was troubled by Britain's history specifically. It felt like her view of Britain's foreign policy – past and present – meant that she struggled to feel affinity with the nation, and indeed made her feel that there was a greater responsibility to share with others *outside* Britain than to share within the nation.

I suggested to them that most of the people I'd met felt that we had a greater responsibility to our fellow citizens than we did to others, and I asked them for their views.

"But how do you define fellow citizens?" Ed said. "Local citizens? Same skin colour citizens? That's the thing isn't it? It's very important how people would define their fellow citizens. My basic view is that people are the same, or at least very similar, and if we could stop identifying the differences between us, we'd realise that we're bloody similar. And one of the ways in which we identify how we're different is that we create national boundaries. It's just part of saying 'we're one thing, you're another thing'. And that's how I think communities can be negative – it looks positive but sometimes it doesn't feel natural to me."

I asked him what he meant by that.

"An example," he said, "would be when you have a national attack and people start getting out the old 'we're British, two world wars and one World Cup, stiff upper lip, spirit of the Blitz' – it's all bollocks, it means nothing, it serves nothing but to divide more. It doesn't bring anyone together who wasn't already together, it's about rallying your troops."

I suggested that I could imagine that some people I'd met might feel disappointment that he and Naomi did not seem to feel a loyalty to the community or to the country. I wondered how they would respond.

"Loyalty to what?" Ed said. "I don't feel disloyal to my country… I'm know I'm being quite sanctimonious and it's theoretical but this is how I would like to feel – I don't feel disloyal to this country, I want to feel loyal to *all* people. So yeah, you might take this as a kind of 'he doesn't love his country' sort of thing, but I do love my country – I just love *countries*. And I'd like to feel that whatever country I was in, I could meet someone who would also want to recognise the 99% of us that are the same."

"I think for someone expressing disappointment at my seeming lack of loyalty," Naomi said, "I'd say the two things are not exclusive. And you feel a national pride in all sorts of ways – you know, I feel really connected to our environment, our geography…"

"But in what other way do you feel proud of your country," Ed asked, "by which I mean the people in it? Being fond of geography is different."

"I suppose pride is the wrong word," Naomi said, "but I feel gratitude to be born in a basically democratic society and pleased that I've been born here as opposed to somewhere like Iran."

"I do feel that," said Ed, "but when I challenge that I realise it's not pride, it's just gratefulness and appreciation."

"And I do feel a sense of community," said Naomi. "I want to be part of this community, and when we think about our business plan we genuinely want to be a positive force."

"And on an individual level," she went on, "I feel that, with the person who is in front of me, I don't want to make their day any worse. I want to have a positive impact on that person."

"And that brings you back to the fact that it is totally normal to prioritise things that are closer to you," Ed said, "and to that extent you feel more connected to a community that is physically closer to you, but I don't know why one would say that goes to the boundaries of a country but then stops. Because your country could be India, which is colossal, or it could be Liechtenstein. It's just absurd – these are totally arbitrary lines."

It seemed clear to me that they didn't want to live in a world where people were defined by the nation of which they were citizens, but based on the conversations I'd had, I still felt that national identity was important. I didn't agree with Ed that Britain's borders were completely arbitrary, but even if they were, they still mattered because they were the boundaries within which inhabitants made collective decisions on matters such as sharing wealth and funding public services. I thought back to Gary Millar, the councillor in Liverpool who had referred to sharing within the nation as 'justice', and felt that as long as there was a British state where decisions about redistribution were made, there needed to be a sense of shared identity to go with it if sharing was to continue.

Thinking about building a sense of the nation as a community, I looked at the Welsh flag up on the wall next to us, and I asked for their view on it.

"It's welcoming to me," said Ed. "It's like 'welcome to our brilliant country'."

"I don't feel quite like that," Naomi said, "because whenever I see a national flag – sorry, whenever I see a *British* national flag – my instant reaction is to align it with the way I see the St George's Cross…"

"I think I'm probably imposing the feelings I have about seeing the St George's Cross," she went on, "which are quite strong, and as a consequence of that, I think when I see a national flag in Britain, I kind of have the same feelings. But I think there is a difference between Welsh national pride and English national pride."

"I think for the Welsh it's about pride in the face of adversity," she continued, "because the historical reality is that they were an oppressed nation, and that oppressor was their neighbour – England. That flag, the English flag, represents oppression across the globe in the way that the Welsh flag will never do."

"You know," she added, "there are lots of ways in which I feel ashamed of being English. Actually living in Wales is one of them because I know that the negative feelings that come from the Welsh are perfectly legitimate. It's not my fault, but it's none the less real or understandable."

"There are reminders everywhere about English appropriation of Wales," she went on. "It's visible in the language: you know, you've got dual place names, some of which don't have any reasons for anglicising them. I think the visibility of that language is something really powerful, so that's why they've had an attempt to rekindle the national language. It's why more children speak Welsh in Wales than their parents do, because there's been such a drive for it. But English is still the first language of Wales, because of our appropriation."

I asked whether she meant that there was more reason to uphold one's culture if one felt that that culture was under threat.

"I think it's seen as a duty, actually," she said, "even reading planning legislation, you are more likely to get planning permission if you are representing Welsh culture or celebrating Welsh culture, progressing the language – those things are very explicitly stated. And implicit in that statement is the reason we're in that situation."

I asked how they would react if the same thing happened in England.

"It would be unnecessary," said Ed, "so I think the point in Wales is that you're thinking of an underdog nation and an underdog identity, and I think it's fair enough to give it a boost. There's no chance of the English thing dying out so it would just be seen as a bit grotesque."

"But then again, I'm not living in one of those communities that feels under threat," he went on, "so I can't really identify with what it really means to have a large number of foreign people come to my town and change it."

"But historically we've been in that situation," said Naomi. "There are some really famous images of the Vietnamese people coming on the boats and being really welcomed by the English. What's different about today compared to back then?"

"Maybe the job market was less threatened," said Ed.

"And I think communities were stronger," said Naomi. "Families don't live close together, everyone's so disparate. People don't feel like they're connected."

"We're all masking insecurity," said Ed, almost as an afterthought. "Security at home – it's only when you're alright in your own head, in your own state of mind and your own feelings about yourself, that you can go out and start doing more positive things more broadly."

I thought about that sense of security at home and in one's own identity, and I asked whether they ever felt the St George's Cross or the Union flag could ever be seen as a positive thing.

"It would require a reclamation," said Naomi, "in the way that the gay community have reclaimed the word 'queer', a huge cultural shift, because at the moment the only time you see that positive pride is sporting events."

"Yeah," said Ed, laughing, "the only legitimate use of the flag is running a lap of honour."

"If I picture the Union Jack non-negatively," he went on, "I see it hanging outside Buckingham Palace or on a formal building, like a posh building, or in a sporting context. Everywhere else, it's negative – it just has those two safe places. If I see it in a shop window or hanging outside somebody's private property, I think 'you idiots'."

"But it's a great thing to work towards," he continued, "because when I go abroad to European countries and see their flag flying, I think 'isn't that nice?' You know, you're in Switzerland, and you see a Swiss flag and you think 'ooh, we're in Switzerland' – you don't think 'nationalist Swiss, just trying to show off', you just think 'that's a nice logo for the country I'm in'. I'd like people to feel that way about our country, to be able to see the flag without having negative spasms."

As we left, I reflected on their sense of shame about the country's history and their discomfort at a sense of special responsibility to, or affinity with, others from the country. I felt that one could accept a transactional relationship with the state, paying taxes for public goods and law enforcement, but that did not seem to be a particularly strong basis for a sense of national solidarity and I wondered whether something richer and better could be found. Thinking back to conversations earlier in my travels, I felt that shared values could play a role in bringing a sense of shared identity and community to a nation of people from a range of different backgrounds. A vision of where the country was going seemed essential to creating a sense of common endeavour, of people working together towards a shared future. But I also felt that if this approach was going to work, the question of Britain's relationship with its past had to be addressed: the view of British history Naomi held was not unusual in my experience and it seemed to make it difficult for her to embrace national pride. Recalling my conversation with Dave in Poulton, I feared it also left her vulnerable to being dismissed as unpatriotic. A measured, nuanced patriotism seemed like a healthy response, but I wanted to explore what impact a strong sense of national identity might have on people from outside the UK before going further.

*****

That evening, I thought about the idea of 'looking out for one's own'. I didn't think it was wrong for people to buy locally – I thought it was in the spirit of community and was environmentally-friendly; I thought it was right to stop multinational companies exploiting local workers, making a profit in the UK while avoiding paying taxes and potentially putting local companies out of business in the process; and I thought it was right for the state to intervene in markets to enable businesses like Dean's to behave ethically without succumbing to competition. The conversations over the course of the day had reinforced my sense that there was a clear role for a 'protective state', supporting local businesses like those I'd seen earlier in the day, making sure multinationals paid their taxes and helping people like those I had met on my travels, particularly young people, to make their way in an increasingly global job market.

Looking after one's own in Welshpool

Once again, it was the cultural issues which were more challenging: Naomi's view of British history and its impact on her sense of affinity to the nation challenged my desire to build a stronger sense of British identity, and I still worried about the UK embracing the idea of simply 'looking after our own'. I agreed with Ed that it was necessary to build a sense of local security before people could cast their minds to global issues, and I feared internal divisions overtaking national debate and preventing social and economic progress if the issues I had identified weren't addressed. Yet I still worried that building a strong sense of 'looking after our own' could lead to prejudice against those who were not 'our own', whether migrants to the country or people living in other countries. Aberystwyth, a centre of Welsh culture, seemed an ideal place to explore this further.

13

Cultural heritage and national identity in Aberystwyth

As I walked up to the National Library of Wales in Aberystwyth the next day, I noticed that all the road signs were in Welsh and in English. The library was in a beautiful, imposing building set at the top of the hill looking down over the seaside town. A stone marked where the library had been opened by King George V in 1911, and as I entered I found a sign which read: *'The National Library of Wales is a repository of treasures and facts. We keep the nation's memory safe.'*

Inside, I got talking to one of the guides.

"We see this as passing the baton," he told me, "holding great works of Welsh literature, art and so on for the following generation."

I took the tour round the archives, and learned that the library had stored many of Shakespeare's manuscripts during World War Two. Now it held six million books and newspapers, 1.5 million maps, 950,000 photographs and 60,000 works of art. In the exhibition area, there were portraits of David Lloyd George, the only ever Welsh Prime Minister of the UK, Aneurin Bevan, the Welsh politician famous for his role in the creation of the NHS, Rowan Williams, the former Archbishop of Canterbury, the composer, actor and singer Ivor Novello, the actor Anthony Hopkins and the footballer Ryan Giggs. Next to the portrait of Giggs was a painting of the Welsh football team which had reached the semi-finals of the 2016 European Championships. The painting was entitled 'Together Stronger' and a note from the artist explained that 'no individual stands out as everyone is central to the success'.

I stepped outside and looked down over Aberystwyth. It seemed to me that it was not just a right to keep Welsh culture alive, but as Naomi had said, a duty. This culture was precious, a gift to be passed to the next generation. Yet when people I'd met in England had talked about protecting national culture, somehow that felt less straightforward. While I felt Ed had gone too far in describing the idea of protecting English culture as 'grotesque', I suspected many people would agree with him that it was more legitimate for a small nation in the shadow of a more powerful neighbour to stand up for itself than it was for a more powerful community to stand up for its culture, with all the risks of exclusion and division which came with it. It did strike me, however, that as I had gone around England, many of the people I had met could not have been described as feeling powerful or secure, even in comparison to minority populations. Perhaps, I thought, it was possible for majority cultures to be insecure in their own ways. I thought back to Blackburn and reflected that I had felt a much stronger sense of cultural security in Whalley Range, the predominantly South Asian area with a thriving community spirit and new mosques at the heart of it, than I had in many of the predominantly white, nominally Christian communities I had visited around the country. Yet I was still worried about the dangers of a strong sense of national culture and identity being used to exclude others and I decided to talk to people from outside Wales to get their views.

*****

As I headed down to the waterside, I saw the Welsh flag and iconography everywhere I looked. At the university, I noticed that the buildings and halls of residence were all named after famous

Welsh figures: Edward Llwyd, Hugh Owen, Pentre Jane Morgan, Carwyn James; the university crest was two dragons over a book; and at the gym on campus, there was a sign with a dragon which read 'Team Aber' and then in Welsh 'Tîm Aber' and a photo of a smiling young man of East Asian heritage throwing a rugby ball. On another poster, the two languages had been fused into a logo which read 'Tîm-ABER-Team'.

I walked down into the town. At the Coopers Arms pub, there were a series of dragons on its outer wall and bunting with dragons on it in the window. There was a certificate proudly displayed in the window celebrating the fact that the pub had been voted the best community pub in the town by the Aberystwyth University Real Ale Society. A taxi marked 'Dragon's Cabs' drove past with a smiling cartoon dragon on its bonnet and a poppy on its hub cap.

In the town centre, I got talking to a Filipino woman who had come to Britain to work.

"We are new here," she told me, "people here friendly."

I pointed to all the Welsh flags which were around and asked her if she found them negative.

"Oh no, no, no," she said, "it's not negative. This is because you are in Wales. If you go to London you notice this as well. It's normal. We have as well in the Philippines, flag display. You go anywhere, they have."

She smiled, thanked me and moved on.

She had stopped near a kebab shop, and I noticed that in the window, they had the Welsh flag and the Turkish flag side by side. I went inside and asked one of the men inside what the symbols signified to them.

"We always respect the Welsh flag, the Welsh people," he told me. "The other kebab house, they think when the Welsh people see the Turkish flag, they get worried but nobody complain to us. The kids enjoy it as well – the kids always ask 'what country's flag is this one?' And I say 'we are Turkish, this the Turkish flag'. I am Turkish but I'm here in Wales – that is why. People say 'oh, the Turkish flag and the Wales flag together, that's normal'. No problem, isn't it?"

I saw that he was wearing a Welsh dragon on his t-shirt. He smiled proudly.

"My son is going to school in Wales," he said. "He is learning the Welsh language and the English language as well, and we are happy."

I told him that some people I had met felt that flags could be used in a negative way to make people feel unwelcome.

"Yes," he said, "I was working in Manchester, we had a kebab shop, and they put the Turkish flag, and maybe people think they are racist for the Turkish flag. But here we have the Turkish flag and ten years, nobody complain for the racism."

I asked whether he was worried about British people being racist.

"No," he said firmly, "definitely not. Some of them maybe not happy, saying 'why do you put a Turkish flag in my town?' But not here, nobody."

I decided to leave it there. I didn't want to push on him the idea that the Welsh flag might be unwelcoming when he clearly didn't feel that. Indeed, he had been worried about imposing the Turkish flag, and it hadn't struck him that the Welsh flag might seem racist. I felt that whoever had designed the kebab shop's signs had effortlessly fused the Turkish and the Welsh flags, suggesting compatibility between the two identities and that one single nationality, important as that identity might be to people, could never alone define who we were.

Down the road, I met a woman her fifties who was originally from England but now lived in Wales. I said that it was striking how many flags and dragons there were everywhere.

"Well, you are in Wales," she said with a smile.

I asked whether she ever worried about associations with nationalism.

"You know they don't burn cottages up here anymore?" she said, smiling again.

"I don't even think about it," she went on. "I mean I'm English born and bred but I've lived overseas for fifteen years and I don't see anything wrong with it. I've lived with Chinese flags, I've lived with Middle East flags and I don't see anything different."

I asked if she felt English people worried too much about it.

"Yeah," she said, "people just need to take a chill pill."

It was starting to get late and I walked towards the promenade, wanting to look out to sea before the sun went down. An EU flag flew in a window, a student of East Asian heritage bought fish and chips from a takeaway and in a nearby house, there were Amnesty International signs in the window: 'Refugees Welcome', 'Protect the Human'. In the window of Llyfrau Ystwyth Books, there were two Welsh flags, bunting of flags from different countries around the world and EU and UN flags, and books of Welsh legends and folk stories. On the notice board in a sweet shop, there was a sign with a Welsh dragon wearing a heart with writing inside it 'Cymru i bawb' – 'Wales for all'. Below it was a note which read 'we support people from every background who live in Wales. We refuse to accept any kind of discrimination or mistreatment of anyone'.

I stopped for a sandwich and noticed a sign in the window which read 'if bringing dogs please keep them on lead and you will be welcome'. In an ideal world, I reflected, a warm welcome would be unqualified and open. But, I reflected, that wasn't Britain right now: not everyone had confidence that people coming to the country would play by the rules. I thought of Chris, the accountant from Preston whose confidence in others had been corroded by what he had seen on the news. Perhaps, I concluded, the things which I had wanted to leave unsaid did need to be spelt out more.

It was getting cold, and it was almost time to head home, but on the promenade, I met a young man, Felix, who was originally from Lesotho but who had lived in the UK for the last fifteen years and was now studying at Aberystwyth University. I asked him for his view about the flags and the Welsh iconography around the town as someone who was not from Wales.

"For me, it's normal," he said, "and I'm also very aware that though it's part of the United Kingdom, it's also quite separate as well. When I was much younger, I started going to a place called Aberdaron, which is quite far north, and there everyone speaks just pure Welsh, and from that you can really see that it's its own country. So I don't feel unwelcome – I sometimes feel I should have learned a bit of Welsh, though here you don't need it so much."

I said I was asking because some people worried about flags being used in a racist way.

"Even the St George's Flag doesn't mean that to me," he said. "To me, a symbol will only ever be a symbol. It can be as meaningless or as meaningful as an individual wants it to be, and it can symbolise whatever an individual wants it to symbolise. A person chooses to impress their own ideology on something and I think the meaning of a flag is based on the context of the time."

"Also," he added, "if that's the only image of the Union Jack that British media chooses to portray, then that's going to be the overwhelming view of it."

I asked if he was saying that the portrayal of the flag in a positive context was crucial to how it was perceived by people.

"I think that's part of it," he said, "but part of it is the person who is perceiving it. For me, I do not see a flag as racist – I see it as a symbol sometimes used incorrectly by people who are racist. So it depends on the viewpoint of the person who is seeing it."

I thought back to Wembley, and the man brandishing the poppy at the woman wearing a burka. Felix had to be right that just because a symbol was misused, one should not stop using it, but I did wonder if there were inherent dangers with symbols of national identity or those associated with military conflict. I thought back to the word Naomi had used: reclamation. Perhaps part of the answer to the questions I was grappling with was to try to take symbols like the Union Flag back from those who misused them.

"I remember the 2010 World Cup," Felix continued. "Pretty much everyone in England had the St George's Flag on their cars. It didn't feel intimidating, and the EDL were more prominent then than they are now, and I saw it purely as 'this is England going to a World Cup, so this is people supporting the England football team rather than the EDL'."

"If I saw you wearing a flag," he went on, "I wouldn't judge you as an EDL member unless I heard you saying horrible stuff. My assumption would be that you were using a symbol – in what context you were using that symbol, I wouldn't know until I'd spoken to you. I don't think that everyone thinks like me, but if a person were to be offended – it's up to the person."

"To me," he added, "to have the attitude of 'don't offend someone' is almost impossible, because people can take offence on the part of people who haven't been offended themselves. It is much easier to have the attitude of 'be kind and don't hurt someone' because hurt is visceral – you know it, you feel it. I know when people have been racist to me it has felt like the ground is swallowing you up. So I won't be hurt by someone having a flag but if someone said something that was hurtful and derogatory and made me feel less than I am, less than a human…"

He didn't need to finish the sentence – his pain at recalling racist abuse was evident. Wanting to think about how such pain could be avoided, I asked whether he felt there was anything the rest of the UK could learn from Wales.

"I don't think Welsh people feel as though their culture is coming under attack," Felix said, "because it's not as diverse as England. So people in Wales still can see a connection from their past to the present – things haven't changed too quickly. The same in large cities where the change in the demographic has happened slowly, the place has got used to it and taken bits of all the different cultures into itself, but still knows who it is. So for example, one of the colleges in Birmingham is called Matthew Boulton College – he was one of the eighteenth or nineteenth century inventors or engineers. So it hasn't hit Birmingham just like that, whereas places where it's happening really quickly, and where all of a sudden people can't see some thread of some form of continuity, that would make you think 'I want to hold onto some thread of who I am'."

I asked whether he felt it legitimate for people to try to hold onto their culture.

"I think it's understandable in its minutiae," he said, "like 'why am I going to go into this shop when I don't know any of the food?' That is understandable. But in terms of culture, I don't think it ever stays the same: if I go back to Victorian England, compared to the Restoration England, you see even with the demographic staying the same, there was a complete culture shift which went from being wild and partying to becoming Victorian and conservative. You cannot hold onto culture, it will change and the meaning symbols have will also change. So it shouldn't be a goal to hold onto it, but if it's there it should be celebrated."

'Celebration' was a good word, I felt. I agreed that culture would inevitably change, but celebration of hard-won freedoms and strong values seemed like a positive way to preserve the good things about a society. Nevertheless, he had seemed a little dismissive of the idea of preserving cultural history, and I asked for his view on the National Library of Wales and its role as the guardian of the cultural memory of Wales. Surely, I suggested, that was a good thing.

"Of course," he said. "I don't know when it was that learning the Welsh language became mandatory, but things like that are a good thing. And holding onto history and documentation of the past for posterity is useful. In terms of the detail of day-to-day life, that will change, so I don't know if it's feasible to hold onto culture in that sense, but in terms of keeping a record of the past, where the country has come from and where it's going, that is valuable.

The main reason I think it's valuable is that it has weight in terms of where you go forward as a country."

"So for example," he went on, "if a government has this idea that they want to intervene somewhere, in some country, and they do not consider that almost every intervention has failed to achieve the purpose that it has been declared for – if you do not keep a record of the mistakes that happened in the past, then you are definitely going to make the same mistakes going forward."

I thought about the conversation in the pub in Poulton and the comparison the men had drawn between David Cameron's decision to call the EU referendum without planning for a Leave vote and the UK under Tony Blair invading Iraq without fully planning for post-invasion. As Felix said, there was a risk of complacency if nations did not remember their history, including the worst moments, but I believed that a wholly negative national story would be an unfair reflection of a nation like Britain which had done a lot of good in the world, had contributed a huge amount to culture globally and had strong values relating to, for example, equality. It seemed to me important to find ways to tell a balanced national story, avoiding both jingoism and negativity, celebrating the good and learning from the bad.

He needed to go.

"Cheers," he said, "see you."

I looked out to sea and thought about what I'd heard. It was clear that the migrants to Wales I had met in Aberystwyth did not feel unwelcome in a place with a strong sense of itself and its history. They did not feel that the flag and national symbols were negative or exclusionary: they could bring their own identities to this place and fuse them with the culture and values of Wales. Of course, Aberystwyth was unique, a bastion of liberal values and Welsh history, with a national library and a prominent university side by side. Nevertheless, it suggested a tantalising possibility: the potential to celebrate a culture without excluding others; to defend that culture while acknowledging that it would inevitably change with time; to establish a common story of where a country had come from and where it was going; to build a sense of a nation as a team and bringing others in to be part of that team. This was the kind of patriotism which I believed the UK needed but I still had questions to address: how could one build a sense of togetherness without excluding or defining against others? What should happen if the shared values of modern Britain challenged the customs and traditions of people from other cultures? And could the worst elements of British history be confronted without losing a sense of national pride? I headed home for Christmas determined to answer these questions in the new year.

*****

I walked down towards the station and in the town centre, as dusk fell, the Christmas lights were being turned on. A large crowd had amassed, many of them holding candles. There were people from all over the world – many of them students at the university – and I looked up and saw signs in a window which said 'Merry Christmas' in different languages: *Nadolig Llawen, Joyeux Noel, God Jul, Wesołych Świat.*

"Let's count down in whatever language you want to count down in," the compere shouted as she prepared to turn the lights on. "Welsh, English, Chinese, Italian… whatever you like…"

As she counted down, people counted down in their own languages, their words different but spoken in unison. As the lights came on, I looked up and saw the Welsh flag flying in the dusk.

14

Upholding shared values in Richmond

I rested over Christmas, convinced work needed to be done to address the issues relating to national identity I had encountered on my travels, but still nervous, particularly about the risks involved in a strong sense of patriotism boiling over into prejudice, division and hatred. I thought Scotland and Northern Ireland, which both had longstanding nationalist campaigns as well as areas with a strong sense of Britishness, would be good places to go to explore my concerns while also thinking about Britain's history and the future composition of the UK. First, however, I wanted to consider the degree to which 'British values' should be imposed on people from other cultures who lived in the UK. As these issues had been particularly apparent in relation to gender equality, I wanted to speak to some experts to get their views, starting in Richmond on the London-Surrey border.

*****

At Richmond Station, England rugby fans were congregating for a match at Twickenham. At a stall in the station, a coffee cart offered 'first class, fast, fair-trade coffee' and two pretzels for £5. In a coffee store, the staff danced with one another and the atmosphere was relaxed and happy. Nearby, a young man handed out leaflets for an organic food store. A homeless man begged by a phone box, a stall collected for Help for Heroes and a long line of black cabs waited for fares.

I had come to meet Gill Frances, a charity leader and grandmother who I knew was a committed feminist with strong liberal values. In her home near the station, we got talking about the Sixties.

"We knew we wanted to do our lives differently from our parents," she told me. "Even into the Seventies, when I had children, I wouldn't leave my children with my mother, or if I did, I'd leave strict instructions and I'd leave all the food prepared. I didn't want a Fifties childhood for my children. I wanted to be much, much more liberal than that."

"For my parents," she said, "it was all about wanting to follow the convention, whereas my generation didn't want to follow the convention. Well, we wanted to follow the convention that was part of the tribe, so my Vidal Sassoon bob became Cathy McGowan long hair, parted down the middle. My hair is basically straight, but I would iron it to get that look. I think my mother would have liked me to have had a 'wash and set', which is what she always did. 'If you just put a little perm in your hair, Gill, it will give it a little lift', she would say, whereas I wanted that very straight hair look."

I asked her what it was about that period which enabled social victories to be won.

"Because it was the first time when young people felt that we had an edge," she said, "we felt that we knew better. I'm a baby boomer – when I was born it was still rationing, so I was brought up with that austerity, and till the day my mother died, she never put the boiler on, she always washed in cold water in the morning. 'It's good for you,' she told me. But we were convinced that things needed to be different."

I wondered how she reflected on today's generation of children and young people in comparison to the revolutionary spirit of the Sixties.

"Ah," she said sadly, and then paused for a while.

"I think it's really tough," she said finally. "I think they have everything and they have nothing."

"My little grandson," she went on, "he's only eight, but every story he reads is about the prince being a hero and it's always the princess being saved, and he will model himself on that. And he's the one who when we're going down a flight of stairs appears and says 'can I help you down the stairs, grandma?' My granddaughters couldn't care a toss! And when the boys play rugby and the girls do ballet, is anyone giving any thought to the story which is being acted out there?"

I suggested that some people I'd met might think that what she was saying about stories and gender was just politically correct, liberal thinking. I asked what her response would be.

"Well, what happens to the little girl who doesn't want to do ballet?" she said, "and what do you do with the little boy's feelings?"

"If you stand outside a German school," she went on, "they don't wear uniform, they all come out in jeans and anoraks, and you have to look closely to work out who's a boy and who's a girl. There's no way you'd do that in an English school. The two genders are brought up in parallel universes and all I'm saying is let's bring that closer together, so that the definition of being a boy and being a girl is a bit closer and that boys have a bigger crack at it, because at the moment, I think girls have more choices about how to be a girl than boys do about how to be a boy."

I asked for an example, and she told me a story which she felt would give a good illustration.

"I was down in town," she said, "and my daughter called and said that they were going away the next day and that my grandson hadn't got any Wellington boots. 'Can you get him a pair?' she said, so I went to the shop, and they had Wellington boots which had camouflage on them, and then boots with some kind of battle going on on them. So I looked at the other ones, and they were little girly type princess-y ones, so I thought 'I can't take them'. So I went to the counter and said 'do you do any standard red or blue wellies?' and they said 'no one buys those any more'. I went all around Kingston looking for the boots, and I finally ended up in John Lewis. And there were some green wellington boots with frogs' eyes on them at the feet, and I thought 'thank God – I can't tell if it's a male frog or a female frog – I'll buy those'. And my daughter said 'mum, what are you like? These cost a fortune'."

"And these manufacturers," she went on, "they're preying on our not thinking, and they're selling clothes that make little boys look like commandos, and little girls looking all frilly. We're being manipulated. Though of course they would say 'we're only producing what we've been asked for'. So you're locked in this poisonous, toxic embrace, and I don't know what to do apart from trying to get people thinking, and they're not going to think about what I've just said because they just think you're being PC."

I suggested that many people, like those I'd met in Blackpool, resented efforts to push cultural change through too quickly. They felt that political correctness seemed to be an attempt to stop them saying or thinking things that in years gone by would have been acceptable, and judged them for things they or their families had once enjoyed. I asked Gill how she thought people like her should respond.

"It's obviously got to be about dialogue," she said. "We've obviously got to find a way to talk in such a way that people don't feel that I am being uppity or lecturing or better than them or that I don't somehow hook something inside them. It's somehow being able to open a dialogue without scratching that sore."

She made me a cup of tea, and told me about her partner, Ivan, who had died a few years earlier. She said he had been very good at standing up for his values.

"He was very good on racism," she said. "He'd lived through apartheid in South Africa and when people would say things like 'monkeys', he'd say 'er, I left South Africa to get away from that chat, no more of that here'. And he'd just move on, and he was very jolly about it."

"I need to find a way to do the same thing, just explain it very simply and not apologetically," she continued. "It reminds me of using words like 'feminism' – you know, people will say to me 'you're not still a feminist, are you?' And I think maybe we could learn from that, because I say 'yeah, of course I am'. You know, I'm the first generation of women who had everything they could have, and I want the same for my children. It hasn't been easy and because we were the first generation to make those advances, we haven't had anyone to copy, but we have had opportunities that our mothers never had, let alone our grandmothers."

"I think we've got to work intellectually as well as emotionally," she went on. "We've got to be emotionally intelligent so that when I'm talking to you, I hook you emotionally as well as working with you using my brain. You'll stay with me as long as you feel an emotional contact with me, but the moment I just operate from my head, the moment I'm no longer emotionally congruent, I lose you, and that's when you might attack me back as PC or whatever."

On the basis of the conversations I had had around the country, I felt that she was right, but I wondered how willing she felt people who saw the world the same way as she did were to make emotional contact when it felt like there was such a cultural divide between people.

"You want to shut people down because they're too dangerous," she said. "I remember watching the Channel 4 News about the sentencing of the Jo Cox killer, and they went to her constituency and they talked to various people. They spoke to two guys in the pub and they were saying 'oh we just need to get England back as it was', 'we've got to make our own laws', 'I think Trump is going to be great'. And I think if I was in that pub, on the day that that court case had come through, and I heard that, I'd probably walk out."

"On the other hand," she went on, "when I went into the pub with Ivan, we went in with the girls – two teenage girls – and some men at the bar started making a noise, and one of them wolf-whistled at the girls, and Ivan wasn't an aggressive man, but he squared himself up against these guys and said 'so which dog are you whistling for?' And these men just shrunk. And he said 'just behave yourselves, otherwise we can't stay in this pub'. And I also wonder whether we liberals should sometimes say 'enough, it's not acceptable, I'm not putting up with that'."

"But I think we might be nervous about that," she added, "because in recent times our confidence has been knocked – and I'm thinking particularly about Islam: the feminist Sixties woman that I am does not like seeing women covered up, I do not like it in my town."

"If I go to another country," she continued, with clear anger in her voice, "I'm happy to cover my head to respect you, but when you're in my country, you better respect my customs. You know, just going around with just two little eye holes… So it's harder for me to be liberal, because I don't feel liberal about that. Or when a friend's father died, he was in hospital and he was semi-conscious and he came round, and the doctor was at the end of his bed, and he said 'what's that black thing at the end of my bed? It's scaring me'. He thought it was the grim reaper, but it was a female doctor, completely covered – she just had her eyes showing. And I think it's perfectly ok for somebody to be upset by somebody shrouded in black when he's very frail and vulnerable."

"Am I being racist?" she asked herself. "It makes me feel confused if I'm then challenging racism myself, because I remember that very strong reaction I had to what happened that day, and I'm furious with the hospital for employing a doctor who the patients couldn't see her face. I don't mind her wearing the hijab at all, but to actually cover herself up completely and only showing her eyeballs while running a public service in this country, I don't think it's right."

"And I also think if you think about the Victoria Climbié case," she went on, "the young girl who was killed by her family in Haringey, they employed social workers with a different values base about the role of chastisement in the child's family. So I think it's perfectly acceptable to ask questions to elicit the values system of the person you're going to employ – when I was working with young people's charities, I always insisted that we ask questions about homosexuality and abortion because I didn't need anyone in my organisation without the right kind of values."

"I think those of us who are on the liberal side have some work to do," she added, "because for all my liberal instincts, there is a part of me which thinks 'this *is* tricky'. I think us liberals are a bit wobbled and I think we need to get it together."

"If we were able to do a rethinking in the Sixties," she asked as we prepared to part, "why aren't we doing that now? Or have we got too fat and comfortable in our £500,000 flats?"

I left her soon afterwards and headed to Richmond Green. As children of different backgrounds played while the sun went down, I thought back on the conversation with Gill. Her view on racism was very clear but, as had been the case throughout my journey, matters of culture and faith seemed much more challenging, particularly when it came to Islam. I wondered whether there was something about the burka in particular – the almost primal desire to see another person's face, the associations it had with gender inequality and unwillingness to engage with others – which made it more troubling for people than almost any other symbol. I had reflected on the issue since the conversation with Howard Williamson in Treforest: while I didn't think that women should be banned from wearing the burka or the niqab, I could see a strong argument for anyone working in the public sector and interacting with service users to be required to show their faces, and for using legislation to ensure that no one was forced to wear any item of clothing if they did not want to do so. The idea of imposing my values on someone from a different culture still troubled me, however, and I decided to explore this further.

*****

My next meeting was with Julia Ellis, a strong advocate of gender equality and prevention of violence against women who I felt would help me to make sense of some of the difficult issues I had encountered on my travels, which so often related to gender. In particular, I wanted to explore the rights and wrongs of getting involved in the traditions, attitudes and cultural practices of faiths and communities which were not my own.

"The way I see it, there are two ends of the spectrum," Julia told me over a drink in a local pub. "One end is that you live in Britain, you get rid of all of your cultural norms and you live by British values, whatever that means. And then the other extreme is about individual choice and liberty – saying, you know, it's fine for somebody to do whatever is culturally appropriate for them and their family – it doesn't matter whether they live in Britain or not. And there is a middle ground which you see in the debate on female genital mutilation: it's clearly something which as a country we don't see as acceptable."

"That campaign has been so powerful," she went on, "because it's been led by survivors from black and minority ethnic backgrounds who are able to say those things which maybe in the past a white female Home Secretary or a male white Prime Minister hasn't. And now you have a very clear line which says 'this is unacceptable behaviour and it doesn't matter that it happens in some people's culture because actually, for women and girls in the UK, it's not ok'."

I asked about the philosophical underpinning of such legislation, with the state trumping customs which went back for generations in the country of origin of the people who practised them.

"Who cares if you can do it somewhere else?" Julia said. "That is a moot point. We as a society very clearly set out what our expectations are of our citizens, and that is what people live to. It doesn't matter if everyone around you thinks domestic abuse is fine and that it's alright for someone to hit their wife or force them to do what they want, because as a society we have decided that that is not ok, and therefore we take action against those people who do it, regardless of what community they're from, where they live, how rich they are. We have decided that these are our red lines of how everybody in our country should be treated, and that applies to everybody."

While it seemed completely fair to say that no community should be singled out and that the same rules should apply to everyone, it nevertheless seemed difficult when the 'red lines' clashed with the long-established practices of some communities. I asked her for her view.

"You wouldn't have the same conversation about burglary," she said, "like 'ah well, in this country they just rob people so that's ok'. Burglary is just illegal, it doesn't matter who you are or where you're from – it's illegal, the end. But because what we're talking about is to do with what happens in someone's home, how they were brought up and what their beliefs are, that creates that sense of a grey area. Like with child sexual exploitation – 'oh, it's just what a certain group of people do' – but actually by being too scared of being called racist, we have sometimes ignored the plight of girls who have been sexually exploited by certain communities, and the people that we have failed there are the girls whose lives have been destroyed – that's not ok."

I agreed that the priority should be the safety, wellbeing and human rights of the individual – in this case, girls at risk of exploitation. Like Gill talking about the Victoria Climbié case and Emma, the youth worker in Blackburn, for Julia the rights of the child clearly came first. While I agreed with her approach, I nevertheless felt nervous about pushing my view on these issues in minority communities as a white, middle class man, and I asked her for her view.

"It's about checking your privilege," she said. "I'm coming from a white, upper-middle class English family – I can't talk about what it's like to be a woman in a Muslim family."

"I think there are sensitivities," she went on, "when people who don't have that experience comment on it without acknowledging the limitations of what they're saying. So sometimes, I might be angry if a guy is commenting on some female issues, as though he knows everything he's talking about. Say, for example, a guy writes an article about street harassment, and I'm like 'you've got no idea what it's like, so don't even start telling me about my experiences…' But actually if someone approaches it like 'I don't know what it's like, but this is the evidence that I've brought together' – that's very different."

"In the same way," she added, "I can't just say 'in a Muslim family, this is how women feel' – I've got no idea, I've never lived it and I would never pretend to."

I wondered what she would say if someone else challenged her and claimed their own authority based on long-held custom or religious freedom. I asked why she felt her view should win out.

"I don't think I get to 'win'," she said, "but I think what we have decided as a society is that this behaviour, wherever it happens, is unacceptable. When we brought in new legislation on coercive and controlling behaviour, for example, we made that decision in exactly the same way that we have decided that burglary is wrong, or mugging somebody on the street is wrong and, you know, murdering someone is wrong – it went through Parliament."

"You might say that by making forced marriage illegal you might be persecuting some communities," she added as we prepared to leave, "but I think the human right to live free overrides anything else."

*****

I decided to follow up on Julia's point about forced marriage by talking to Aneeta Prem, the founder of Freedom Charity, an organisation set up to work with young people across the country to prevent them being forced to marry against their will. I told her about the issues I was grappling with and asked for her view.

"When you look at abusive practices like forced marriage," she told me, "many people tie it up in culture and I think in the past, people in the UK have been very worried about that, and that's why I think many types of crimes have been allowed to go unchallenged."

"When I do try to challenge people about forced marriage," she went on, "people have said to me 'this is our culture, we can't give a girl her freedom because if we did, she would be promiscuous and by actually finding her a husband early on, there's no risk of her mixing with men, there's no risk of early pregnancies'. And they say 'it's our culture to do this'. So I think culture and religion is almost a mask that people are putting on, and it's really important to say 'this isn't about culture and religion and just focus on the child and what's right'."

I asked what forced marriage was really about if it was not a cultural issue.

"I think it's about control," she said. "I think it's about parents and families believing that they know what's best for their children and not allowing their children – and women in particular – to make their own choices. And I think it's about male dominance and keeping 50% of the population in servitude. You know, if you tell young girls 'you are going to be disowned, you will have no contact with your family if you don't do this', a lot of them will go through with it. We rescued a young person who simply wanted to complete university and go and get a job as a teacher. That's not something that anyone should have a problem with – it's something we should be proud of – but her family believe they have an absolute right to choose her life for her and they feel that family honour is more important than her happiness. Her family have actually told her that she was only allowed to go to university because, as a commodity, they would get a better match for her if she had a degree."

I suggested that given that social mores and expectations must have influenced the family's behaviour in the example she had given, it wasn't easy to completely detach culture from the family's approach in such circumstances.

"It's not easy," she said, "but you have young people who are educated in the UK, have the same expectations as the friends they go to school with – having a university education, having a career – then having that freedom to choose taken away; that can't be right. Now some young people may want to get married and that's absolutely fine, and if they want an arranged marriage, no one has an issue with that – but when there's a level of force and coercion, that's when it's wrong – someone being forced to do something against their will cannot be right, and forced marriage is quite brutal: the levels of domestic violence are much higher, suicide rates for young Asian girls are three times higher than the norm. So what gives a parent or a community the right to tell them that's what they have to do?"

"We're seeing an increase in the number of girls of thirteen or fourteen being taken out of school," she went on, "sent back to their country of origin, forced to marry, often a first cousin, and they're not allowed to return to the UK until they're pregnant. Their child is then a UK citizen and then they apply for a spouse visa – so they're really manipulating the system so that others can come to Britain. And the pressure on that young girl to make that marriage work, even though she's been taken abroad against her will, is extreme. And that's not just one or two, that's hundreds, thousands of girls in the UK each year."

"It's not just in South Asian communities," she continued, "we're having more and more cases from the travelling community and the Mormon community. There are over 90 countries where forced marriage is reported in the UK. So though it would be easy to say it's a South Asian issue, it goes far wider."

I asked her why some communities might be affected more than others.

"If you go to some areas," she said, "they do seem to have disproportionately high numbers of cases, and that's to do with the demographic and the fact that the people there have held on to their traditions from their country of origin."

I thought back to the Comedy Carpet in Blackpool and how difficult it had been for the people there to concede that elements of a culture which had been part of their past were now considered unacceptable. While the circumstances were very different, there seemed to be a parallel with people being told that the culture of their country of origin was not acceptable in Britain, and I could see how both instances could be painful for people. In both instances, I thought it was important to be sensitive to the discomfort people might feel when their cultural traditions were challenged, but that such sensitivity should in no way inhibit efforts to uphold shared values like equality or basic human rights.

"Also," Aneeta went on, "you've got 'community elders' – and I'm saying that very tongue-in-cheek – who seem to be having a real influence in what happens. They're holding onto their traditions of where they came from, what happened to them when they were growing up, but I also think they're trying to hang onto these values and customs because it gives them status and power."

"The same with men in families," she went on, "they feel out of control and are seeing things change. They need to be in control of something, so they start with women in their families."

I asked whether the fact that she was female and her family was from India gave her more authority than a man like me, who had no connection with South Asia, to talk about issues like women in South Asian communities being forced to marry.

"Well I was born in Bethnal Green," she said, "and I think it is an issue for all of us in the UK, and all of us have to stand up, not just people who are brown. These issues have escalated because in the past people have been scared to deal with them. The police have let people deal with it themselves and it's just getting worse. I think we need to challenge it and see it for what it is."

"I think the problem we're seeing now is many communities becoming more introverted," she went on, "where many young people are saying that they don't want to become friends with other young people just because of the colour of their skin and their religion. And I don't think we've seen this before to this degree – maybe we did during the Sixties but now we're getting a different kind of backlash where people are scared of each other and that's bringing a whole new series of hate. At the same time, you have attitudes becoming more entrenched in some minority communities, people are less westernised and less willing to accept British values."

"So we've got big issues to deal with," she continued, "and we can't let political correctness get in the way. I'm not saying that people should forget their traditions and religions, the things which enrich us – I believe that if people come to the UK they should be able to maintain their culture and traditions from back home but they should embrace the best of the UK, and that's a real marriage and partnership. And that also means that when people are using culture to justify abuse, we have to be able to robustly challenge that without anybody being called a racist."

"I've spoken to many people in authority like headteachers and police officers," she added as we prepared to leave, "who have said 'I'm afraid to deal with that person because the first thing they're going to do is play the race card' or 'I can't raise that issue because it's too politically sensitive'. So you've got white British men like yourself, middle class men, often in positions of authority, almost apologising for who they are, when in fact if we're going to make any progress on these issues and make this a safer place for us all to be, we all need to work as one."

*****

That evening, I reflected on the conversations with Gill, Julia and Aneeta. I had started with Gill talking about gender-neutral Wellington boots for children and ended discussing with Aneeta how to make sure that young women were free to make their own choices about who and when to marry. The continuum between the conversations happening in very liberal circles and those taking place in more conservative communities seemed vast and, if Aneeta was right, cultural divides were becoming more entrenched. I had assumed that over time integration and attitudinal change would happen naturally, but she had suggested this wasn't necessarily the case and that things could go 'backwards'.

While I was conscious of impinging upon people's freedoms, like Julia and Aneeta I believed that we should have some very basic standards as a society on what was acceptable and unacceptable, and I felt that if those standards were established through a democratic process and were grounded in human rights and shared values, they should have primacy over community and faith customs and practices. I knew that Julia was right that I should be conscious of my ignorance in relation to other people's cultures, but as Aneeta had said, that should not stop people like me having a view about what was happening in Britain and standing up for what I believed in. After all, I wanted the UK to be a true community in which everyone, whatever their background, felt a responsibility to one another. Furthermore, Aneeta had suggested that some people involved in abusive practices would use culture as cover for what they were doing and that there was a danger that people in positions of authority – often white men – would be put off intervening as a result. This was not something I wanted to happen, and the key it seemed to me was to be careful to apply shared values and standards absolutely fairly and equally to everyone in British society, including both the majority community and minority communities.

The principle of treating all communities equally appealed to me, as I had been worried about the way Muslim people and South

Asian communities had been singled out for criticism during my travels. While focusing on one community felt instinctively wrong, I did think that it was possible that some communities might have more challenges on issues like gender equality than others because of the way those communities had developed. Aneeta had provided important insight into why communities might develop differently, referencing people not wanting to let go of the traditions of their country of origin, elders whose power depended on a firm set of cultural traditions and some men wanting to maintain their control and ascendancy by taking away women's freedom. These were complex circumstances, and I agreed with Julia that it was critical to apply the same standards to everyone; never indulging prejudice but at the same time not shying away from identifying where specific communities had a problem.

As I prepared to go to Scotland, I reflected on how much I admired the moral courage of the women I'd met. I was determined to have the same, and while I would remain conscious of what I didn't know about the culture and heritage of different communities within Britain, I wouldn't let that stop me standing up for what I believed in. I wanted to ensure that a very basic set of values relating to freedom, equality and prevention of harm to people were equally applied in all communities. That, I felt, would be right for the people in those communities – giving every one of them, particularly girls and women at risk of abuse, the freedom, security and rights to which they were entitled – and would also help to build a sense of shared values in the country which meant something because they were not just articulated, but also upheld. From the conversation with Aneeta, such efforts were desperately needed: if she was right, there were growing cultural divides in the country which would be further exposed if nothing was done.

15

Civic nationalism, monarchy and history in Scotland

My first stop in Scotland was Edinburgh and in the gardens by the Scottish Parliament building at Holyrood, visiting schoolchildren of different backgrounds enjoyed their lunch in the afternoon sun. It was a glorious day, and the hills overlooking the Parliament were a beautiful green. Around me, the children mixed with tourists, locals walking their dogs and employees from the Parliament and the Palace of Holyroodhouse, the Queen's official residence in Scotland, which was just across the road.

At the Parliament shop there were books on Scotland and Scottish history for sale alongside children's stories of Scottish mythical creatures and Scottish folk and fairy tales. There was a book called *My First Scottish Weather*, with a young girl on the front holding a tartan-pattern umbrella in the rain. The tea on sale was from the Wee Tea Company, and the jewellery, textiles, gifts on the shelves were all made in Scotland. Scottish folk music played in the background. Across the road, at the Palace of Holyroodhouse shop, there were cushions on sale with the Union Flag and aprons with the royal crest and the words 'God Save The Queen'. Footage of the 2011 Royal Wedding was playing on large screens dotted around the shop.

Nearby, I saw a man in a t-shirt with the word 'Yes' in the middle of the stars of the EU flag and I went over to him.

"I'm wearing this with pride," he told me. "Unfortunately, we have become a nation which has accepted handouts from south of the border, we've lost our pride, and we need to restore that."

"We actually think that as a united Europe, all of us can bring much more," he went on, "and we would much rather that you misguided people south of the border would have followed us in voting to stay in. But, see, leave it the hands of the Tories, and we will end up with all of the workers' rights taken away and we'll be back to the days of Maggie Thatcher, the Poll Tax, strife in the streets, miners and the police fighting each other."

"We want to determine our own fate," he went on, "and as long as we stay together, that won't happen. All of us want to be determined by our own abilities or lack of them. And I want England to be in control of England's destiny – if you really don't want to part of Europe, fine, but the Scots voted to remain… The Union Flag is not an England flag – the Cross of St George is an England flag. You fly it with pride and let us fly our flag with the same pride."

"You just can't accept that you're not very good at everything," he continued. "We accept we're not very good, but there's only 5 million of us – there's 60 million of you."

"Well, actually," he added, "there's only 50 million of you – the other ten million are immigrants who you don't want anyway. We're a different kettle of fish, we want to see as many people come into our country as possible. There's a lot of you who voted for Brexit because of detestation of foreigners. We don't have an issue like that."

He had kept using the word 'you' to describe the English and the words 'we' and 'us' to describe the Scottish, and I asked him why he didn't identify with England and the UK at all.

"I'm a republican," he said. "I don't want to have a Queen, I don't want to see any form of royalty, I don't want to see anything that has been gifted as a consequence of birth. I want people to gain what they gain on their abilities, and I think the majority of what I would consider to be right-thinking Englishmen would think the same. Unfortunately, you voted for a Conservative government – so you're obviously not that right-minded."

"The majority of nationalists are socialists at heart," he went on, "so we want to see a country which seeks to give the best opportunities to everyone. We do not want to see a country which wants to go back to the grammar school days, to the days of Eton and Harrow. I don't want to see David Cameron and his cohorts in power. I don't want to see anyone who went to Eton getting a chance to be something that they don't have the ability to be."

As I headed for the station, with Glasgow my next destination, I wondered why it was that he wanted as many people to come to Scotland as possible when so many people in England felt differently. I was also keen to find out whether his view on immigration was reflective of Scotland as a whole. I thought back to Alex Smith in London and his disappointment that the commercialism of Manchester United's owners belied the values for which he felt the club stood, and wondered if the reality of modern Scotland would live up to the welcoming, inclusive vision the man I had just met had painted.

At the station, I could hear a bagpiper playing 'Flower of Scotland' and there were quotes from Sir Walter Scott all around, including one which caught my eye.

"Breaths there the man, with soul so dead,
Who never to himself hath said,
This is my own native land."

*****

When I reached Glasgow, I headed for Ibrox, the home of Glasgow Rangers, a football club traditionally associated with a strong sense of British identity. I had been really taken by what the man in Edinburgh had said about Scotland being a welcoming place for people from all over the world and I wanted to know how real that was, and whether there was anything the UK as a whole could learn from it. Ibrox, a poorer area of the city which I knew housed a large number of refugees and asylum seekers, seemed a good place both to test out what he had said and to reflect on what Britishness meant.

By Ibrox Stadium, a boy walked past in a Union Flag hoodie and in the window of the chip shop was a poppy and the words 'support our troops'. There were stickers and graffiti on the walls from Rangers supporters all around. 'Glasgow Bears', read one sticker depicting a roaring bear in front a Union Flag. 'We will follow you win, lose or draw', read another.

Around the corner, I got talking to a local woman in her forties called Lisa.

"There's so many drug addicts round here that I would not trust my best friend now," she told me. "I'll just say hello and goodbye to people – that's it. If could leave, I would. I hate being here, I hate being Glaswegian: every day on the TV someone's been shot, someone's been stabbed."

"There's been ten people stabbed in Glasgow in the past ten days," she went on. "One boy, he got stabbed just there, right in front of me."

She pointed around the corner.

"Why can't they just have a fight," she added, "a wee normal fight, a little fisticuff?"

Around the corner, by the Subway station, a couple of young women shouted, and Lisa turned abruptly. She was obviously a little on edge.

"Crack is a big thing in Glasgow," she said after a moment, "and I'm not a racist person, but it's the Syria and Sudan boys who have brought it in. You've got the boy racers with their brand new cars and they give the cocaine to wee boys to deliver. And the police won't go after them."

"There are boys that have opened up shops doing barbering or doing courses," she went on, "they want to better themselves and that's fine. But that house there, you've got fifty people in that house. You've got people sleeping in the garage next door. Syria, Sudan, Romanian people – I don't say the word 'hate' but I can't stand them, they're so rude."

"This guy was smoking crack cocaine on my landing," she continued, "and he started hassling me and I said to him 'excuse me, if you touch me one more time, I will bite your balls off and send them to your wife as a pair of earrings'. And he said 'You white bitch', 'You Scottish bitch' and I was like 'I'm a Scottish bitch who's going to knock the fuck out of you'. And he said 'don't answer me back, my wife don't answer me back', and I'm like 'I ain't your fucking wife'."

"And don't get me wrong," she added, "there's people here who would batter their wives as well, but it's not the same as how I was brought up."

She told me a disturbing story of a case of child prostitution and trafficking which had happened nearby which she said had been led by men from Glasgow's migrant communities. She told me the police had been called and that a group of girls, some as young as twelve, had been freed. As she finished the story, a couple of men walked by, and when they had passed, she turned back to me.

"They're the ones sleeping in the garage," she said, "and they're working. They're getting the bru – the benefits – they're getting DLA."

I asked her what she thought about the campaign for Scottish independence and whether it would make a difference to the issues she was describing.

"Nicola Sturgeon is an arsehole," she said, "but people vote for her because they want Scotland to be Scotland. Their picture is this amazing country, meeting different people from different countries, eating different food, but if you get behind the scenes, into the dirty, nitty-gritty bit of it, it's no' like that."

She wished me well and went on her way.

Around the corner, I got talking to two women, one in her sixties, one in her twenties, sitting on deckchairs outside their tenement building enjoying the sunshine. Beside them, a toddler played in a walker. I asked for their views on independence.

"I'm no' for it," the older woman said firmly. "I think we should be our United Kingdom, I don't think we should be separate from England."

The younger woman nodded strongly in agreement. I asked them in which ways being part of the UK was preferable.

"Everything," the younger woman said, "in regards to trade and stuff. Just together as a country."

"We've no' got enough money to cope financially on our own," the older woman said, "because we'd lose our pound."

"For us personally," the younger woman said, "there's also a sense of Britishness. It's a British identity not a Scottish identity."

I asked what being British meant to her.

"The whole thing," she said. "The whole thing of being British."

I suggested that Nicola Sturgeon would say that there was a unique Scottish identity which was distinct from British identity.

"Aye," the younger woman said, "but we can still maintain it while still being British. There's little bits of England which keep their identity while still being British."

I asked what it was that could keep British identity together with so many separate identities coexisting within the country.

"I don't know really," the younger woman said. "I think it's ever since the World Wars, they united the country."

"The soldiers went and fought unitedly for Britain," the older woman said. "And that wee saying 'United we stand, divided we fall', do you know what I mean – why should we try and divide it?"

"If Scotland leaves," she went on, "we would lose our monarchy. She says we'd keep it, but how long can you trust her?"

I asked if by 'her' she meant Nicola Sturgeon. She nodded.

"I can't stand her," she said. "I would never vote SNP. I'm a Unionist."

I asked what being a Unionist meant to them.

"Supporting the Union," the younger woman said.

"I'm a Christian," the older woman said, "and this is a Christian country and I think we should maintain our Christian country."

I asked how that would change if Scotland became independent.

"I don't know," she said. "I would just want to make sure it never happens."

The child made a noise, and she turned to him.

"What is it darling?" she said, "you want a drink?"

She gave him a sip out of a drink and turned back to me.

"I saw her the other day," she said, "Nicola Sturgeon."

I asked if she'd spoken to the First Minister.

"I wanted to," she said, "but I'd of ended up in jail. I'd have been lifted if I said what I felt."

"I just don't like her," she went on. "She's trying to divide the country. She keeps saying she speaks for the people of Scotland – she doesn't speak for me, she speaks for herself."

"The country was very divided after the independence referendum," the younger woman said, "and those bridges are just starting to get built up again because it did ruin people's friendships and relationships. And now she's starting it all up again, all so she can try to make her utopia."

"That's what they want it to be," the older woman added, "but she's a nutcase. These people voting for it, they're all dreaming of *Bonnie Scotland, Braveheart*. It's a pipe dream."

"I think we should still have our Queen," she went on, "for Queen and Country. She's been there for a lot of years."

"You might not physically have it," the younger woman agreed, "but you feel like you've got a bond with them. They're there, you know, they're our heads of state. That's how I feel, like they're the ones for us."

"I was just thinking about the way my gran felt about them as well," she continued. "My gran absolutely loved the Queen and that kind of gets passed on. My gran was a pure matriarch of our family, and you can see the similarities with the Queen."

"Because the Queen's the head of our family," the older woman added.

The remark struck me, and I wondered how the women would feel when the Queen died.

"We were brought up to respect the royal family," the woman continued, "because my mum did. And when she passed away, we were getting rid of a lot of stuff from her house, and the amount of royal stuff, going back to the Queen Mother, was unreal. My mum just loved the royal family."

"I always remember my mum talking about when the Queen had her first coronation," she went on, "and they were all huddled round televisions watching it. It's history, isn't it?"

As I left Ibrox, I reflected on the conversations I had had there: the sense of Britishness I had found seemed to be built on heritage rather than a vision for the future or a sense of what people actually had in common. I was left thinking back to the Rangers supporters' sticker – 'we will follow, win, lose or draw' – and I wondered whether such unhesitating loyalty could be relied upon forever and what would happen when the day came that the Queen died.

The conversation with Lisa had also made me think about the risks of trying to tell a story of welcoming integration and collective identity as the man in Edinburgh had done: if people like Lisa had an experience which differed from that story, it felt legitimate for them to be cynical. I knew Ibrox was exceptional – a very poor area relative to much of the country – but if the vision of Scotland the man in Edinburgh had provided did not apply in testing circumstances, I wondered how real it actually was.

As I headed to the Subway, I noticed a series of stickers which had been stuck onto walls and bins near the station. Each of the stickers was in the same shape with writing in the same font.

'If you hate white people and the United Kingdom, vote Nigger Sturgeon, Socialist Negro Pakis (SNP)', one read.

*****

I headed north, and in the Kelvingrove Park area of the city, I met a man in his sixties. He told me he wasn't in favour of independence. I asked him why.

"Because together, Scotland and England has done so much for the world," he said. "We built an empire together, we gave Christianity to the world together and we gave democracy to the world together. Split the two of us apart and it will destroy the rest of the world."

I started to ask him a question about his view on Nicola Sturgeon saying independence was the best way forward for Scotland but he interrupted me before I could finish.

"Nicola Sturgeon is a communist," he said. "She's only got one policy and that's the destruction of western society. She's not my First Minister."

"You should ask her how many of these Syrians are Christians," he went on. "I can tell you what the answer is – the answer is none – they're all Muslims. And you watch them on TV, marching through Europe, these so-called children, it's all young men, being drafted in to form jihadi groups for the future, to form sleeper cells. The Muslims plan to take over Europe, and they plan to take over Britain too and Nicola Sturgeon has welcomed them with open arms."

"If she wants more people, she should encourage young people to have families," he continued, "not stop the allowances after women have two children maximum. I know why they're doing that in England, because it's all Muslim families and they have ten children."

"Nicola Sturgeon wants Muslim children," he added. "She wants to change the ethnic group. She doesn't see any difference between a Muslim jihadi or a Scottish person. Did you see those jihadis on the television the other day? Do they resemble you or me? Obviously not, they're all Muslims – they're not British."

I said that many Muslim people made a very positive contribution to British society and would consider themselves as British as him and me. Thinking back to my conversations earlier in my journey, I gave the example of Sadiq Khan as a Muslim person born in Britain making an outstanding contribution to British society.

"That's right," he said, "your Mayor of London is the first one. He's a Muslim, he's ruling a population that's larger than Scotland. That should tell you something."

I asked what it should tell me.

"It tells you that Muslims are taking over," he said.

"What makes a nation," he went on, "is a fundamental belief in what you are as a people. You can't flood the country with Muslims and say 'these are our people'. They are never our people – they're not our flesh and blood; they don't have our DNA. That's what makes a nation."

I suggested that people had come from all over the world and settled in the UK over centuries.

"Aye," he said, "my ancestors came from Poland. I'm very friendly with the Polish people that came here and they're very nice people. When I was a young man, I went to sea in the merchant navy and I sailed alongside Polish men that came over after the Second World War, and they were the best men under the sun. I knew some of the women as well and these are Scottish people. But you wouldn't get any one of these people singing the songs of Nicola Sturgeon about bringing in the Muslims, opening up your doors. The SNP are boasting about a family of Muslims they've sent over to the island of Mull – Muslim people on an island in the middle of the ocean. Now these are ethnically different people – the Europeans are not ethnically different."

I asked what was wrong about a Muslim person who shared Scottish values settling in Mull.

"Oh yeah," he said sarcastically, "they share Scottish values… I'll believe you son, but thousands wouldn't."

He walked off laughing to himself.

I sat on a bench and thought about what he had said. His attitude about people from abroad seemed to be the antithesis of the view of the man I had met in Edinburgh, and I reflected that while my aim was to bring people together, there was ultimately a battle between the nationalism based in ethnic heritage he had described and the inclusive patriotism based in shared values which Alex Smith had talked about when I was in Wembley. Alex has used the word DNA to talk about values which could be embraced by anyone, while the man in Glasgow had taken a literal interpretation, suggesting that tribes were ultimately united by ethnicity, and had used that interpretation to argue that Muslim people could never be 'our people'. For all my hope of building a sense of a united nation and finding common ground between people, I knew these two definitions of nationality were incompatible, and I knew which one I wanted to underpin a future sense of Britishness.

I walked around the corner and saw a mosque. Outside was a sign advertising the 'Ahmadiyya Muslim Fun Run' in Kelvingrove Park which was raising funds for the Glasgow Children's Hospital Charity. The website given was from an organisation called 'Muslims for Humanity'. Nearby, I saw a note scrawled on a wall: *RIP Asad Shah*, it read, a reference to an Ahmadi Muslim shopkeeper from Glasgow murdered the previous year in a sectarian attack carried out by a Sunni Muslim from Bradford. I looked up the case on my mobile phone. According to Shah's killer, Tanveer Ahmed, Shah had "disrespected Islam". Shah's family had said that the shopkeeper had been "everyone's friend", a man who showed each person he met, no matter their background, the utmost kindness and respect.

*****

The next day, I headed to nearby Anderston. I had heard Nicola Sturgeon talk about a sense of 'civic nationalism', an identity and set of values which were open to everyone whether or not they were born in Scotland and I wanted to hear more about it, so when I saw an SNP office in the middle of a housing estate, I knocked on the door. The local MP, Alison Thewliss, opened it and agreed to talk to me. I began by asking her how she would characterise 'Scottishness'.

"For me," she said, "it's very different to the little Englander attitude of Brexit, of pulling up the drawbridge and being against other people. It's much more open and outward-looking. For the SNP, that's a vein which has run through for a long time, so when Winnie Ewing got elected in 1967, she famously said 'stop the world, Scotland wants to get on'. We want to co-operate, we want to collaborate, we want to be speaking to other countries and making a contribution to the world. And it's certainly not about that kind of take things back to the 1940s or 1930s or whatever rose-tinted, backward-looking attitudes people want to take. We want to be a modern, inclusive society where we have technology as our driving force. We want to invest in our people, we want to invest in our economy, science, things like that – so it's that inclusive, outward-looking, civic nationalism, welcoming people, not chucking them out."

I asked her what civic nationalism meant to her.

"It's about shared values and a commitment to social justice," she said, "which we can see fraying quite badly south of the border. That sense of community, solidarity, looking after your neighbour seems to be diminishing and I feel very sad about that:

my husband is English and my in-laws live in Derby, and they were quite upset by the Brexit vote because they voted to remain and they couldn't believe their neighbours had voted otherwise. But there is that divergence – the way that Scotland is voting, the social attitudes that we have, the way in which we are seeking that social justice. You know, there have been cases where families have come to settle in Scotland and the Home Office wants to kick them out, and we've got newspapers saying 'how dare you kick out people who have come to live here and make their home here?' Whereas the narrative south of the border is that we've got too many people coming in."

"We need immigration here," she went on, "because historically we've had depopulation in many parts of Scotland, particularly the Highlands and way up north. So why wouldn't we welcome people who want to bring their skills and build their lives here? It's of great value to Scotland to have talented people come here."

"That sense of Scottish identity extends to people who have come here," she added. "So I was at a reception for the Sikh community a few weeks ago, and the chap I was speaking to was like 'Yeah, the Sikhs in Glasgow are really Scottish' – wherever they've come from, Scotland is their home and they're gunning for Scotland."

Thinking back to the man I'd met the previous day, I asked how one could prevent civic nationalism turning into prejudice or hatred of those who weren't of that nationality.

"I think they're two very different attitudes," she said, "and you just shouldn't pander to those kind of racist attitudes, because the more you play to the tabloids about immigration figures, the more you have 'go home' vans, the more you build that narrative. You know, if you think of all the people in Scotland who went to other parts of the world, who are we now to say 'you can't come in here'? We've contributed to other countries, we've helped to build and grow them and people who come here by and large work hard and contribute to this country."

"They're doing all kinds of things to the benefit of the UK," she went on, "and I don't think that's well enough recognised. That's something we've been conscious of here – there has been cross-party consensus on welcoming refugees and asylum seekers to Glasgow. We've had a banner on the City Council building saying 'Glasgow welcomes refugees'."

I asked her about my experience in Ibrox and the concerns about immigration which I had heard. I wondered how she reconciled that with her vision of being positive and inclusive.

"I think it's just about keeping explaining to people," she said, "because if you've never sat down and chatted to someone who has come through that experience, you're not going to know what they've been through. So the Scottish Refugee Council are doing a 'cup of tea with a refugee' initiative at the moment because once you break down those barriers, that starts those conversations. Similarly if you've got your kids in schools together, you can start to have that conversation: 'did you know the situation in the place that that person has come from?' People do pick up things from the tabloids or hearsay, so it's continuing to say 'actually, this is the situation and this is why we need to continue to welcome people and support them'."

"In Glasgow," she went on, "the children of asylum seekers went to the local schools and they actually brought up the levels in the local schools – they were improving outcomes for local children because they were excited about learning and saying to the other kids 'why aren't you excited about learning?' It changed attitudes, and it became a very international community – and that's not to say that everything is perfect and all attitudes are as perhaps they would be in an ideal world, but it is about changing those conversations."

Her remarks about education took me back to previous conversations in England where I felt there was a sense of people from long-established, predominantly white communities, feeling that they were being usurped by 'outsiders', with educational performance of people from migrant or minority backgrounds being emblematic of that changing status. I wondered whether she thought that was an issue in Scotland.

"It's about how you manage that and how you bring everybody along," Alison said, "because it's an amazing opportunity for learning and changing attitudes."

"Asylum seekers are dispersed pretty widely across Scotland," she went on, "including to Bute, which is pretty rural and pretty far away from where people had come from. And there's a guy who had come there and opened a barber shop, and everyone was out celebrating – you know, he's come here, he's set up his business – brilliant."

"And that's not to say that there aren't challenges," she added, "of course there are. I see a lot of asylum casework through my office: people coming from pretty desperate circumstances, and it's a pretty difficult process for them as well, so it's about saying to people 'you know what, there's a lot more to it than you might think'. So it is challenging and difficult, but if you do it right and you set yourselves up to say 'the government is supporting this, all the parties are supporting this' and you do it with communities rather than just imposing people onto communities, and you do all that you can in terms of fostering integration – to run interfaith events and to welcome people in different ways – you can move forward. Above everything else, we have an obligation to help people as a nation. A lot of the issues that are occurring in the Middle East and elsewhere are a direct or indirect result of the actions of the UK government, so we most definitely have an obligation to help people wherever we can."

I wondered if she had any lessons for England on how to build a positive, welcoming patriotism rather than a dangerous, divisive nationalism.

"It's just about having the genuine civic pride in the place," she said, "and I think the difficulty in England is that it has been claimed by groups that you don't want to be any part of – the English flag has been claimed by the EDL and it's just about reclaiming that and saying 'you know what, that's not yours – we are proud to be English' and not making it that negative, destructive attitude. So if it is your football team or your rugby team or whatever, it's about celebrating that. It's about celebrating St George's Day in a positive and inclusive way and saying 'that's ok'."

I was conscious of her time, but given my experiences the day before, I did want to ask her for her view about people who didn't buy into her vision for an independent Scotland.

"There are people who have a very strong attachment to being part of the UK," she said, "and that's perfectly understandable – I can absolutely see where people are coming from on that, but the reality is that with Brexit, with a Tory government for who knows how long, the question is whether your attachment to the UK, and the romantic notion of what that is, is more important than the welfare of your neighbours, of the economy, of the future for young people? You can see the direction that Britishness is going in – do you want to be part of that or do you want to do something else? Is it this historic tie or is it future prospects? Because looking at the way the UK is going, I don't see great hope in those future prospects."

*****

As I prepared to finish my research on Scotland, I went to meet Alan Hamilton, a Scottish writer in his forties who now lived in London. Over a cup of tea, the rain pouring outside the café in which we met, I asked him if he felt there was a distinct Scottish identity.

"I do believe that Scottish people look at the world slightly differently to English people," he told me. "There's a pragmatism and a puritanism which is strangely still in the Scottish culture which isn't part of English culture at all. I think that religion in Glasgow and down the West Coast definitely plays a far larger part in identity than you would imagine – not necessarily to actual church attendance mind you – and far more than in English life. And that sense of sectarianism – whether you identify as Protestant or Catholic – is part of Scottish identity, informing a sense of puritanism regardless of which side of the divide you fall."

"I also think Scottish people are far more self-identifying than English people," he went on. "With English people, there's almost an apologetic note when you go abroad – 'I'm sorry I'm English' – whereas Scottish people are very proud, and feel that by self-identifying as Scottish, they're guaranteed a warm welcome. In the same way, if you went into a bar in any town in England, and you didn't know anyone, you could stand all night having a drink and not get talked to. That's very different from Scotland – regardless of where you're from, someone will start talking to you. Scottish people are just more garrulous than English people."

"I think Scotland has maintained an outward-looking vision which England has lost," he continued. "Obviously Britain built an empire based on the backs of oppressed people around the world. It hardly makes you popular. And England has just gradually become more insular, whereas Scottish people have that sense of being European. Now that's not everyone – I don't know if people in Ibrox would necessarily turn round and go 'oh, I feel European' – but even the poorest kids get taken to Stirling or Edinburgh, and you're made aware that we did once play on the world stage and make a difference in the world, and I don't think we've forgotten that."

"The British Empire is recent enough," he added, smiling, "that people in England still have a mentality – which I don't think Scottish people have as strongly – that they're still a big player in the world, not a small, windswept rainy island on the edge of a continent. And I tell you what, looking out of the window, that's where I feel like I live."

I asked why he was smiling.

"Because people get really riled up about it," he said, "but do these empires ever last forever? Of course they don't. Does the Ottoman Empire still exist? Does the Alexandrian? Or the Mongol or Roman? No. So it seems futile to try to hold onto it."

"As much as they were part of the Empire," he continued, "I don't think Scottish people want to hold onto it. I think they think of it like it was *English* expansionism and *English* failure. It's not true – if you look at history, so many of the Empire's chief architects and proponents were Scottish and I think Scotsmen and women have travelled around the world and made a massive contribution to the world, but I think now there is that humour of a small country who knows how to laugh at itself, and is modest, and is realistic about its place in the world."

"So I do think that we are a distinct tribe from English people," he added, "but then you get into trouble by defining your identity in opposition to things. I think English people think there's a hatred of the English because our football matches against England are our biggest matches: well of course they are – because, and it's a ridiculous thing to say, but we were conquered by England hundreds of years ago, and people don't forget that cultural flow of history."

I asked to what extent he felt Scottish identity was defined against England.

"I think that the gallows sense of humour that people have got," he said, "the pragmatism, the sense of being perpetual losers in sport, being perpetual strivers to punch above our weight, all of these are created by many things, one of which is having a more successful neighbour to the south. It's not a chip on the shoulder, it's looking over and saying 'yeah, you're successful, but we're fine as we are'."

"It's a totally personal view," he went on, "but I just find people friendlier. The thing with the Syrian refugees seemed amazing to me: in small islands around Scotland, Syrian refugees were essentially parachuted into communities, and all of those communities rose to the challenge of integrating those people while also respecting their culture and what they've been through, and I think that's a testament to what Scottish people are like. It goes back to First Footing, when people go round to people's houses on Hogmanay – you take a piece of coal and a bottle and you knock and people invite you in. It's a piece of coal for the fire and something to drink, and you go from one house to the next. I think that sense of an open door and a welcome and a drink is just part of Scotland."

"I also think Scottish people are maybe less private," he continued. "You know, people will say 'my door's always open, come round'. And I think tea, weirdly, is almost a bigger ritual in Scotland than in England. So for example my gran would always be horrified if we went round to someone's house in England for a cup of tea and they wouldn't give you anything with it, because in Scotland, you would never have a cup of tea without a biscuit or a piece of cake."

"My gran lived in a nursing home in West Lothian until she died," he added, "and in that nursing home it was the same sort of community. In the street where she lived, there was that same sense of community, she knew all of her neighbours, they all did things for her. So when she got frail, every single one of her neighbours, even those who'd only been there for a year, all did stuff for her, all went in to see if she was ok, went up the street and brought her messages – you know, your shopping, a loaf of bread or some milk. She was 95 and living on her own but we never worried because we knew that her neighbours would look out for her, always."

I suggested that what he was saying meant that Scotland's sense of community wasn't just a romanticised myth painted by Scottish nationalists.

"It *is* real," he said. "I don't think it is a myth, I don't think it's romanticised – I think that's what a lot of people think is really important about Scotland, it's the fact that we are still a community.

I mean it might help that there are only five million people and it probably is changing – like for example my friend lives in Edinburgh, in a tower block and I think he knows his immediate neighbours to say hello to, but it's not like where my gran lived."

I asked why he felt things were different in England.

"If you think about the last forty years in terms of terrorism and headlines," he said, "you had the IRA bombing campaigns in the Seventies and the Eighties, and when I was growing up that was a very real and present danger with the bombs in Manchester and Warrington and in London – and that was reflected in the press. And then there's been global terrorism, and I think we've become very fearful, and I think the press have sensationalised it, and I think that's affected how people interact. I remember the week after the 7/7 attack getting the train and still feeling afraid. I think that's a totally justifiable fear, but the constant coverage of it makes you feel that there are things that you have to protect yourself from and an inevitable consequence of that is that it changes your mind-set. Not consciously, but you suddenly start to make different decisions and you become a little bit more conservative, more reticent and anxious."

He needed to go, so I asked him whether there was anything England could learn from Scotland in terms of building an inclusive and non-confrontational sense of nation.

"I don't know," he said. "I think the Tory government has stoked nationalism, and made a scapegoat of the EU. But when that's gone, who's the next scapegoat?"

*****

In a pub in the West End of Glasgow, an area well-known for being associated with students, professionals and people from around the world, I met Hannah Patterson, a lawyer in her thirties and my final interviewee before I headed to Northern Ireland. I asked her if the positive attitude towards immigration I had heard about really existed.

"We'd like to think that it does," she said, "and in some areas or some parts of Scottish society it probably is stronger than in other parts – but we do still have real problems with sectarianism, racism and homophobia."

"There are also many parts of the country where the population is not particularly diverse and therefore where these civic values haven't particularly been tested," she went on. "Proportionately, the immigrant population in Scotland is significantly smaller than in England so I think it's easy to say that Scotland embraces those who choose to live here regardless of their background, but I wonder whether there is really much concrete evidence for that. I think the best that could be said is that it's a worthy aspiration but that it's more being used for political spin to distract from any negative connotations of nationalism."

"And in fact," she added, "part of me thinks that the strong sense of Scottishness derives to an extent from an inward-looking perspective – and that actually the more outward-looking or inclusive a country becomes, inevitably the more diluted the sense of national identity becomes. I'm not sure how easy it is to have the positive aspects of both – to have a strong sense of national identity and be open-minded and inclusive as far as 'outsiders' are concerned."

"In the same way," she continued, "it's hard to see the strong anti-English sentiment which was apparent in some parts of the population during the campaign for the independence referendum as consistent with the claims to civic nationalism."

I asked if that meant she felt the SNP didn't always practise what they preached.

"I suppose you have to distinguish between the party and those who support it," she said. "There is a group within the latter which has a reputation for targeting and abusing those who don't share their views, most commonly through social media. There was definitely an atmosphere during the build-up to the independence referendum which led to some being afraid to voice their support for the Union publicly. That didn't sit comfortably with the principles of democracy and the lack of tolerance seems contrary to the spirit of inclusivity."

I asked whether there was anything the rest of the UK could learn from Scotland in terms of building a strong sense of national identity and solidarity while avoiding the traps into which she suggested the SNP had fallen.

"It seems that it may have become more acceptable to be proud of being Scottish than of being English," she said, "which helps create the solidarity and community. That could be because we are the 'wee brother' and so that sense of solidarity is perceived as being less threatening or aggressive. I think being a smaller country also makes it easier to foster a stronger sense of community."

"My sense," she went on, "is that events of recent years involving terrorism and extremism may have created a greater suspicion of both neighbours and strangers in some parts of England – which must have had a detrimental effect on the sense of community – than is found in Scotland – which has been fortunate enough not to have the same direct experience of these issues."

"I suppose what I'm saying is that the context and circumstances perhaps make developing a stronger sense of solidarity and community in England in particular more of a challenge," she continued. "So a starting point might be overcoming the perception that these are not positive aspirations – eliminate the association with superiority complexes or exclusion of others."

"For what it's worth," she added, "you do see the sense of solidarity and bond with the UK emerging strongly in Scotland during times of celebration like royal weddings and the Olympics, and in times of tragedy like terrorist attacks. It plays into the nationalist agenda to distinguish Scotland from the rest of the UK, including in terms of solidarity and community spirit, but I'd say we have far more in common than we do that is different."

*****

The next day, I got on a bus to Stranraer, from where I would catch a ferry to Belfast. As the bus went through towns and villages full of dilapidated, grey sandstone housing from another era, I thought back to Lisa, the woman in Glasgow living in the tough reality of a poor area with many new people coming into it. It wasn't exactly the Scotland that the man in Edinburgh had described, and I did think there was a risk of nationalists painting a romanticised picture of Scotland – 'utopia' as the woman by the tenement building in Ibrox had put it. I feared that if the reality didn't live up to the vision, people would justifiably be cynical and proponents of the vision would be discredited.

Alison Thewliss had been more realistic than the man in Edinburgh, I felt, but the attitudes I had heard on the streets of Glasgow were still quite inconsistent with the values she had set out in relation to immigration. I could see how much she wanted her civic nationalism to be shared by her fellow Scots: she clearly wanted Scotland to be an inclusive, welcoming country and she also clearly believed that depopulation meant Scotland really needed inward migration. Yet I wondered whether some of the people I'd met would ever feel the same way as her: whether it was damage done by fear-provoking headlines, as Alan had suggested, or the kinds of direct negative experience which Lisa had described, many of the attitudes I'd encountered felt deeply engrained. I still thought it was important to try to build a stronger vision of what Britain was for and about, but my experience in Scotland had taught me that the vision had to be realistic both in its description of the modern day and in its aspirations for the future.

Civic nationalism, monarchy and history in Scotland

As I reflected on my conversation with Alison, I did feel she had fallen into the trap of defining Scottishness against Englishness rather than in its own terms but the comparisons with England she and Alan had made were still very challenging for the future of the Union. I thought back to her remark about the foreign policy mistakes of the UK government, deftly distancing Scotland from them even though, as Alan had said, Scottish people had been at the heart of the Empire and more recent wars. While support for independence seemed to have slipped since the EU referendum, I could see how easily in the years to come the nationalist movement could define itself against the Conservatives, Westminster, the 'Little England' mentality and the worst of British foreign policy, painting England as an insecure, unwelcoming neighbour 'pulling up the drawbridge' and trying to cling to old glory. If Brexit went badly, it would, I felt, provide the SNP with more evidence of the 'divergence' of which Alison had spoken.

I believed that the opportunity for the SNP was particularly acute because despite spending a day in Ibrox, an area traditionally associated with the UK, I hadn't heard a convincing argument about Scotland's future in Britain or an attractive story of modern Britishness. There was an economic argument for the Union and a strong sense of loyalty, tied to history, religion, past wars and to the monarchy, but I did wonder if the latter might fade a little, particularly given how linked it was to the Queen personally. Similarly, I imagined that the role of religion in Scottish life would diminish, and I didn't think that war was likely to be the uniting factor it had been for past generations. Hannah had suggested there was more in common between England and Scotland than that which divided the two nations, but I felt work needed to be done to demonstrate that commonality. Her suggestions about trying to eliminate a sense of superiority and exclusion which came with a strong sense of national identity seemed a good place to start.

As I boarded the ferry, I thought about the lessons from Scotland on how a strong and inclusive sense of identity could be built in a multicultural nation. Scotland was, as Hannah had said, a smaller nation in which immigration was much lower than in England; and she and Alan had both commented on the fact that corrosive impact of 'domestic terrorism' – with a threat from within as opposed to an external enemy the whole country could unite against – had been felt far more in England than in Scotland. Building a stronger sense of community in a larger, more diverse and warier nation would be difficult, I felt, but it was important, and I couldn't help thinking that building a stronger sense of security – in all senses of that word – lay at the heart of the challenge ahead.

These were difficult social and political questions, but as the ferry sailed to Belfast, I felt the biggest question which I still hadn't answered was more personal: whether, given my reservations about British identity boiling over into xenophobia and nationalism and about the worst elements of British history which people I had met on my travels had mentioned, I could personally feel comfortable in embracing patriotism in the way Alison had suggested. Northern Ireland seemed the best possible place to confront those fears.

16

Symbols, sectarianism and reconciliation in Northern Ireland

On my first day in Northern Ireland, I headed into West Belfast, where I was shown around the largely-Catholic Falls Road area by a local man, Sean, a strong supporter of Irish nationalism.

"It's a very diverse part of the city," he told me as we drove around, "especially from the Middle East and Africa – Sudan, Somalia. We've got a lot of refugees living here and nobody has got a problem with anybody."

Given the issues about people coming into the UK from abroad which I had encountered on my travels, I asked him why he felt this place was untroubled by immigration.

"The people in this part of the city were also refugees once," he went on, "so there's this kind of rapport with Syrian people and Palestinian people. You have to understand the mentality of the Catholic-Nationalist-Republican people: they embrace all walks of life into their community because for hundreds of years, they went through the same scenario."

We reached a huge mural commemorating the hundredth anniversary of the Easter Rising and another commemorating the IRA hunger strikes, and then a large mural of Nelson Mandela next to a set of Palestinian and Irish flags flying side by side.

"Within Catholic-Nationalist-Republican areas," Sean told me, "they will always have sympathy with the minority of people who have been looking for independence, and this is why within these communities, the Palestinians have very big support."

"95% of the murals in Nationalist-Catholic-Republican areas are not in a paramilitary attitude," he went on. "They have changed over the years because the people have moved on from the conflict. Unfortunately in the Protestant-Unionist-Loyalist areas, they do have more paramilitary-style murals on the walls, showing gunmen and sectarian attitudes on the walls."

"In some Protestant communities, Catholics still aren't welcome," he added. "Fifteen, eighteen years ago, people from Eastern Europe flocked to Belfast, but when the Protestant community realised that Poland and Lithuania were Catholic countries, those people were burned out."

I asked him why he felt things were so different in Protestant communities.

"They're frightened of change," he said, "that's all it is. You have to understand the Protestant-Unionist-Loyalist people, because from 1922 they controlled things – that's nearly a hundred years ago."

"The British wanted to keep control of the North of Ireland," he went on, "so they moved Presbyterians and Protestants and Unionists into the North from Scotland, Wales and England and they set up a Protestant government. That meant that Catholics were always going to be second-class citizens."

"Belfast was one of the richest industrial areas in the UK at one time," he continued, "and that's why the British wanted the North – you had the second largest shipyard in the world, you had the cotton mills, you had the linen factories, you had the aircraft factories, coal... The Protestants controlled all of the industries, and Catholic people weren't allowed to get employment because of their faith, they weren't allowed to learn their Irish language, their culture or their history. They lived in overcrowded housing and when a

Protestant young lad left school at fourteen, he was guaranteed employment, whereas a Catholic young lad, he stayed in education because he couldn't get a job."

"In 1968," he added, "there were rumours that the IRA was using the civil rights movement as cover to re-establish itself so the police force, with the help of Loyalist mobs, attacked the civil rights movement, and then every Catholic home within two-and-a-half kilometres of where you're standing right now was burned to the ground. And there's your connection with the refugees, because there wasn't enough places to put up the people who were fleeing from their homes, so they had to flee to the south of the border, to Europe, to the Americas…"

We stopped at the Greater Clonard Martyrs Garden, dedicated to Republicans who had died during the Troubles. I looked at the main plaque on the wall.

'This plaque is dedicated to the people of the Greater Clonard who have resisted and still resist the occupation of our country by Britain. We acknowledge with pride the sacrifices they made. Their deeds of bravery and resistance are un-equalled. We, the Republican ex-prisoners of the Greater Clonard, salute you and your reward will only be a united Ireland.'

I asked him for his reflections on the last line.

"It's only less than a year ago that 56% of people in the north of Ireland said they want to stay within Europe," he said. "They done a poll here two weeks ago, and it's gone up to 63%. There was only one political party which voted to leave Europe, the Democratic Unionist Party – the DUP – even though tens of thousands within the Unionist community voted to stay with Europe."

I asked whether he felt that the DUP's decision was self-defeating given the uncertainty about Northern Ireland's future which the Brexit vote had created.

"I don't have to say that," he said, "even their own people are saying it."

"We have 1.8 million people living in the North and the DUP average 220,000 votes," he went on. "Sinn Fein came in 1,800 votes behind them… The Unionists have lost their majority in politics in the North. The whole geographics have changed, the attitudes of the people have changed. A lot of Eastern European people who moved here, they're now into their tens of thousands, and they're now citizens of the North, and they will be able to vote in a referendum because they've been here twenty years. And the majority of those people want to stay in Europe. So Sinn Fein may get their way sooner than you might think."

I suggested that there was a substantial population in Northern Ireland who felt a strong sense of British identity.

"It's all down to the majority of people," he said, "and that's the way it is. Change doesn't hurt no-one. Of course the Protestant-Unionist-Loyalist people find it hard because they've had it for 80 years."

I asked him what he meant by 'it'.

"Power," he said.

"It's only a matter of time," he went on. "Change is around the corner for everybody on the island of Ireland. Massive change. Why should people want to be part of a British Empire that doesn't really exist anymore, because every other country that Britain had power over has gone independent and bettered themselves? The days of the Empire have gone, and it's self-inflicted."

He sat on a bench, vaping and enjoying the sunshine. I suggested that he seemed very relaxed, as if he felt that what he wanted was an inevitability.

"Don't forget," he said, "that since the referendum, 850,000 people here have applied for Irish passports and the majority of those are from the Protestant-Unionist-Loyalist community. Within those communities, there are more people learning the Irish language than there is within Republican communities. They've realised in the last five years that the Irish culture should be shared by everyone. So a united Ireland should not offend or scare anyone. We won't take away their British identity, we won't take away their Protestantism. It's just that we'll have all these identities, and we'll all be European at the same time."

I suggested that the people would no longer be British if Northern Ireland became part of a united or federal Ireland.

"But the Empire is gone," he said, "this is the island of Ireland. This doesn't belong to the British people. But nobody wants to take people's identity away. People will still be able to fly the Union Jack."

But, I suggested, they wouldn't be British citizens.

"No," he said, "but that's the future. It's move on time."

As I left him, it was hard to know how representative his view was, but it did seem clear that demographic and political change, including the Brexit vote, had put the status of Northern Ireland back into question, and with it, the question of what being British would mean in the future. I decided to focus next on communities which felt a strong sense of British identity.

*****

That afternoon, I headed to the Shankhill Road, a part of Belfast traditionally associated with the Protestant community. There were Union Flags everywhere and large murals dominated the streets. I walked past one commemorating the hundredth anniversary of the Battle of the Somme, and further down the road was a war memorial in the grounds of a pub: the British flag flew high above a small cenotaph and beyond it a sign on a wall read 'no surrender'. Nearby was another memorial plaque, with a wreath in red, white and blue. On another building, there was a huge tribute to the Queen over a two-story building: 'Belfast, Shankhill Road, the heart of the Empire, salutes Her Majesty on sixty glorious years'. Next to it, there was another huge mural, this one depicting a woman, Ulster, holding a sword in one hand and waving the Union Flag with another. Beside it was 'a message from Ulster to England':

"Thou mayest find another daughter with a fairer face with a gayer voice and sweeter smile and a softer eye than mine, but thou canst not find another that will love thee half so well."

Just off the main road there were memorials dominating the sides of buildings to members of Loyalist paramilitary groups who had died in the Troubles. The memorials looked just like memorials to the British army. *Lest we forget*, the memorials read, *at the setting of the sun and in the morning, we will remember them*. There were insignias for the different paramilitary groups which those who had died had represented, all of which had the Union Flag in the middle. Nearby, I saw the anti-Catholic slur 'Fenians' scrawled on a wall and a mural of men with balaclavas and machine guns in front of a British flag. It felt like the antithesis of the welcoming patriotism I had found in Aberystwyth. Here, the strong sense of identity felt aggressive and the Union Flag felt like it was at the heart of that aggression.

I headed to East Belfast, another strongly Unionist area. The first house I saw had red, white and blue wreaths outside and further up there was an Ulster Volunteer Force (UVF) flag. Outside one home, a Union Flag duvet and pillow covers were drying on a washing line as children played on a trampoline. At a bus stop opposite a supermarket, there was a three-storey UVF mural with two men in balaclavas holding guns. Beside it was the message: '*We seek nothing but the elementary right implanted in every man, the right if you are attacked to defend yourself*'. Nearby I saw an Ulster Defence Association mural. It read:

'*The UDA was formed in 1971 as an umbrella for Loyalist vigilante groups to defend Protestant community from IRA violence. They remain today.*'

A Union Flag flew next to it and a young girl and her mother walked past. I couldn't help but wonder about the damaging impact that paramilitary symbols would have on a child, and whether the Union Flag would be tainted by association.

Nearby, I got talking to a man in his fifties called Sam, who told me he was a local historian.

"For us in East Belfast," he told me, "the Troubles started on the 27th of June 1970. The Provisional IRA came over to St Matthew's Chapel on top of the Newtownards Road here, and they took over the chapel, and as the bands and lodgers came back from a parade, they opened fire on the marchers. Two people were killed and another hundred were injured."

"Then there was the murder of the three Scottish soldiers in March 1971," he went on. "Young lads, out on the beer, were set up by what was called a honeytrap – the IRA sent a couple of good-looking girls down, invited them to a party, and when they were on the way to the party, members of the IRA were waiting and all three were shot in the back of the head. They were seventeen, eighteen and nineteen, two brothers and their best friend."

"If you asked 100 people what Bloody Sunday was," he continued, "I guarantee they could tell you, but if you asked 100 people what Bloody Friday was, they couldn't. Bloody Friday was the 21st of July 1972. The IRA detonated 36 car bombs in Belfast city centre in the space of two hours but because it happened in Belfast, nobody cared and the Protestant community was left to defend itself. All the vigilante groups came together and they said instead of having all these different vigilante organisations, we'll combine and create one, and that was the birth of the Ulster Defence Association."

I looked at all the paramilitary iconography around and asked if he felt there was a risk of the violence coming back.

"No," he said, "definitely not. Nobody wants to go back to the way it was – on either side, Republican or Loyalist. It's all scaremongering – there certainly aren't men in the shadows wanting to go back to it. Not a hope."

I asked why, if that was the case, the murals had not come down.

"People are still very proud," he said. "Sinn Fein have attacked the Protestant culture, and one of the main aspects of Protestant culture is bands, parades, the Orange Order, things like that. Whenever those attacks were being made, people fell back – they didn't bring guns into it, but they made sure that you know where you are. The murals are part of that – it's propaganda: 'this is our area'. It's just basically keeping your history and your culture alive, but there's no threat."

I said that I found the portrayal of the paramilitaries in front of the Union Flag quite aggressive.

"Well," he said, "a painted man has never shot somebody."

"It was part of their history and people don't want history rewritten," he went on. "Sinn Fein and the IRA are very good at propaganda and they're slowly but surely rewriting their history. They went from sectarian terrorists to peacemakers all of a sudden, but we want to make sure that the world doesn't forget the two-and-a-half thousand people they slaughtered. So you will get murals that will depict that – there's no way we want to allow history to be rewritten."

I asked how children might respond to the murals depicting men in balaclavas toting guns.

"When you've had something there so long, you don't even notice it," he said. "An outsider might be shocked, but local people wouldn't even notice it was there any more. It seems strange to see a thirty-foot gunman but kids wouldn't even know they're there. We become sanitised to it – you just walk past without a blink of the eye. But no one wants to go back to how it was – there were hundreds of people killed on streets like this. The war was always about maintaining British culture and identity, but it's a new battlefield now, the battlefield is all about politics."

Across the road, at the Union Jack Souvenir Shop – which proudly proclaimed itself 'British by birth-right' on its sign – a message in the window read 'show unity of purpose – vote Unionist'. There was no sense of which Unionist party people should vote for or which policies were being supported beyond maintaining the union with the United Kingdom, and I thought back to the slogan on the Rangers supporter sticker I had seen in Glasgow: we will follow you – win, lose or draw.

Inside the shop, a flag of a soldier at dusk and the words 'lest we forget' was on sale, along with pins and flags of various different paramilitary groups, photos of the Queen and royal memorabilia, poppy pins and more. I thought back to the Loyalist paramilitary slogan talking about the 'elementary right' to defend oneself if under attack. As the man I had just met had said, the 'war' was not fought with guns in the main any more, but the aggressive defence of culture and identity was still there. The Union Flag and the poppy had, it seemed, come to symbolise that defence, and I found the threatening use of those symbols deeply troubling.

As I left the shop, I thought back to Naomi in Welshpool who had talked about the idea of 'reclamation' and bought a small Union Flag pin badge for myself. I felt that if I was going to truly embrace patriotism and Britishness, I couldn't just have a utopian view of what that meant. I had seen in Scotland how important it was not to present an unrealistic view of the country or to pretend it was something which it wasn't. I felt that one had to present and embrace a fair and balanced view of the totality of the nation, not a selective view emphasising either just the good or just the bad. I didn't like the aggressive use of the Union Flag I had seen in Belfast, particularly behind images of men toting guns and wearing balaclavas which children would walk past each day, but I felt if I could embrace a Union Flag here, where I was at my most uncomfortable with a strong sense of Britishness, then I really could accept it warts and all. I wanted to finish my conversations in

Northern Ireland before coming to a final view, so I put the pin in my pocket and headed for my next meeting.

*****

I had arranged to meet Andrew Fleming, a man in his twenties who I knew had worked on the campaign to leave the European Union, at a café in East Belfast. I started by asking him for his reflections on the night the referendum result came in.

"I was at the count," he told me, "and I never thought it would happen. And then the Sunderland result came in, and as the night went on and things started to look a bit more positive, all the faces on the Alliance Party and the SDLP, Sinn Fein fell – so it was great."

"For me," he went on, "it was a question of why should we let somebody else have control over certain aspects of our laws, whether it's immigration policy, trade policy, whatever it is. I felt if we left, we would be free from their grasp and we would be free to strike trade deals with countries around the world without being told 'oh, you can't do that'. It's just so much easier for an independent country to make a trade deal."

"I think British people don't have the same attitudes as people on mainland Europe," he continued, "we just don't have this idea of forever integrating into this thing. And there's the whole immigration thing as well – I don't think people like the idea of a big influx of immigrants coming into the UK in numbers that are unsustainable."

I asked why people might want immigrants to leave.

"I think amongst really working-class people," he said, "they might have a sense of Polish people taking their jobs maybe. And maybe they've seen places in England change and been worried about that, especially with the whole Islamic threat. There's probably lots of different reasons, but people are British and proud and they don't want anything interfering with it. I don't think that everyone would have thought like that, but I do think people want to maintain their culture, maintain their identity – people don't like the idea of possibly being overrun by foreigners."

"I think many people voted Leave in order to regain control of immigration," he went on, "and to have the ability to deport criminals that should rightly be deported but perhaps cannot be deported due to refusal from the EU or human rights legislation. In particular, I believe many people voted to leave amongst English working-class communities living in towns and cities where there are concentrated hot spots of Muslims and/or other groups which have immigrated over the years. I think the indigenous populations in these areas now feel like they are now outnumbered and perhaps feel that the immigrant population are replacing the indigenous population, or at least they fear that happening. It's not a concern here but there's some parts of England where Muslim immigrants literally outnumber English people, and it's become so dense, and there are certain mosques that have been set up that have been radicalising Muslims for a perversion of Islam – Islamist terrorism if you like. You've got people walking around enforcing sharia law on people who are not Muslim – who do they think they are? But the bottom line for me is that we should have control over our own immigration policy."

He had talked about people who were traditionally in a position of ascendancy in England now feeling outnumbered by people who were different from them. I asked if there was any parallel with the Protestant community in Northern Ireland, who felt threatened by the Catholic population according to some of the people I had met.

"I think there is an element of that amongst Protestants who see the population of people of the Catholic religion growing faster than Protestant," he said, "but what Unionists, particularly the DUP, need to do if they are to defeat Sinn Fein is to sell the Union to Catholic people. I believe many of them would buy it, but as long as the DUP continue not to do this, they will continue to inadvertently push Northern Ireland out of the Union. The DUP are nothing more than an Ulster nationalist party due to their Protestant-only image and their reactive nature, which makes Sinn Fein's job very easy – they play the equality and respect card and voters come out in their droves."

"The Protestant population is declining," he added, "and it's long overdue that Catholics should be brought into the Union. Unionists need to lead the way in stopping using the terms 'Protestant' and 'Catholic' when it comes to identity and instead sell the benefits of the Union to Catholics."

We talked for a while about how sectarian identity politics was undermining progress in Northern Ireland, with the power-sharing executive regularly suspended and progress on all manner of different issues held up by political parties focussed on shoring up power for themselves and 'their' communities. It seemed an important lesson for the rest of the UK to learn and I wanted to explore it further, but time was running short and I wanted to hear more about Andrew's views on the EU before we left.

"The other reason for me campaigning to leave was that I saw this EU being this project," he told me, "and if you look at its history, the EU has slowly been eroding the idea of the nation state, very slowly and subtly, almost in stealthy ways – no borders, single currency, things like that – and it seems like their endgame is that all the member states are the EU, they are the European Union, it's all one state. The Schengen arrangement – thankfully the UK and Ireland are not part of it, because if we were we'd be an awful lot worse off in terms of security. Thank God we've got passport controls because there's a massive security issue in Europe at the moment."

I asked him why national identity was important in his view.

"Well why should we just give it away," he said, "to become this big massive united one state of Europe? This cult of all these former countries becoming just one country… It would be forcibly erasing all these countries – their past, their history, their heritage, everything. People say it's a progressive thing to do, being part of this bloc, but why is it a bad thing to want to negotiate your own trade deals? It's just crazy, you know."

"So you ask why national identity is important," he went on, "but why is it not important? I don't really know where to start with your question. It's important because it's our past, it's our history, and we should never forget it. And if you're proudly British, that's your identity and surely you want to keep it. Because the pursuit of a United States of Europe, this all becoming one nation state, it really takes away your identity because suddenly your replacing Britishness and taking on this European identity that's been manufactured by the EU. No, you're not European – you're British, you're French, you're Dutch, you're whatever, and everybody should embrace their identities and embrace their histories, and it's not about the British beating the Germans or the French or whoever, it's just that we want to keep our identities thank you very much, we don't want this one state thing."

"If you're a patriot," he added as we prepared to leave, "you embrace your identity, you want to preserve it, you want to keep it, you don't want people to take it away from you, and it's not about not accepting immigration, but at the same time, people shouldn't just be allowed to come in and set up sharia courts all over. What the hell's that all about? That's not British. But instead it's 'oh sorry, yes sir, you go ahead because I don't want to be called racist' – it's right that we make sure that we're welcoming people but for God's sake, we've got to fucking stand up for ourselves."

As I left him, I thought about the parallels between what he was saying about immigration to the UK and the sectarian divide I had witnessed in Northern Ireland. While the circumstances were different, in both cases it seemed people were seeking to defend and uphold their culture and preserve their way of life. I felt this was a universal human instinct which, if it wasn't handled carefully, had the potential to be very dangerous indeed: my experience in Northern Ireland was that social division was both extremely damaging in and of itself, but also that it also came to dominate politics and stymied progress in other areas. Based on my conversations around the country, I felt this was a danger of which the rest of the UK needed to be acutely conscious.

*****

That evening, I headed to the Belfast Friendship Club, a community initiative which ran out of the Common Grounds café in the south of the city, a multicultural area including many students from the nearby Queen's University. There I met the group's co-ordinator, Stephanie Mitchell, and talked to her about the Club and how people could be brought together in difficult, divided times. I had been reflecting particularly on the insecurity I had found on my travels and I wanted to think about how this could be overcome. As we sat outside the café in which the group was holding its regular Thursday meeting, its members chatted and danced inside.

"The Belfast Friendship Club started life in 2009 in response to unprovoked racist attacks in the south of the city," Stephanie told me. "Our agenda is to welcome people who are new to the city for any reason at all, but it's equally for locals, people who are more settled here. We now have between thirty and sixty people every week, and at least twenty nationalities, all walks of life, and five to ten people each week will be new. Mostly they're brought by friends, family members or classmates – usually there's a word-of-mouth connection."

"We don't have a strata," she added, "and that creates a sense of solidarity. We're all members, and, as the co-ordinator, I'm the only person who has a paid role."

I asked her how she felt a sense of solidarity could be built.

"By doing," she said. "We don't talk about it, it's just what we do.

So for instance, if somebody here needs a listening ear, somebody will come alongside you and listen. Or if somebody needs help in some way, someone will go to them. When people see one another operating like that, that sense of human warming is tangible – it brings out the best in people."

"Another key distinction," she went on, "is about solidarity and not charity. And that is the thing which makes a huge difference: to do something when you're motivated by solidarity is very much about equals. It's very much an equal relationship. With charity, I am doing things for you – I am bestowing my kindness upon you because you need my help. If I do something with you in the spirit of solidarity, I'm doing it in the same spirit that I know you would do it for me – so there is an equal relationship between us."

"Our members are changing all the time," she added, "but the DNA remains the same. That's what transmits itself, the DNA – it seems to convey itself from person to person."

I reflected on what she had said about DNA. She was talking about a sympathetic approach and set of values which could be taken on by anyone regardless of their background, as Alex Smith had done talking about Manchester United. It was the antithesis of what the man in Glasgow had said about British people being those who were 'our DNA, our flesh and blood', where national identity was only open to people of one ethnicity. I asked whether there were lessons from the Club for the UK more broadly, particularly for people who felt their identity was under threat.

"I'm not particularly familiar with any religious tenets," she said, "but there is often a remit to welcome the stranger – and that's not an easy thing to do, because we are inherently afraid of people who are different for reasons that go back to our survival. So one of the things we began to do seven years ago is a programme called Small Worlds, where we take a little taste of our diversity here at the Club out into communities, to youth groups, schools and community groups all over the country, giving people an opportunity to meet someone different in a safe environment. That addresses myths, misunderstandings and media perceptions in a way only meeting someone face-to-face can do, because when you've looked into somebody's eyes and heard their story, you can't think the same way about that group anymore. It's not something we can force people to do, but bit by bit, slowly-slowly, change can happen."

"I think you also have to provide an environment in which people are accepted for who they are, not who you might want them to be," she went on, "because when you think about it, where do we experience unconditional welcome? You have to be a particular way to go into lots of different environments, you have to conform, and that may mean hiding certain aspects of who you are. And our families are not always particularly accepting – they may not like the way we are, they may wish we were different, and so I think to experience being welcomed into a space, genuinely, for who you are and accepted for who you are, can be something of a novelty."

I was reminded of Charlotte Bull all the way back in Darlington, saying that an ideal world was one in which everyone felt loved. I suggested to Stephanie that she was saying something similar.

"Love is not too strong a word," she said. "I think that that is probably one of the single most important things that happens here on a weekly basis. The nature of how you are greeted makes a huge difference: you never know what somebody has come from or is going to, so it's always helpful to just be aware of our complete level of ignorance. It's too easy to make assumptions about people, so the nature of welcome is a very powerful thing. That genuinely warm welcome is twinned with no expectation on the person to be a certain way here: there are so many different ways to be in this space – you can sit in a corner with a cup of tea, quietly, for the whole evening, close your eyes if you like. You don't have to be the life and soul of the party, you don't have to talk to anybody, you can just be there. It sounds so naff when you describe it, but what's wrong with 'love of fellow man'?"

"Talking about love is not something we're particularly good at," she went on, "particularly the English – and I say that as an English person. But that acceptance makes so much possible and from it comes more, so when you start to model it, it actually generates itself."

"That's what you see in there," she added, motioning towards the people enjoying themselves inside.

She needed to get back and we headed inside. A man from Yemen was leaving, and she gave him a two-stage handshake and fist-bump which they had obviously practised together. She hugged a Palestinian man as he departed and beside me, people from Spain, Ukraine and Somalia chatted; a woman knitted, board games were out and on the turntables a woman played music from the Fifties and Sixties. A couple of members were talking about organising a 'More in Common' lunch in memory of Jo Cox, and in the middle of the café a man from Syria, a woman from Zimbabwe and two British women danced to 'Why Do Fools Fall in Love?'

*****

That evening, I sat in a pub in the centre of Belfast while a group played folk music on a guitar and fiddle and thought back over the last couple of days. Sean, the man in West Belfast, had felt the writing was on the wall in terms of the break-up of the United Kingdom. He felt now that the trajectory was inevitable – quite when and how it would happen he didn't know but he felt sure that change was coming. He said that Protestant people didn't need to worry, that their identity wouldn't be taken away, but I didn't believe that the people who shopped in the Union Jack Souvenir Shop would feel that way, just like I didn't think those people who I had met on my travels who were worried about the way Britain was changing would simply accept it. I thought back to the Loyalist paramilitary message stating that people would defend themselves if they were threatened and Andrew's suggestion that we had to 'stand up for ourselves' against the use of sharia law in the UK. The situation in Belfast, with its history of violent sectarian conflict, was obviously unique, but there were enough similarities for me to think that there was trouble ahead for the whole of the UK.

While my most significant worry was about the possibility of ethnic and religious prejudice and violence, cultural defensiveness also seemed dangerous and counter-productive from a political perspective. I thought Andrew had been right that the best course of action for Unionists in Northern Ireland was to make their cause non-sectarian and seek to appeal to every Northern Irish citizen, not just Protestant people. As he had said, the DUP's close affiliation with Protestantism played into the hands of opponents of the Union as did, I felt, its support for Brexit, with its knock-on impacts on Northern Ireland's border with the Republic of Ireland. I thought back to Alison Thewliss in Glasgow describing a 'civic nationalism' which was open to everyone in Scotland, no matter where they or their family was from. The lesson for supporters of the Union, it seemed to me, was that retreating into an ethnic or religious definition of the nation was not only exclusionary, but ultimately self-defeating.

Stephanie had provided some ideas on how to bring people together in an open, mixed community like South Belfast. The Friendship Club seemed to be underpinned by a belief in the intrinsic good of human beings: that if people felt secure, welcomed and accepted then positive relationships across ethnic, sectarian and religious boundaries could blossom. But, I felt, the depths of anger and fear I had encountered and the willingness of others to play on divisions made this a difficult reality to deliver in areas like inner-city Belfast and many of the other divided places I had seen around the UK. Building a sense of security amongst people who were feeling under threat and sensing that their power was being usurped was, I felt, the key.

*****

Symbols, sectarianism and reconciliation in Northern Ireland

The next day, I headed to Hillsborough to meet Robin Eames, the former Archbishop of Armagh and Primate of the Anglican Church in Northern Ireland, who knew the Protestant community of Northern Ireland as well as anyone, and who had been closely involved in the Peace Process.

"During the Troubles, I was a frequent visitor to paramilitary prisoners at the Maze Prison," he told me, "and the contrast was interesting. The Loyalist prisoners were still drilling with cardboard guns, they were still answering commands – left, right, march. Come into the Republican wing and what did you find? Tutorials, bookshelves packed with philosophy, political theory, history, visiting teachers, external degrees being sought. And that contrast was the first thing that alerted me to what the future would bring. And that's exactly what has happened: when the Good Friday Agreement came and the prisoners flooded out, the Republicans brought their books with them, the Loyalists brought their cardboard guns."

"Even to this day," he went on, "in Loyalist areas there are people who owe their status in that community to the UDA days. And now there's another generation growing up, who never lived through it, and the question is would they ever want to go back to that? Part of me says 'no, they won't' but part of me says 'don't be so emphatic'."

"Loyalism is based on basic Protestantism," he continued, "which says 'you live by rules': if you infringe on those rules, you must re-establish those rules, and if you can find someone who will take the lead in that, well and good, but if you can't, you take the lead yourself and you re-impose the rules. Translate that into a community that has unemployed people who because of their past will never be employed, people with only basic education skills: put that all into that mixture and then add Brexit, the border, distrust of Westminster and distrust of local politicians seen to be feathering their own nest, you've got a very, very dangerous vacuum. What Cameron did was to throw a smoking grenade into the middle of this, this little place which is on a knife-edge because of our history, and damn it all, the grenade blew up."

"The new generation that I've talked about don't necessarily want to go to early graves as their forefathers did," he added, "but they do not want to feel that they are going to be swept aside in a united Ireland in which their rights will be swept under the carpet. Nor do they want to see a united Ireland in which their identity is not recognised. One theory on your side of the Irish Sea is that the IRA gave up the struggle because they couldn't win and that is the greatest tripe that anyone ever said. They ended it because they saw another way of achieving a united Ireland – a political way, the Gerry Adams, the Martin McGuinness way."

I suggested that trajectory could be threatening to people who felt a strong sense of British identity.

"Stop for a minute," he said, "and ask yourself – what is the British identity? The Crown, the Protestant cause, a United Kingdom? The Crown is largely symbolic; Scottish independence is being considered, Northern Ireland is up for grabs… So what is the British identity? To cut a long story short, I believe the British identity here is anything that isn't an Irish identity: 'I am British because I am certainly not Irish'."

I asked whether he felt that was the sentiment people in East Belfast were expressing by flying their flags.

"At one level they're saying the British identity is the orange sash and the bowler hat and the marching on the 12th of July," he said, "and in one sense they're saying 'the erosion of that identity is when we're not allowed to parade through a Catholic area, beat our drums and blow our trumpets.' Another one is to say 'God Save the Queen, you're welcome your Majesty and we should get Westminster to give us more money'. The Union Jack, yes, is probably flown more in this part of the United Kingdom more than anywhere else, but I wonder what they mean by British identity and I wonder what it is that will become their identity after Brexit. There is confusion about what Britishness means, there still is fear that this identity could somehow be eroded. Then you say 'ok, eroded from what?' and they flounder."

"Protestantism and Loyalism is really built on the negative: we are this because we're not that – we're this because we're not Republican, we're not Roman Catholics." he continued. "So your friends in East Belfast with their Union Jacks and their murals, they chant 'we're British, we're British, we're British' because they don't know anything better. But it's only I think when Brexit comes that they're going to be asked fundamental questions about what their identity is. How will the post-Brexit Britain work for unemployed Loyalist Protestants of East Belfast? Will people there say 'I'm British, but what have I got out of it? I've not got a job but I can wave a flag'."

"Now," he went on, "the biggest percentage of people who have applied for Irish passports since this carry-on began, who are they? Northern Ireland Protestants. So is the Union Flag a flag of convenience, or is there something deeper there? I wish I knew the answer, but I do wonder whether there's a sneaking feeling amongst the Protestants that 'we don't want to be treated the way that we treated the Catholics'. One of the things that was known as a catchphrase in hot, rigid, Loyalist areas was 'look at them Catholics, they're breeding like flies'. What did they mean by that? That 'they' would out-populate 'us' ultimately – 'look at those Catholics, they're breeding like flies and we'll be the minority'. Jump up to the next scenario, which was 'we don't want to happen to us in a united Ireland what we did to them'."

I wondered why the DUP had backed Brexit when it seemed to open up the possibility of a united Ireland, the very last thing that they wanted.

"I think they were confused," he said. "I think they made the decision because Europe was basically Catholic – not just numerically, but Catholic in its philosophy. I cannot overemphasise to you how deep this reformation Protestant ethos goes – it's frighteningly deep. I've seen it. I've seen women with bibles in their hands throwing stones at Catholic children going to school. I've seen police having to be called out to protect a school bus of Catholic children going to a Catholic school because that bus was passing through a Loyalist area. It's terribly, terribly deep. I have devoted my life to countering it, but it's there, it's there. So is that the reason why the DUP did as they did? I don't know."

It seemed an important lesson on how politics of identity could become not just dangerous but also self-defeating. Thinking about how to avoid this happening in the rest of the UK, I asked how one could build a sense of identity which was not defined against another group.

"You dwell on the positive to the extent that it's better than the negative," he said, "and you show an attractiveness to the positive which is not represented by the negative, because it's worthwhile and because it contributes to the greater good. And I think unless a community can somehow identify a common ethic – that may be religion, that may be wanting to do good in a society – unless they can identify with that they're just going to continue to splinter."

I could see what he was saying about attractiveness and it sounded reasonable, but I also knew that some of the people I had met on my travels would find it hard to talk positively about Britain and Britishness without feeling a sense of shame at what had been done in the country's name in places like Northern Ireland. I asked him how Britishness could be the attractive identity he had talked about given the way many people felt about the country's history.

"First of all," he said, "you don't rewrite the past. There is a great tendency for people to rewrite the past but you can't rewrite the fact that the famine took place in Ireland and that Britain – or England I would say – greatly ill-treated the people of Ireland and drove them into immigration into the United States. Coming up to more recent history, Catholics resent very, very much events like Bloody Sunday.

One response is to rewrite the past, one response is to acknowledge that it happened and to move on. There is a new generation coming through and that's where the hope lies. We need to say to them that the past is the past and that they have a bigger contribution to make in the future."

That to me seemed the key point: no one should be bound by the past, I felt, but reconciling with that past and learning from it seemed essential if a nation was to move forward. As my final day in Northern Ireland neared, I knew where I had to go to explore how possible that reconciliation was for me personally.

*****

The next day, I headed to the city of Derry/Londonderry – Derry to many Nationalists, Londonderry to many Unionists. I caught a taxi from the railway station to the Bogside, a centre of Republicanism in Northern Ireland throughout the Troubles from where Martin McGuinness had directed the operations of the IRA, and where fourteen Catholic people had been killed by British security forces on 'Bloody Sunday'. As we crossed the bridge from the station, which was on the south side of the River Foyle, and headed towards the predominantly-Catholic area north of the river, the driver told me a bit more about the city.

"Most people on this side of the water we're just entering would be Catholic and they'd all say they're Irish," he told me, "and on the other side of the water, where we just came from, they'd say they're British. It's mad. There's too much of the past getting brought up all the time."

"I had a wee nephew killed in the Troubles," he added, "but there's no grudges. You need to learn from the past but not get held up by it. The only thing that you should worry about is the future."

In the Bogside, an unremarkable-looking residential area, a woman was walking her dog and birds ate abandoned rubbish. There were Sinn Fein posters all around.

The taxi driver dropped me off at the Bloody Sunday memorial.

"Where you are right now," he said, "is where Hugh Gilmour was killed."

At the memorial, I saw that Gilmour had been seventeen when he died, one of fourteen people killed on Bloody Sunday by British security forces. The memorial read 'Their epitaph is in the continuing struggle for democracy'. A wreath in front of the memorial was in the green, white and orange of the Irish flag.

Across the road, at Free Derry corner, I stood under the iconic message – *You are now entering Free Derry*. There were Palestinian flags all around an island in the road and in the middle flew a flag which read 'Irish Republic'. Near it was a quotation from James Connolly: "The Irish people will only be free when they own everything from the plough to the stars".

I headed up to the border with the Republic of Ireland, which would one day be the border between the UK and the European Union, an anonymous straight of road a couple of miles out of the city. In the area where once there had been no man's land between the UK and Ireland, there was now a travelling circus; where the British army border base had been was now a car showroom; the old Customs and Excise building was now a fireplace store. Down the road I saw a poster of a man with a gun, and it took me a moment to realise that it was not a paramilitary mural but an advert for a local paintball centre.

I headed back to the station and took the train to the airport. On the table next to me a father played with his baby daughter, while the girl's mother took photos. As they did, I looked up David Cameron's 2010 statement in the House of Commons, responding to Lord Saville's Bloody Sunday inquiry in which the then-Prime Minister apologised for what had happened:

> "I am deeply patriotic. I never want to believe anything bad about our country. I never want to call into question the

behaviour of our soldiers and our army, who I believe to be the finest in the world. And I have seen for myself the very difficult and dangerous circumstances in which we ask our soldiers to serve. But the conclusions of this report are absolutely clear. There is no doubt, there is nothing equivocal, there are no ambiguities. What happened on Bloody Sunday was both unjustified and unjustifiable. It was wrong.

These are shocking conclusions to read and shocking words to have to say. But you do not defend the British Army by defending the indefensible. We do not honour all those who have served with such distinction in keeping the peace and upholding the rule of law in Northern Ireland by hiding from the truth. What happened should never, ever have happened. The families of those who died should not have had to live with the pain and the hurt of that day and with a lifetime of loss.

A state should hold itself to account and we should be determined at all times, no matter how difficult, to judge ourselves against the highest standards. Openness and frankness about the past, however painful, do not make us weaker, they make us stronger."

I reached for the pin in my pocket and reflected that awful things had happened in Britain's history and that the nation had to reconcile itself with that fact. Bloody Sunday was a clear example of something that was terribly wrong and which had resulted in unspeakable pain and loss. But David Cameron – no 'apologist' or 'traitor' – had said sorry on behalf of the government and the nation, and the obligation now, I felt, was to learn from history, to stop such things happening again in the future and to do good in the world. I understood why some people I'd met were ashamed of what had happened, but I felt that shame was ultimately wasted energy; I preferred to try to learn and to look forward. If the taxi driver could do so in spite of the loss of his nephew, then I had no excuse.

As I headed to the airport, I saw a message inscribed in large letters on the side of a pub. It read: *'A nation that keeps one eye on the past is wise. A nation that keeps two eyes on the past is blind'*.

*****

There was a hen party near me on my flight back to London and as they chatted happily about the forthcoming wedding, I thought about love and wondered about what Stephanie had said about acceptance. While she wanted everyone who entered the Friendship Club to be welcomed warmly, I didn't think she was suggesting that any of her members were perfect. No doubt every member was flawed in some way, yet they were still accepted. It seemed to me that the same applied to a nation – we should not seek unquestioning love of the country, I felt, but something more nuanced: acceptance of the nation for all its history, not just the good parts; of the flag in spite of the fact that it had been, and sometimes still was, used aggressively; and, for all our differences and our flaws, of one another. I thought back to what Robin had said about attractiveness and about not denying history. It struck me that part of loving something was accepting its imperfections, and that 'warts-and-all' acceptance, appreciating and celebrating the good, not hiding from the bad but learning from it, was richer and truer than blind loyalty.

I knew that some of the people I'd met would think differently: I knew they would be troubled by the idea of patriotism, of 'looking out for our own' and where that might lead, and would always look at the British flag and remember it being used aggressively. I didn't blame them but I hoped those who saw things differently at least recognised that the issues I had identified weren't going away. It seemed to me that our only choice was whether to engage with those questions responsibly or leave ill-feeling to fester and let others take advantage. Doing nothing, I felt, could leave vulnerable people at risk, undermine the sense of solidarity on which so much depended and lead to divisions dominating politics and preventing progress in other areas. I also reflected that those who were troubled by the idea of building a strong sense of Britishness would be left open to unfair but nevertheless harmful accusations of 'talking the country down' or 'being unpatriotic' and could see their arguments undermined as a result. Working to build a measured, balanced patriotism, rooted in both pride and reconciliation with the country's past, was the most powerful way I could imagine to counter such accusations.

As the plane came in to land at Luton Airport, I looked down at the green fields of Bedfordshire. In one rectangular field, someone had mowed a horizontal line, a vertical line and two diagonal lines intersecting in the centre of the field and forming the unmistakeable shape of the Union Flag. Across the aisle, one of the members of the hen party pointed it out to her friend and as she did I saw a tattoo on her arm: 'this isn't the end, it's the beginning', it read.

Conclusion

As I wrote up my notes from my travels, Theresa May triggered Article 50 and then called a general election in which the Conservatives lost their Parliamentary majority as Labour's vote share grew significantly. In order to form a government, May entered a deal with the DUP which was criticised for putting the Good Friday Agreement at risk and for wedding the government to a party with very conservative views on homosexuality and abortion. While this political upheaval was unfolding, a string of terrorist attacks were carried out in London and Manchester and a fire ripped through Grenfell Tower in London, killing scores of people. Britain at the end of my travels seemed even more troubled than when I had begun, and once again, the biggest challenges the country faced seemed to come from within.

While my experience was in no way representative or systematic, I was determined to use what I had learnt to help address the problems the country faced. As a starting point, I felt that there was plenty of opportunity to bring people together on economic matters: there was clear consensus, for example, that there were big issues relating to free markets and free movement from which some people had benefited and others had not. While Dan Naylor, the public affairs expert I had met in Whitehall, was no doubt correct that migrants had made a big net contribution to the British economy, free movement of people was widely seen as part of an economic model built on low-paid, insecure work which did not prioritise preparing British workers, and young people in particular, for the jobs of the future. At the same time, there was clear anger across the board about multinationals making a profit in Britain and not paying their fair share in taxes.

I couldn't help feeling that Labour's increased support at the 2017 election reflected a widely-held feeling that Britain's economic model was not working, a feeling reinforced when I visited post-industrial communities and found huge, unanswered questions about their social and economic future, and when I met young people anxious about jobs and student debt. At the same time, I shared the anxiety expressed by Dean, the business owner in Welshpool, about the national debt and whether the country would be able to pay it down, because the Britain I saw on my travels was struggling. Many town and city centres had been redeveloped but there was a sense, encapsulated by Sam, the man selling joke books in Blackpool, that the authorities had to some degree been 'painting on rust'.

When exploring how Britain should respond to the economic challenges it faced, I was pleased to find much common ground amongst the people I met. There was widespread support for the idea that the state should act as a shield against the worst impacts of globalisation, ensuring that the economy was made to work more effectively in the interests of all people, not just those at the 'top'; making certain that rich individuals and multinationals paid their fair share in tax; redistributing opportunity around the country; retraining those whose jobs had been put at risk by globalisation; and investing in education, particularly vocational education, to prepare young people for the jobs of the twenty-first century.

Yet I felt more work needed to be done to make the case for solidarity and sharing in the country. "We should never have to beg," Gary Millar, the Liverpool councillor had said in respect of the Westminster government giving money to deprived areas of his city, but his argument had, I felt, been predicated on a belief that the country was a coherent community in which people felt a special responsibility to share with one another. As I travelled, I had heard many concerns which I felt could, if they were not addressed, put that sense of a coherent community at risk, and I felt that those who wanted a greater sense of solidarity had a responsibility to try to create the social conditions in which people felt ready to share. In my view, that meant having a convincing response to the very difficult cultural divisions which had dominated my journey.

By far the most commonly-raised cultural concerns related to immigration. Some of these, such as the belief that migrants were taking jobs or putting a strain on public services, were on the surface economic. Yet I felt that the deepest anxieties were about identity, community and values: worries about a lack of integration, not just in areas with large numbers of recent migrants but also in places with more established minority communities; a feeling that the state had failed to stand up for shared values or against those who wanted to do harm to the country; and the belief that rapid change, particularly relating to customs, cultures, languages and religions meant that many people felt that the country was changing in a way that they didn't like, that their culture and way of life was being eroded and that no one was acting to stop it. All of this, I felt, contributed to the strong sense of 'us and them' which I had encountered on my travels.

It was an unavoidable truth that this sentiment was expressed far more strongly and regularly in relation to Britain's Muslim population than any other community, particularly in areas where South Asian and white communities lived side by side but led parallel lives. Whether or not the cultural divides which people described were as deep as they perceived, the strength and consistency of concern seemed to make for a dangerous situation composed of multiple issues. The covering of women's faces, for example, seemed emblematic of fear about a very different culture and set of values, particularly in relation to gender, existing unchallenged in Britain.

Conclusion

The people I met also raised concerns about sharia law and those who preached hate or threatened violence in the name of Islam, implying that the Muslim community lived not just in parallel with the rest of British society but potentially in conflict with it. Even those people I met who acknowledged that extremists were small in number and not reflective of the wider Muslim community still felt that the actions of that small number of people had eroded trust and cohesion more broadly. I also remembered what Aneeta Prem, the forced marriage charity director I had met in London, had said about some people becoming more 'introverted' and cultural divisions becoming more entrenched. For these reasons, I didn't think that it could simply be assumed that greater integration would naturally happen over time: thorough, long-term work was, I felt, needed to address the issues I had identified.

At the same time, I couldn't help but feel that the widespread concern I had heard about Muslim people was in part rooted in insecurity amongst the majority, predominantly-white population. The success of mosques while churches were closing, the desire of people of South Asian descent to get on and succeed in education, prosper in work and get involved in politics shone a light on some of the challenges facing more established communities. Not only were people in established communities often finding life difficult, but they were also watching some minority populations thrive and feeling their power and ascendancy drift away. It felt like a toxic combination which, if stoked, could cause unrest in communities and put British Muslims at particular risk. The Islamist terrorist attacks in London and Manchester clearly exacerbated that risk, and I worried that the attack on Muslim worshippers near to Finsbury Park Mosque and a string of hate crimes against British Muslims and people of South Asian heritage was a portent of dangers to come.

The social and cultural challenges I had identified weren't just to do with immigration and integration, of course: the divisions between rich and poor, Left and Right, liberal and conservative, between those who felt British and those who saw themselves as European or global citizens, felt entrenched and often angry. At the same time, I believed the campaigns for a united Ireland and Scottish independence would resurface in the coming years, seeking to challenge the bonds of Britishness and to define against 'little England', the Westminster elite and Brexit. I felt that too much of the response making the case for the Union lay in history rather than the present or the future, and I worried about the weight carried by the Queen personally as a symbol of unity. Reliance on a woman in her nineties seemed a risky place to be, yet it was hard to know where else to look in terms of uniting people: the government, and politics more widely, was discredited, while many of the institutions which could have brought people together at a more local level were struggling, with funding cuts affecting local government and community organisations, and churches seeing their congregations diminish.

I feared the direct impacts of Britain's divisions – from the potential break-up of the Union to the risk of violence in communities – but I also feared that those divisions would colour British politics for years to come, distracting from some long-term issues like funding pensions and social care and inhibiting the achievement of positive outcomes on others, such as our future relationship with the EU. I believed that Northern Ireland showed the potential impact of cultural division dominating politics, with self-defeating decisions made on the basis of appealing to one community's supposed interest and achingly-slow progress on matters of huge importance to people's lives as parties vied for cultural as well as political power. If the UK as a whole was to avoid the same fate and address the long-term challenges it faced, starting with building the best possible future relationship with the EU, I believed we needed a new political settlement for the post-referendum era. In my mind, this meant combining the steps on education and the economy for which I had found broad support early in my journey with efforts to address the cultural issues which had been so evident around the country.

In order to address those cultural issues, I felt that the country needed a stronger sense of shared identity, common values and the future towards which it was heading. While some of the people I had met on my travels clearly felt a sense of shame at the country's past mistakes and current iniquities and were wary of the dangers of nationalism and xenophobia, I believed those fears needed to be overcome if we were to rebuild our society. It seemed to me impossible, for example, to talk about solidarity and sharing without also trying to build a sense of what people in the country had in common, and why that meant they should look after one another. Building a sense of the nation as a true community where people were bound together by more than simply being in the same place at the same time seemed an essential task for the years ahead.

The challenge of building a strong society which wasn't homogenous or held together by a common faith, which was welcoming to all while clear in its values and which maintained the freedoms which its people held so dear was significant, however, and I didn't know whether it was even possible. I didn't know if the strongest community I had seen on my travels – Blackburn's South Asian community – only thrived because of a widely-shared faith, because it was largely homogenous or because there was an engrained attitude that people there, many the children and grandchildren of migrants or migrants themselves, had to stick together and work especially hard to succeed. The lessons from the unique circumstances of Scotland and Northern Ireland were similarly limited, and I wondered whether it was possible for multi-cultural, multi-faith Britain as a whole to find the same spirit as some of the stronger communities within it.

Yet my experience of a multi-cultural community in Aberystwyth, apparently thriving under the banner of the Welsh dragon, suggested that something like what I was looking for was possible: a place with a clear heritage and sense of identity but which was welcoming to those from outside. Aberystwyth was not a typical place, of course: it was a relatively affluent university town which did not face many of the same challenges as other parts of the UK. 'Welshness' also had fewer of the negative associations with empire that Britishness did and, since the country's language and heritage had been threatened in the past, there was a clear justification for conscious efforts to uphold the Welsh cultural identity. While these circumstances meant that the Welsh model could not simply be applied to the UK as a whole, the fact that so many people from abroad were thriving in a place with a strong sense of history and identity did give me cause for hope.

I knew that trying to build a stronger sense of national identity in the UK as a whole would be hard, but I felt that shared values were the key. Chris, the accountant in Preston, had talked about Britishness being about values rather than heritage, and based on my largely positive experience of meeting people around the UK, I believed that the vast majority of British people could live up to a set of values focussed on respect and care for one another. I felt that a clear articulation of a set of shared values which everyone in society worked towards embodying was needed and that over time, this could form the basis of a stronger sense of national identity which was not based on heritage and which did not need to define against others. While not religious myself, I felt that Christian values like charity, compassion and sharing, along with key tenets of the other religions, cultures and value-systems which made up modern Britain, should provide the basis for a Britishness which welcomed people of all faiths and none.

Yet I knew that if Britishness, and the values which underpinned it, were to mean anything, some difficult issues would need to be confronted, not least in relation to customs being practised in the country which were not in line with shared values and human rights. I felt that as long as standards and laws were developed democratically in line with shared values and human rights principles, and as long as they were applied equally and sensitively in both majority and minority communities, there was a fair way forward which provided equal treatment, equal protection and equal rights to everyone in the country. Emma, the youth worker in Blackburn who wanted to understand more about the communities she worked with but ultimately prioritised the rights and wellbeing of the young people she supported, provided a role model in that respect, seeking to build bridges while at the same time reinforcing the primacy of human rights and values like gender equality.

For my own part, I had come to the view that most people, whether they were from a majority or minority community, would naturally want to uphold their values, their identity and their heritage, but that every culture was on what the sisters in Blackpool had called a 'curve', which meant that that it would evolve over time. I believed that while people should be expected to move with the times and embody the values of modern Britain, they should not be judged too harshly as the changing world challenged long-held values and norms. Respectfully explaining to people why change was happening, as Len in Blackpool had said, seemed to be the key to positive cultural evolution.

Like the sisters in Blackpool, I believed that this evolution could and should include learning from people from other countries, recognising that British culture was not perfect and that there was much we could learn from abroad. At the same time, I believed that while Britain should be welcoming to people coming in from other countries and that those people should not be asked to forget their cultural identity while living in Britain, there was a special responsibility on people coming into the UK, particularly those coming from cultures which did not have as strong a commitment as Britain to values like gender equality, to learn about and uphold the ideals for which the country stood. I believed that the vast majority of migrants already lived up to this responsibility, providing the basis for a rich sense of 'us': a community united not by ethnicity but by shared values and a shared culture which would inevitably evolve over time, with those who came to Britain from abroad playing their part in that evolution. I felt this sense of one community in which everyone had a stake provided the basis for a comprehensive response to those who when discussing heritage and religion talked in terms of 'them and us'.

Yet the nationalism and racism I had seen on my travels suggested there was still much work to be done and I worried that even the most sensitive attempts to build patriotism could be used to exclude those who did not 'fit in'. I thought of the man at Wembley brandishing the poppy at the woman in a burka, and reflected on the words of the judge sentencing the murderer of Jo Cox. Mr Justice Wilkie had said that patriotic sentiments could have resonance but in Thomas Mair's mouth were "made toxic". I felt the judge was right that patriotism was a very powerful double-edged sword, and I could understand that some of the people I had met wanted to steer clear of it. Yet the aggression I had witnessed at Wembley and the unsettling conversations I had all around the country reminded me that the dangers I was worried about already existed. I knew there were people with malign intent ready to take advantage of the feelings I had encountered, and to use them to foster hate and gain political advantage. I decided that it was better to take on those who sought to incite hate or to use it to get votes than to leave them to it.

I still worried that going too far to encourage a sense of 'us' in Britain would lead to people feeling less of a responsibility to those beyond Britain's borders. Yet I felt that the desire to 'look after one's own' was a natural human instinct which should not be judged or denied. Looking out for each other and, by extension, the national interest did not mean that British citizens were more valuable than people from other countries, but simply that Britain was a community in which people felt a special responsibility to one other and exercised that responsibility in various ways, including by sharing resources and opportunities through the state. I also felt that if people could feel more secure in their history, culture and identity then they would be less likely to hold ill-feelings towards people of other backgrounds and would be more likely to want to make a contribution to the world. That sense of security was, I felt, the key not only to healing Britain's internal cultural problems but also to gaining public support for strong, positive international partnerships, including with the EU, in the future. Patriotism and internationalism could, I believed, go hand in hand.

If a new, modern patriotism was to be built, I believed consideration would have to be given to the way people thought about Britain's history. On my travels, I had found a big split between those who subscribed to a notion of British greatness, linked to the country's history, its military prestige and its record of global power, and those who were so ashamed of the country's history that they felt little affinity to it. Both approaches were counterproductive in my view: a story of un-nuanced greatness led to arrogance, complacency and repetition of past mistakes, while I felt that blanket shame was an unfair and unappealing response to a country which had done terrible things but accomplished great things too. I came to the view that there was a middle ground between the two: a celebration of all the wonderful things which Britain had achieved and the values for which the country stood alongside reconciliation with the past and a willingness to learn from the mistakes which had been made. Arguments that Britain should learn from its history had sometimes been dismissed by some on the Far Right as coming from people who "talked Britain down" and "didn't really love the country". Embracing a new, nuanced patriotism would, I felt, head off such tactics in the future, enabling a proper, balanced debate about Britain's future role in the world.

Having spent a long time worrying about what I'd heard on my travels and how to respond, I became increasingly excited at the idea of a richer sense of national identity built in a shared set of values and shared vision of Britain's future. That, after all, seemed so much fuller and deeper than an identity based on a one-dimensional national story which said nothing about who people were and what they had in common. I felt that the country could do so much better than a nostalgic view of the past or a utopian vision for the future, blind loyalty or ethnic and religious prejudice. The best response to that kind of prejudice was, I felt, to show what a true love of country, and of one another, looked like.

All that was needed was a symbol for the sort of national community I wanted to work towards and the kind of patriotism that I wanted to build. I knew that for some of the people I had met on my travels, the Union Flag would always have connotations of racism and nationalism but I did not want to see it in that way: I wanted it to be a symbol of our community, of an acceptance of the nation and of one another. Embracing it did not mean excluding others or condoning the worst of British history and the inequality which still existed in the country, but rather accepting the country for all its flaws and imperfections, appreciating the wonderful things about it, learning from its mistakes and fighting to make it better.

The flag could, I felt, be the symbol for that fight and for the Britain we wanted to work together to build: a self-assured country which had the strength to admit and learn from its mistakes; a state which protected its people from the worst impacts of globalisation but which still played a full role in the world; a nation which put great emphasis on educating and training its people, particularly the young, so that they were ready to respond to the challenges and opportunities of the changing world; a cohesive community where people were willing to share not just resources but also opportunities because they felt a responsibility to one another; a society which

Conclusion

stood up for its values and for human rights without fear or favour; and a home where people were treated equally and no one was judged on the basis of their heritage. This was, I believed, the new settlement Britain needed for the post-referendum era, constituting a crucial step for our wonderful, troubled country as we entered a new stage of the British Journey.

A note for readers

My travels around the country were predominantly a personal journey and this is a very personal book. It isn't an objective analysis: it says nothing about historical trends or how Britain has got to where it is; it is unrepresentative in all manner of different ways; it makes a number of assumptions which would not be permitted in an academic study; it sacrifices verbatim transcription of what people said for brevity and accessibility; and details have often been changed, for example to protect people's identity where they spoke to me in confidence. Given these flaws and the obvious potential for some of the content to be upsetting and offensive, some friends advised me not to publish the book at all.

In the end, I decided to publish for two reasons: first, because the experiences I had played a big part in forming my thinking about what I should do next and in the months and years to come, as I seek to address the difficult issues covered in this book, I would like to be as transparent as possible about the experiences which have shaped my views. I know that those experiences have been partial and unrepresentative but I suspect that even independent-thinking academics, who pride themselves on following the evidence wherever it takes them, will have had unrepresentative experiences in their lives which have shaped the way they see the world. This is, after all, what makes us human and I'd like at least to be open about that.

My second reason for publishing is that what I saw and heard on my travels scared me and I wanted to share my fears. I worry both about the direct impacts of the divisions I encountered and about the issues raised in the book coming to dominate our politics if we don't get a handle on them quickly. I fear that if we don't, these divisions could undermine our efforts to address the other major challenges the country faces, starting with our future relationship with the EU. I trust my instincts that we've got a very significant set of social and cultural problems on our hands and I hope that reading this book might shake a few people into action. Even if they don't like my recommendations, just accepting the scale of the issue we have would be a start.

That is why I have chosen to include in the book the repeated concerns I heard about Britain's Muslim and South Asian communities. It gives me no pleasure to do so, but I believe that what I heard does reflect a deep problem in our society and I don't believe we can afford to sweep our problems under the carpet: the lesson from doing so in the past is that it only stores up trouble for the future. I hope this book will play some small part in bringing the issues we face into the open so that they can be addressed, and that the value of doing so outweighs the dangers of describing divisions as plainly and frequently as I do.

In short, my methodology and presentation are completely open to critique, but that does not mean that the issues aren't real and don't need to be addressed. As I seek to play my part in responding to these issues, I believe this book will help me to be as transparent as I can be about my values and experiences. I hope readers will take what I have written in that spirit.

Joe Hayman, London, August 2017

Acknowledgements

I am grateful to Haroona Ashraf, Shabaz Ashraf, Jenny Barksfield, Sajid Butt, Kat Craig, Gerry Czerniawski, Neela Doležalová, Luise Fitzwalter, Juliana Franco, Carol Greenwood, Ian Hepplewhite, Joe Kenyon, Clare Laxton, Adam Murray, Aneeta Prem, Peter Riddell, Marc Rooney, Frances Ross, Alex Smith, Hibo Wardere, Shoqo Warsame, Howard Williamson, Sarah Woodcock, Guuleed Yaasin and, most of all, my family for their advice and support in the process of writing this book.

The book would not have been what it is without the contributions of the people I interviewed, to most of whom I was a complete stranger approaching them out of the blue. Whether or not I agreed with them, I am very grateful for their willingness to discuss difficult topics so openly.